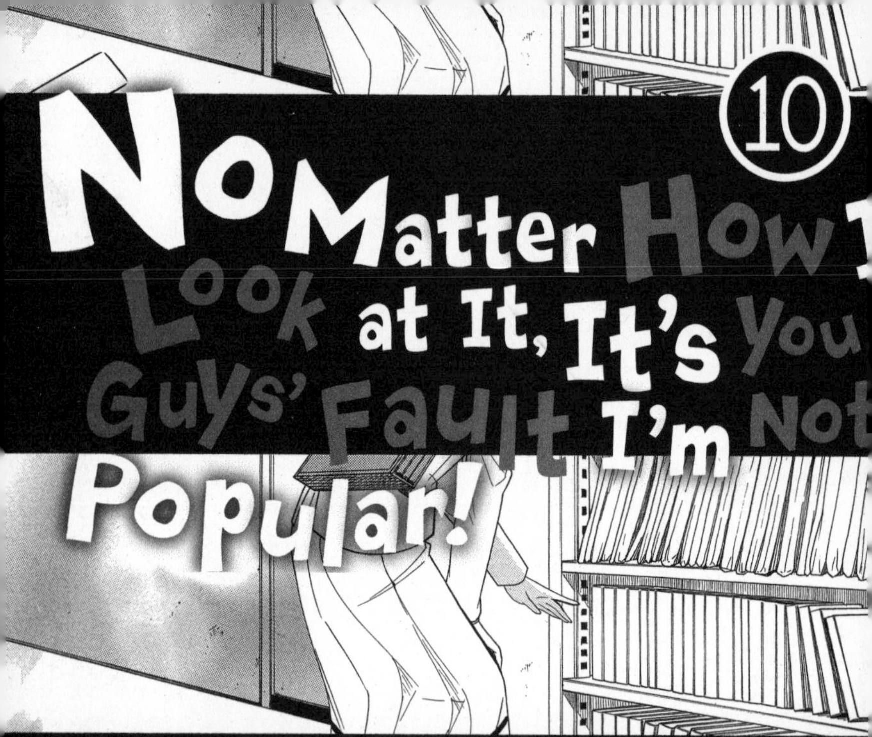

No Matter How I Look at It, It's You Guys' Fault I'm Not Popular!

10

Presented by
NICO TANIGAWA

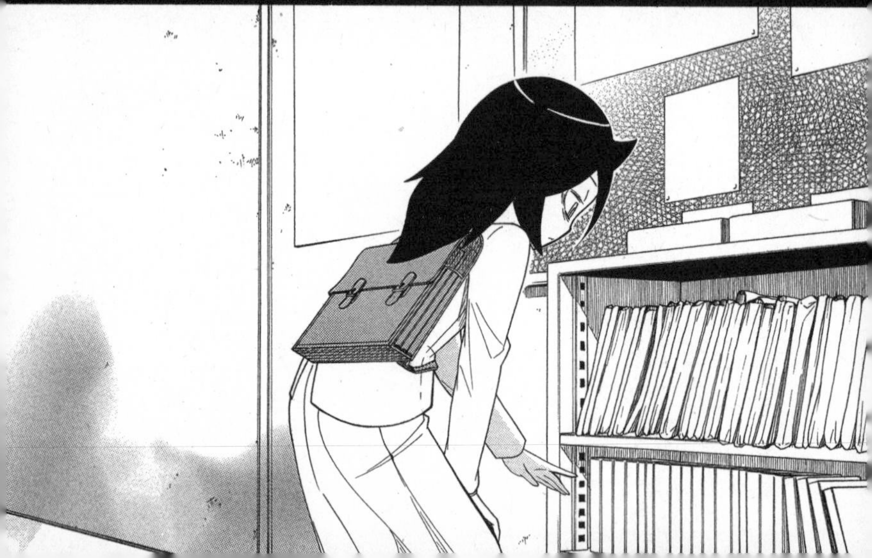

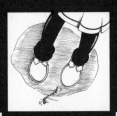

...AWW, IF I'D BEEN A WORM, I WOULD'VE HAD A MAN FROM THE GET-GO AND DEFINITELY HAVE HAD S●X, NOT TO MENTION KIDS...

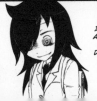

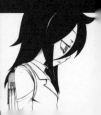

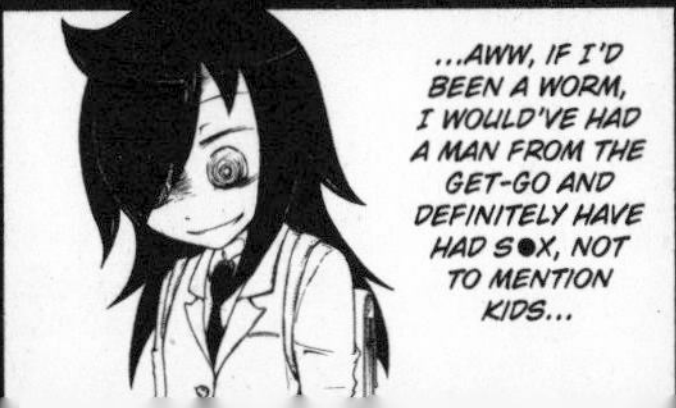

FAIL 89: I'M NOT POPULAR, SO I'LL FORGET SOMETHING.

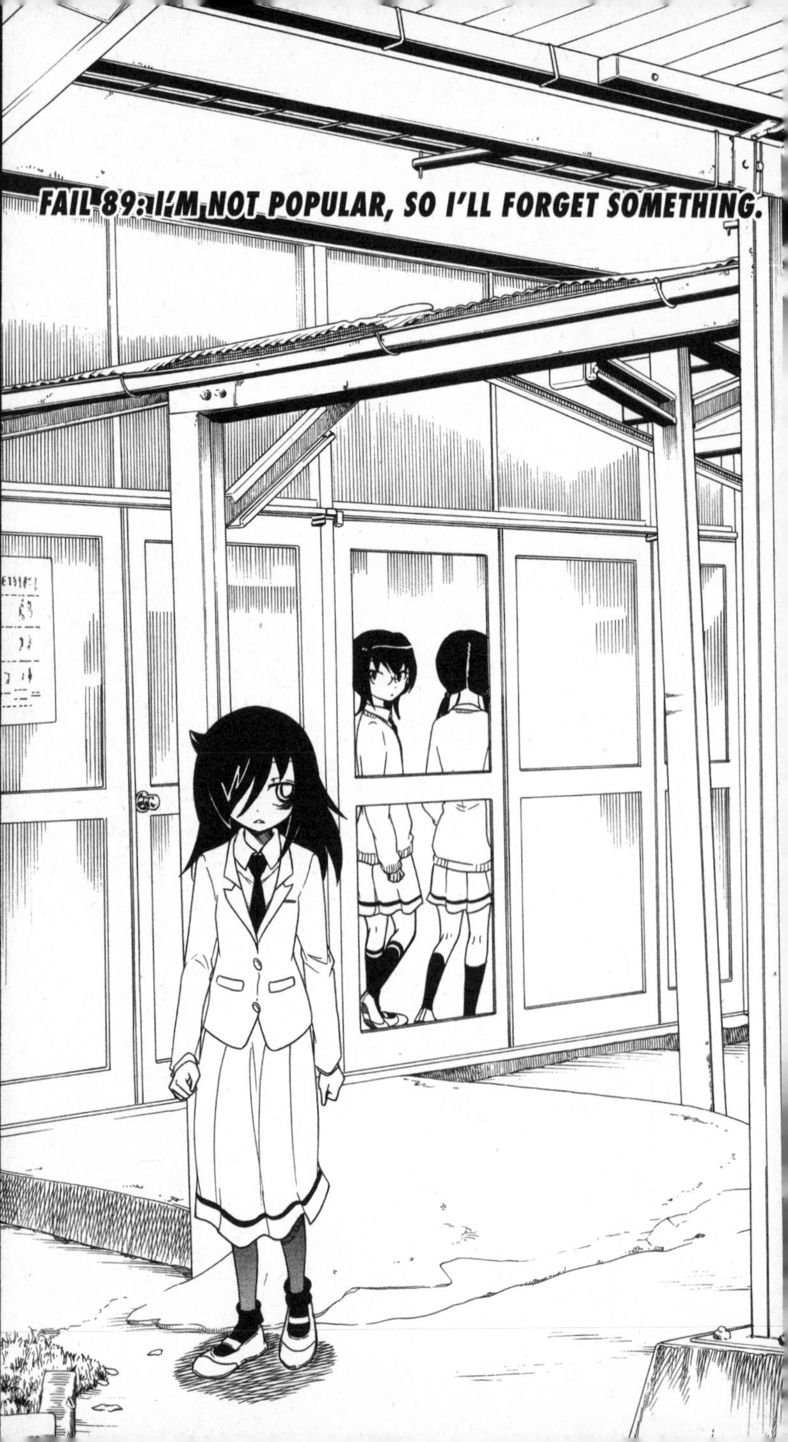

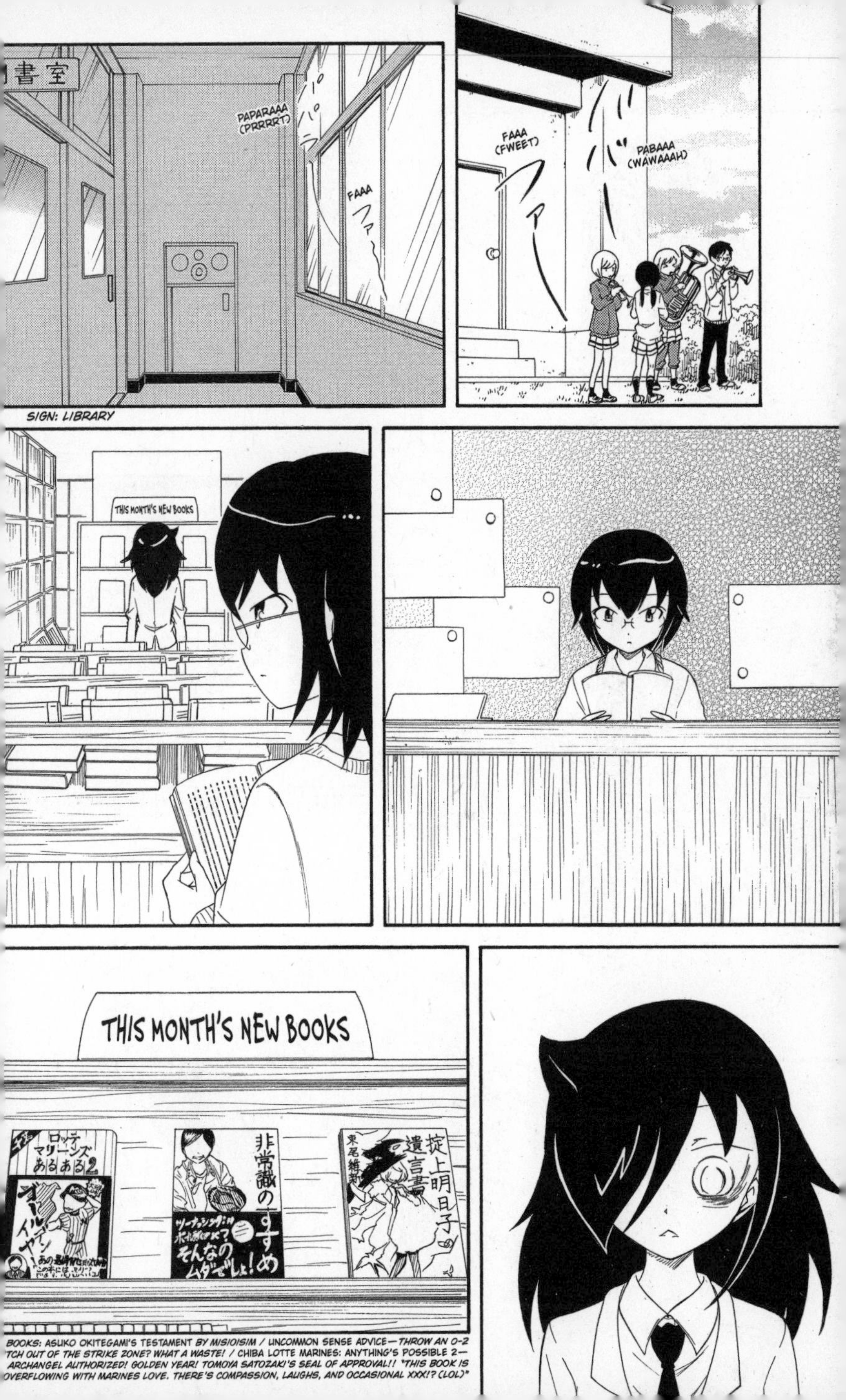
PABAAA (WAWAAAH)
FAAA (FWEET)
書室
PAPARAAA (PRRRRT)
FAAA
SIGN: LIBRARY
THIS MONTH'S NEW BOOKS
THIS MONTH'S NEW BOOKS
掟上明日子 遺言書
東尾維新
非常識のすすめ
そんなのムダでしょ!
ロッテマリーンズあるある2
BOOKS: ASUKO OKITEGAMI'S TESTAMENT BY MISIOISIM / UNCOMMON SENSE ADVICE—THROW AN 0-2 TCH OUT OF THE STRIKE ZONE? WHAT A WASTE! / CHIBA LOTTE MARINES: ANYTHING'S POSSIBLE 2—ARCHANGEL AUTHORIZED! GOLDEN YEAR! TOMOYA SATOZAKI'S SEAL OF APPROVAL!! "THIS BOOK IS OVERFLOWING WITH MARINES LOVE. THERE'S COMPASSION, LAUGHS, AND OCCASIONAL XXX!? (LOL)"

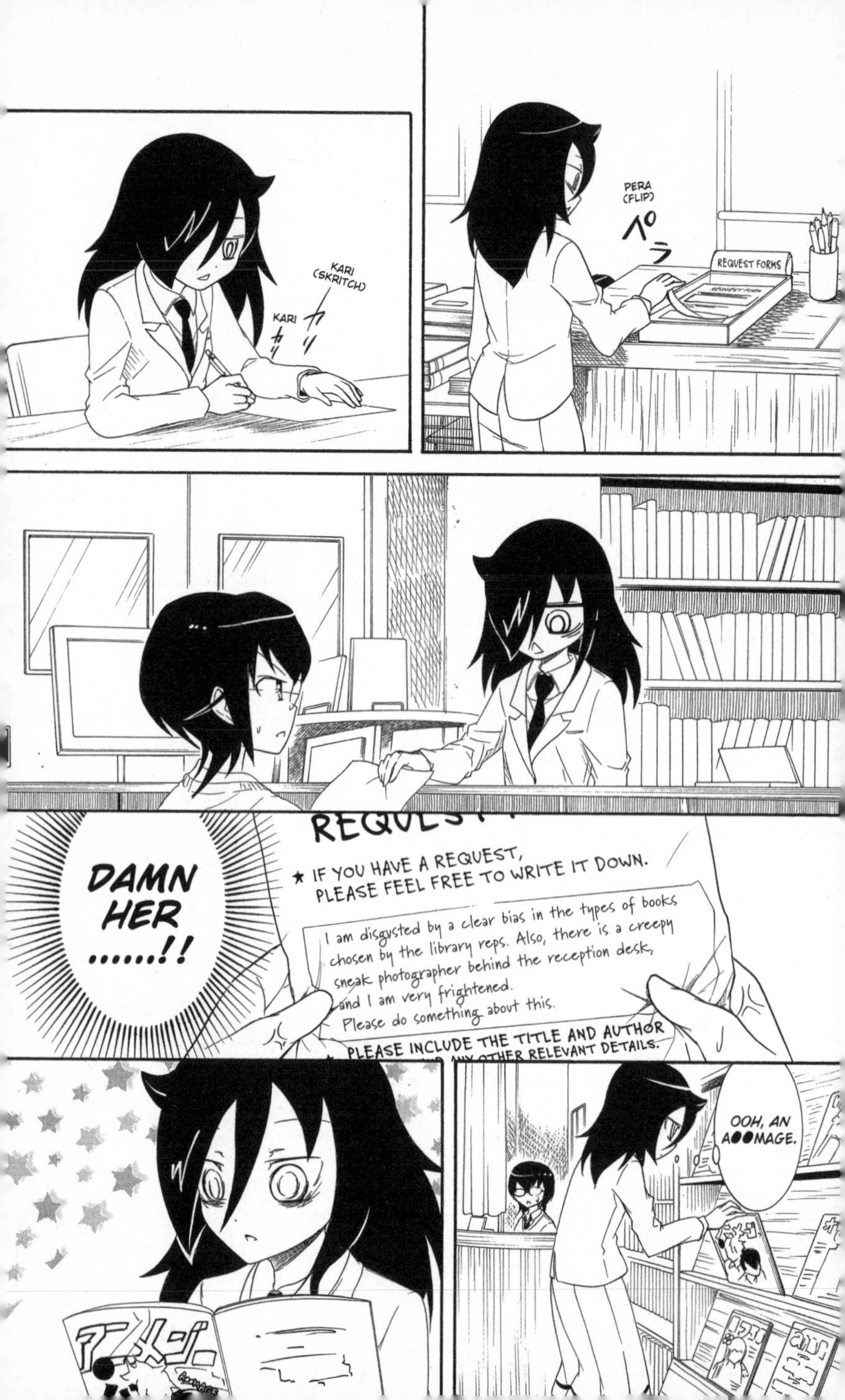
PERA (FLIP)
ペラ
REQUEST FORMS
KARI (SKRITCH)
KARI
カリ
カリ
REQUES
★ IF YOU HAVE A REQUEST, PLEASE FEEL FREE TO WRITE IT DOWN.
I am disgusted by a clear bias in the types of books chosen by the library reps. Also, there is a creepy sneak photographer behind the reception desk, and I am very frightened.
Please do something about this.
PLEASE INCLUDE THE TITLE AND AUTHOR
ANY OTHER RELEVANT DETAILS.
DAMN HER ......!!
OOH, AN A●●MAGE.

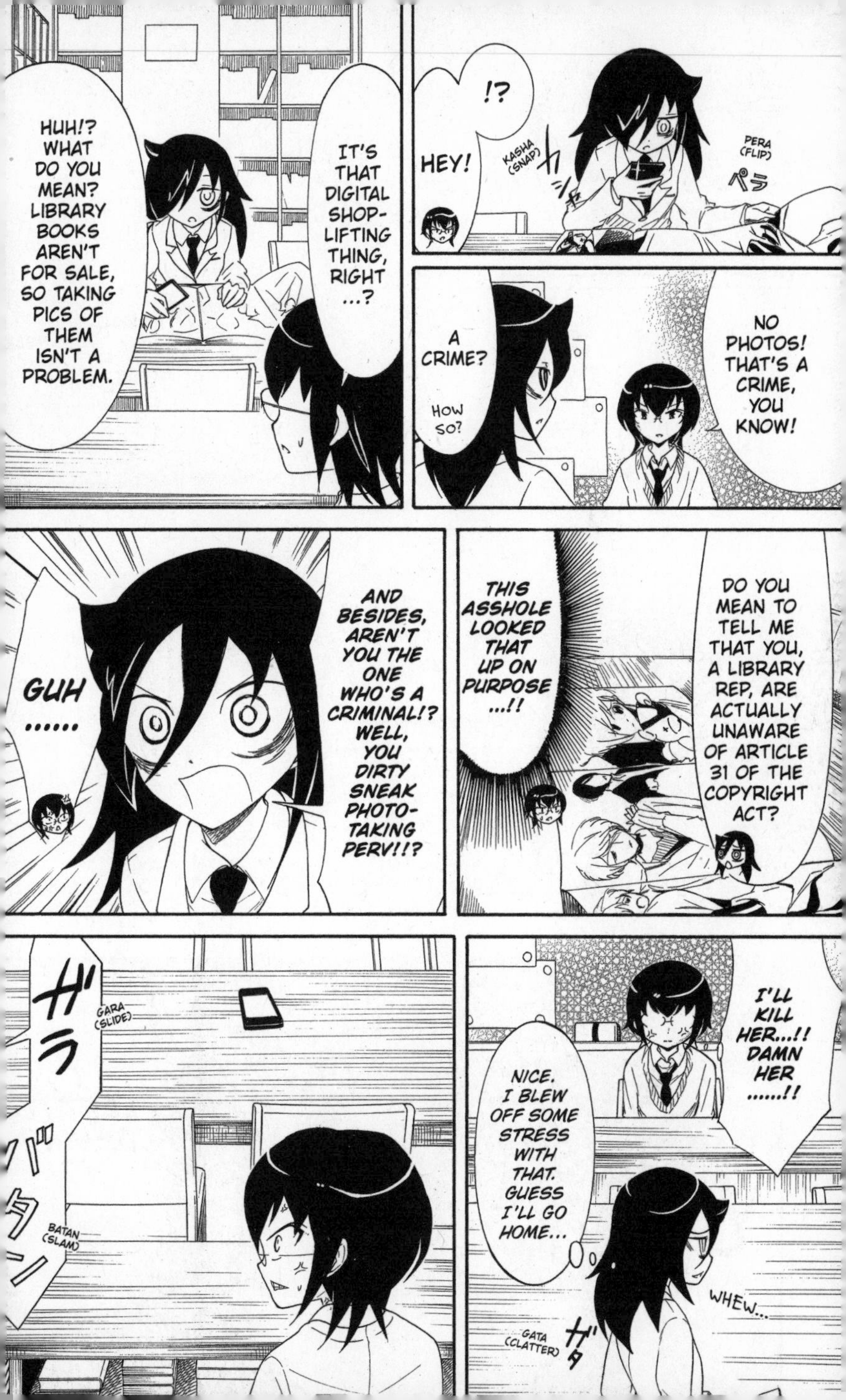
PERA (FLIP)
ペラ
!?
HEY!
KASHA (SNAP)
カシャ
NO PHOTOS! THAT'S A CRIME, YOU KNOW!
A CRIME?
HOW SO?
IT'S THAT DIGITAL SHOP-LIFTING THING, RIGHT ...?
HUH!? WHAT DO YOU MEAN? LIBRARY BOOKS AREN'T FOR SALE, SO TAKING PICS OF THEM ISN'T A PROBLEM.
DO YOU MEAN TO TELL ME THAT YOU, A LIBRARY REP, ARE ACTUALLY UNAWARE OF ARTICLE 31 OF THE COPYRIGHT ACT?
THIS ASSHOLE LOOKED THAT UP ON PURPOSE ...!!
AND BESIDES, AREN'T YOU THE ONE WHO'S A CRIMINAL!? WELL, YOU DIRTY SNEAK PHOTO-TAKING PERV!!?
GUH ......
I'LL KILL HER...!! DAMN HER ......!!
NICE. I BLEW OFF SOME STRESS WITH THAT. GUESS I'LL GO HOME...
WHEW...
GATA (CLATTER)
ガタ
ガラ
GARA (SLIDE)
バタン
BATAN (SLAM)

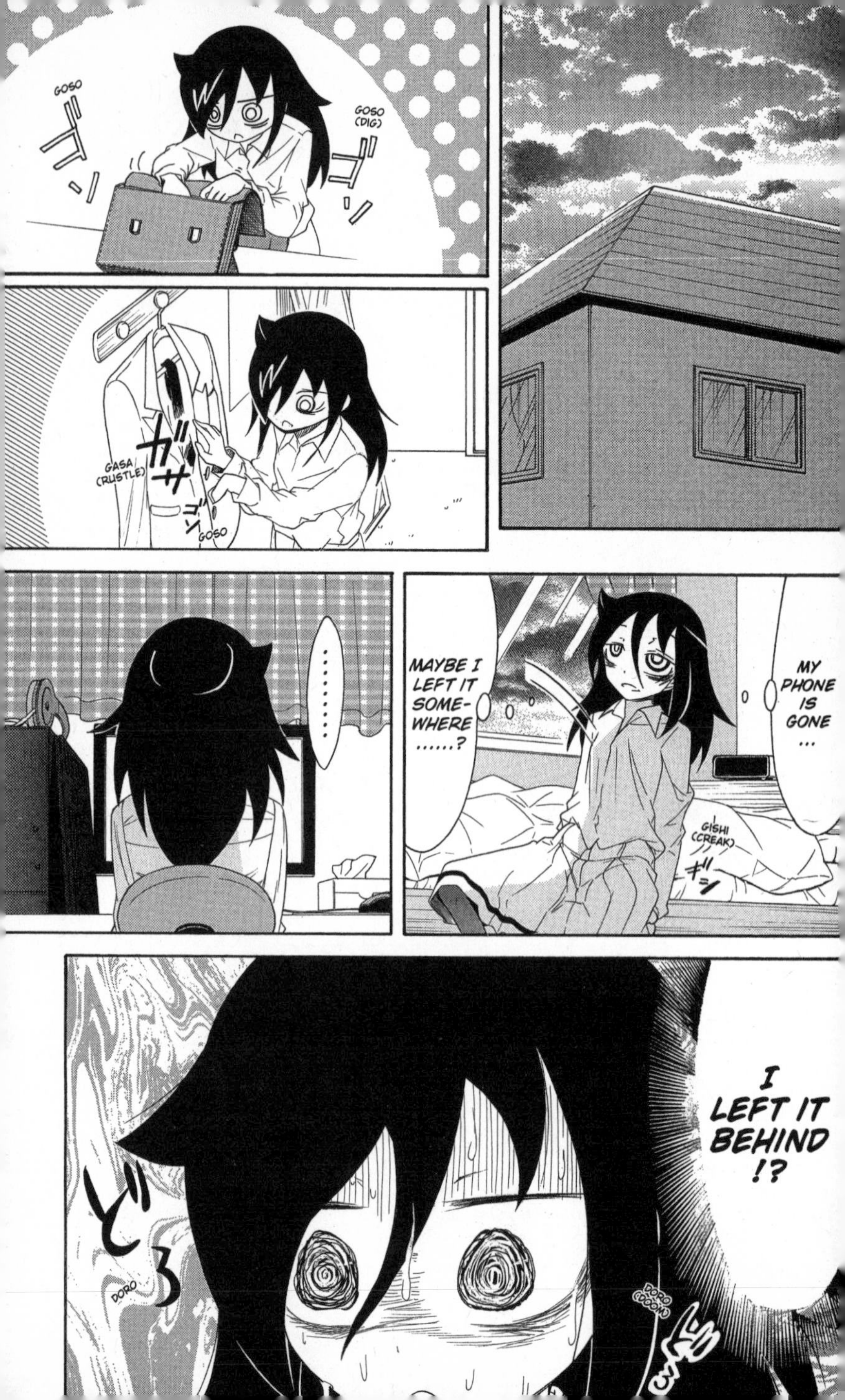
GOSO
GOSO (DIG)
GASA (RUSTLE)
GOSO
MY PHONE IS GONE...
MAYBE I LEFT IT SOME-WHERE......?
GISHI (CREAK)
......
I LEFT IT BEHIND!?
DORO (DOOM)
DORO

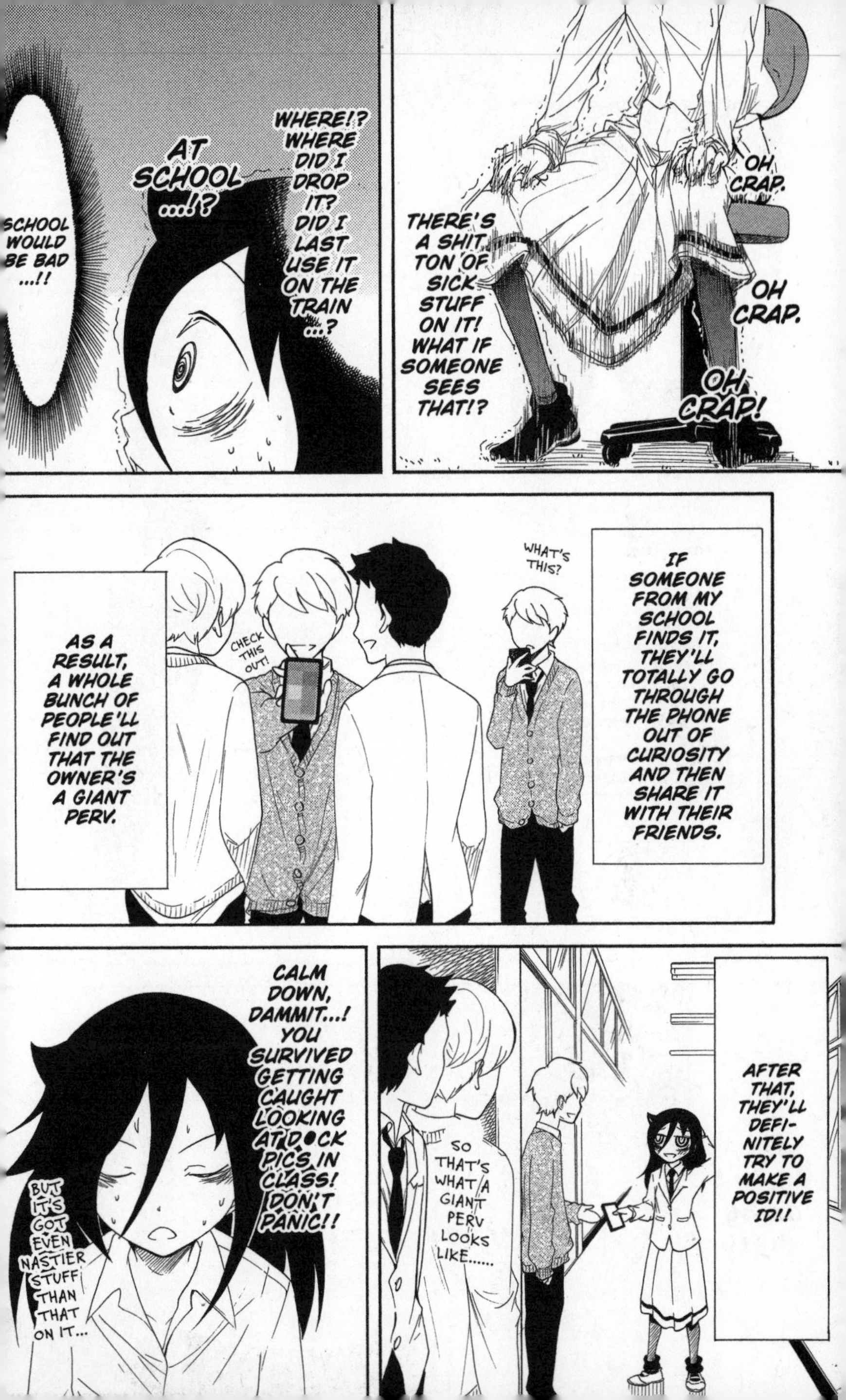
OH CRAP.
THERE'S A SHIT TON OF SICK STUFF ON IT! WHAT IF SOMEONE SEES THAT!?
OH CRAP.
OH CRAP!
WHERE!? WHERE DID I DROP IT? DID I LAST USE IT ON THE TRAIN ...?
AT SCHOOL ...!?
SCHOOL WOULD BE BAD ...!!
IF SOMEONE FROM MY SCHOOL FINDS IT, THEY'LL TOTALLY GO THROUGH THE PHONE OUT OF CURIOSITY AND THEN SHARE IT WITH THEIR FRIENDS.
WHAT'S THIS?
CHECK THIS OUT!
AS A RESULT, A WHOLE BUNCH OF PEOPLE'LL FIND OUT THAT THE OWNER'S A GIANT PERV.
AFTER THAT, THEY'LL DEFI- NITELY TRY TO MAKE A POSITIVE ID!!
SO THAT'S WHAT A GIANT PERV LOOKS LIKE......
CALM DOWN, DAMMIT...! YOU SURVIVED GETTING CAUGHT LOOKING AT DOCK PICS IN CLASS! DON'T PANIC!!
BUT IT'S GOT EVEN NASTIER STUFF THAN THAT ON IT...

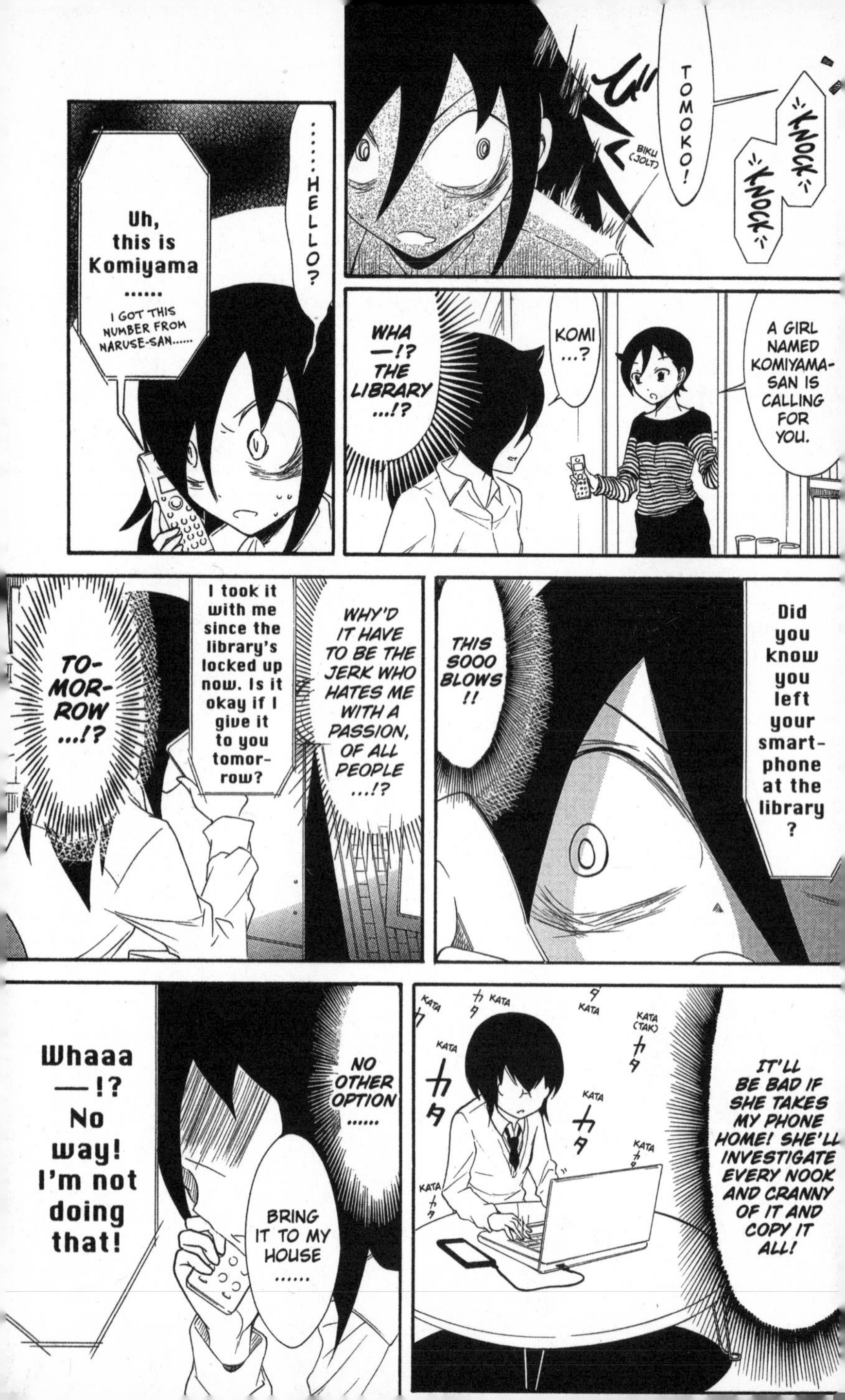

KNOCK
KNOCK
TOMOKO!
BIKU (JOLT)
A GIRL NAMED KOMIYAMA-SAN IS CALLING FOR YOU.
KOMI ...?
WHA—!? THE LIBRARY ...!?
......HELLO?
Uh, this is Komiyama ......
I GOT THIS NUMBER FROM NARUSE-SAN......
Did you know you left your smart-phone at the library?
THIS SOOO BLOWS!!
WHY'D IT HAVE TO BE THE JERK WHO HATES ME WITH A PASSION, OF ALL PEOPLE ...!?
I took it with me since the library's locked up now. Is it okay if I give it to you tomor-row?
TO-MOR-ROW ...!?
KATA KATA KATA KATA (TAK) KATA KATA KATA KATA
IT'LL BE BAD IF SHE TAKES MY PHONE HOME! SHE'LL INVESTIGATE EVERY NOOK AND CRANNY OF IT AND COPY IT ALL!
NO OTHER OPTION ......
BRING IT TO MY HOUSE ......
Whaaa—!? No way! I'm not doing that!

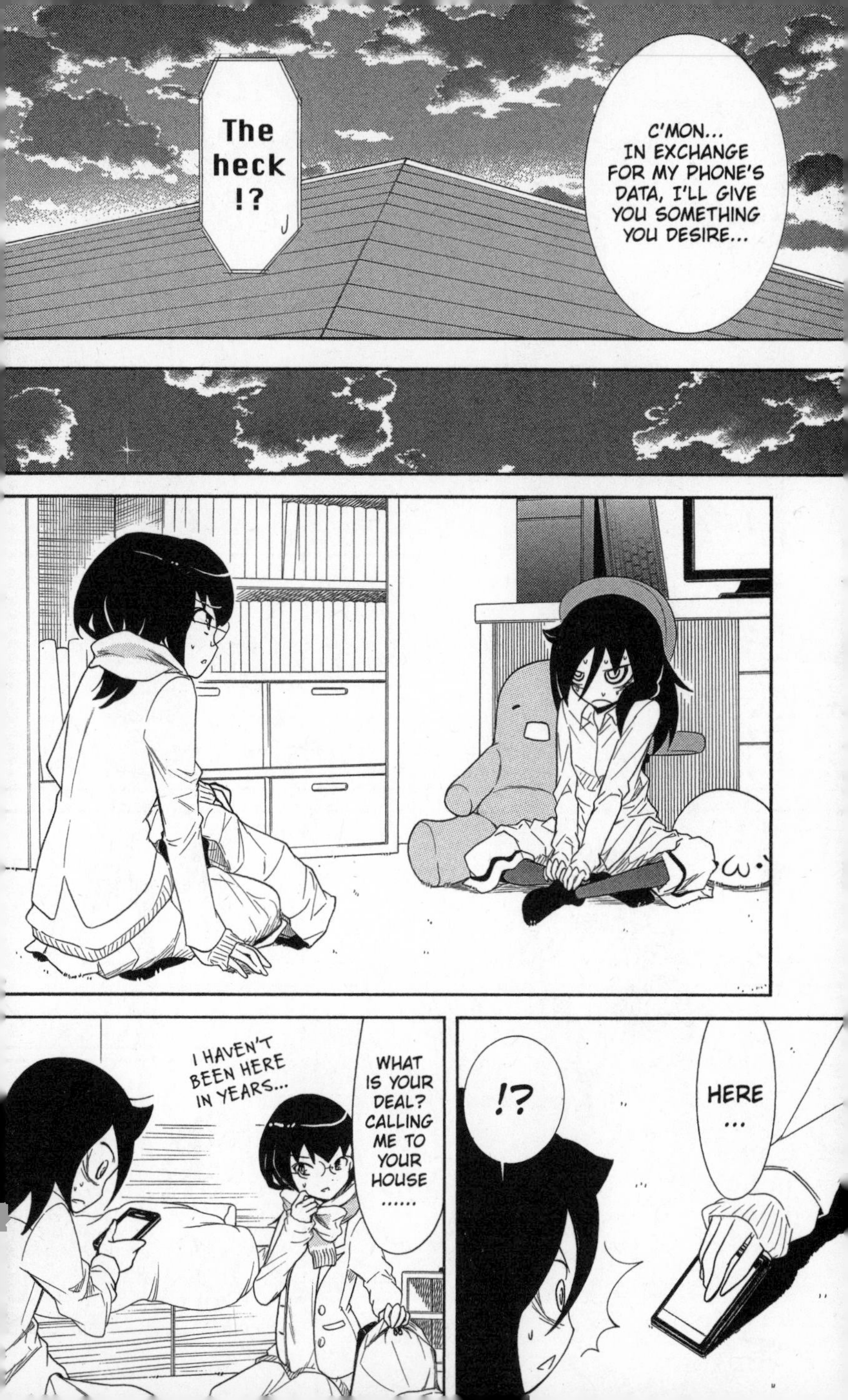
C'MON... IN EXCHANGE FOR MY PHONE'S DATA, I'LL GIVE YOU SOMETHING YOU DESIRE...
The heck !?
HERE ...
!?
WHAT IS YOUR DEAL? CALLING ME TO YOUR HOUSE ......
I HAVEN'T BEEN HERE IN YEARS...

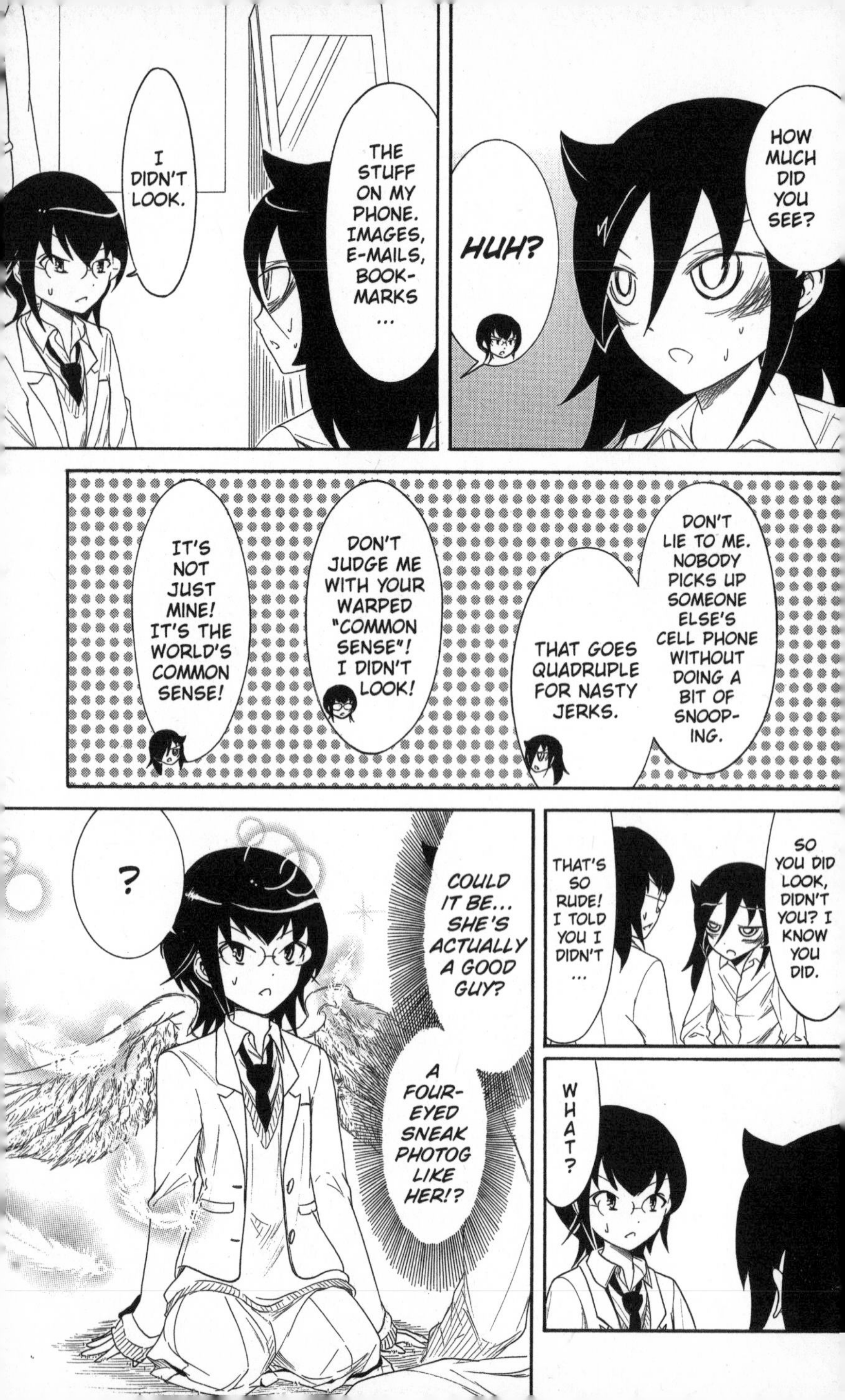
HOW MUCH DID YOU SEE?
HUH?
THE STUFF ON MY PHONE. IMAGES, E-MAILS, BOOKMARKS...
I DIDN'T LOOK.
DON'T LIE TO ME. NOBODY PICKS UP SOMEONE ELSE'S CELL PHONE WITHOUT DOING A BIT OF SNOOPING.
THAT GOES QUADRUPLE FOR NASTY JERKS.
DON'T JUDGE ME WITH YOUR WARPED "COMMON SENSE"! I DIDN'T LOOK!
IT'S NOT JUST MINE! IT'S THE WORLD'S COMMON SENSE!
SO YOU DID LOOK, DIDN'T YOU? I KNOW YOU DID.
THAT'S SO RUDE! I TOLD YOU I DIDN'T...
WHAT?
COULD IT BE... SHE'S ACTUALLY A GOOD GUY?
A FOUR-EYED SNEAK PHOTOG LIKE HER!?
?

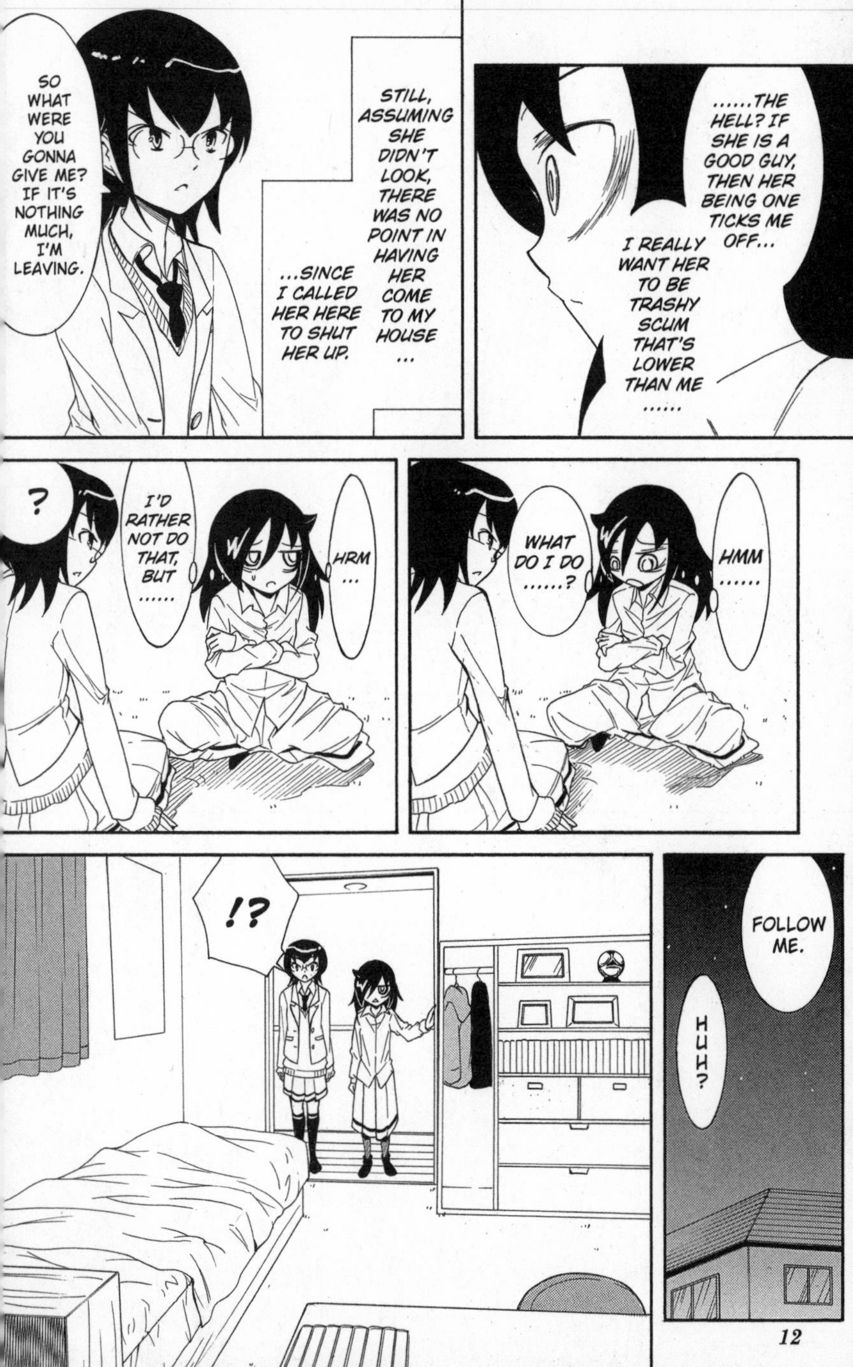

......THE HELL? IF SHE IS A GOOD GUY, THEN HER BEING ONE TICKS ME OFF...
I REALLY WANT HER TO BE TRASHY SCUM THAT'S LOWER THAN ME ......
STILL, ASSUMING SHE DIDN'T LOOK, THERE WAS NO POINT IN HAVING HER COME TO MY HOUSE ...
...SINCE I CALLED HER HERE TO SHUT HER UP.
SO WHAT WERE YOU GONNA GIVE ME? IF IT'S NOTHING MUCH, I'M LEAVING.
HMM ......
WHAT DO I DO ......?
HRM ...
I'D RATHER NOT DO THAT, BUT ......
?
FOLLOW ME.
HUH?
!?

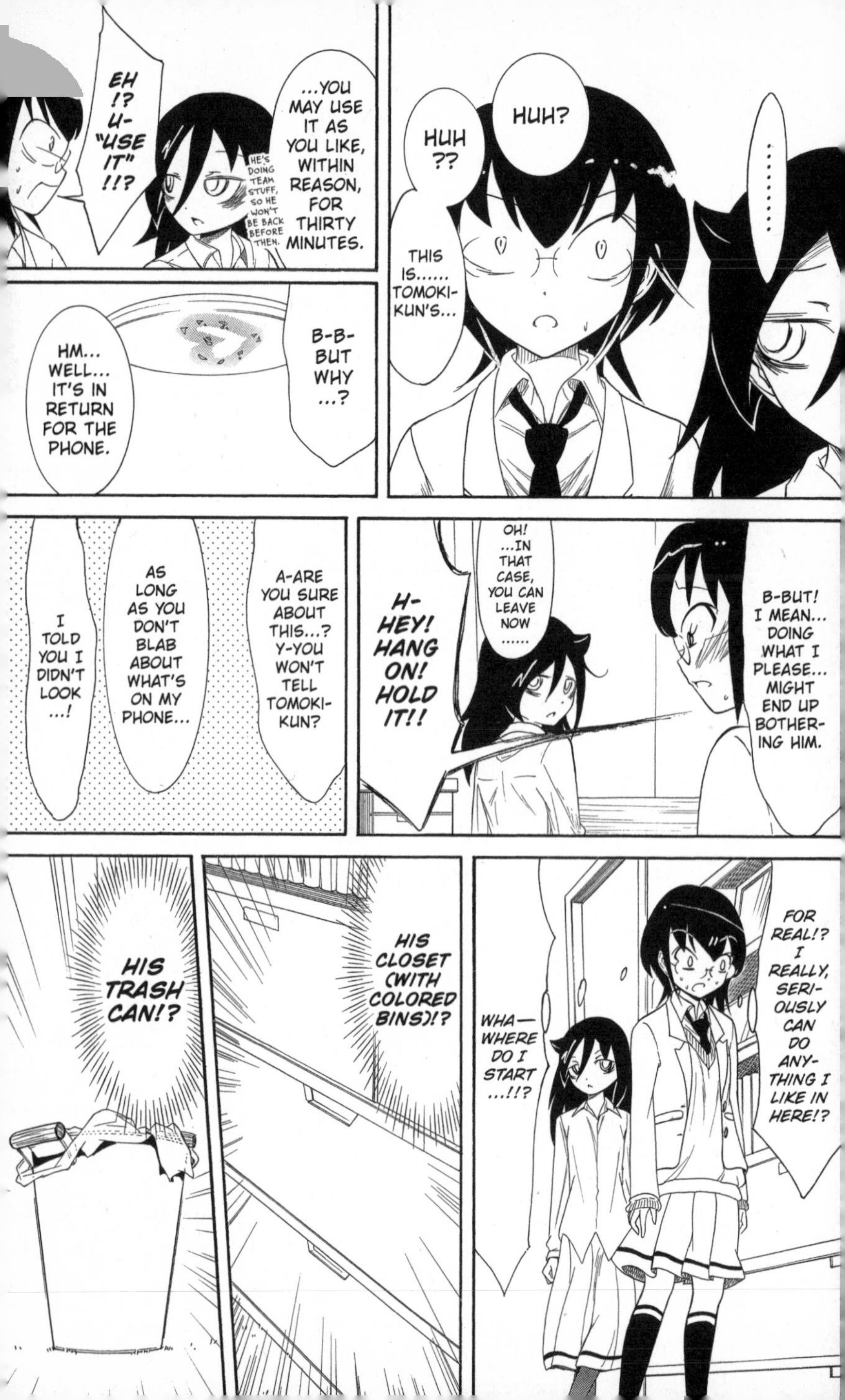

......
HUH?
HUH ??
THIS IS...... TOMOKI-KUN'S...
...YOU MAY USE IT AS YOU LIKE, WITHIN REASON, FOR THIRTY MINUTES.
HE'S DOING TEAM STUFF, SO HE WON'T BE BACK BEFORE THEN.
EH !? U- "USE IT" !!?
B-B-BUT WHY ...?
HM... WELL... IT'S IN RETURN FOR THE PHONE.
B-BUT! I MEAN... DOING WHAT I PLEASE... MIGHT END UP BOTHERING HIM.
OH! ...IN THAT CASE, YOU CAN LEAVE NOW ......
H-HEY! HANG ON! HOLD IT!!
A-ARE YOU SURE ABOUT THIS...? Y-YOU WON'T TELL TOMOKI-KUN?
AS LONG AS YOU DON'T BLAB ABOUT WHAT'S ON MY PHONE...
I TOLD YOU I DIDN'T LOOK ...!
FOR REAL!? I REALLY, SERIOUSLY CAN DO ANYTHING I LIKE IN HERE!?
WHA— WHERE DO I START ...!!?
HIS CLOSET (WITH COLORED BINS)!?
HIS TRASH CAN!?

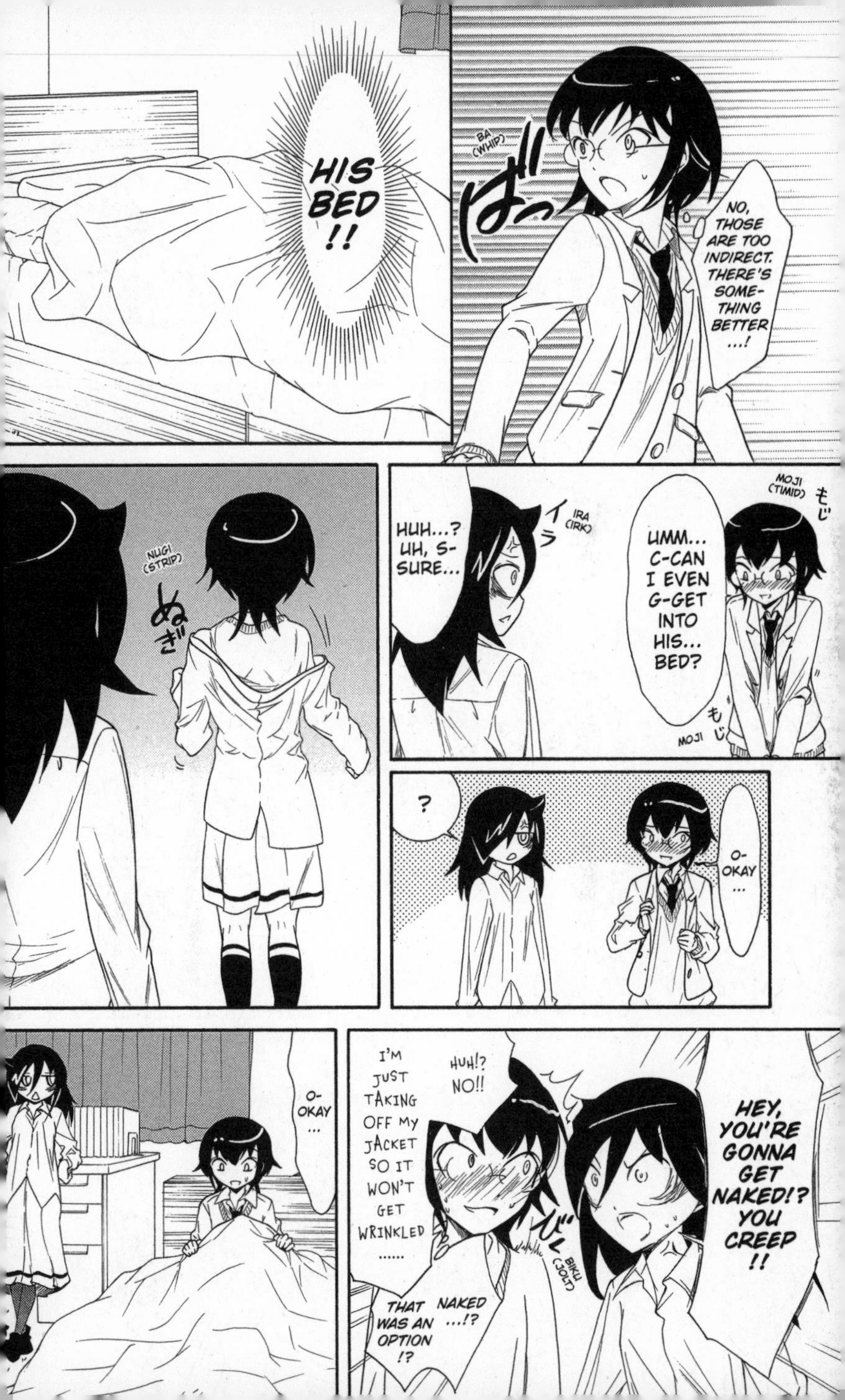

BA (WHIP)
ばっ
NO, THOSE ARE TOO INDIRECT. THERE'S SOME-THING BETTER ...!
HIS BED!!
MOJI (TIMID) もじ
UMM... C-CAN I EVEN G-GET INTO HIS... BED?
IRA (IRK) イラ
HUH...? UH, S-SURE...
もじ MOJI
O-OKAY ...
?
NUGI (STRIP) ぬぎ
HEY, YOU'RE GONNA GET NAKED!? YOU CREEP!!
HUH!? NO!!
I'M JUST TAKING OFF MY JACKET SO IT WON'T GET WRINKLED ......
びくっ BIKU (JOLT)
NAKED ...!?
THAT WAS AN OPTION!?
O-OKAY ...

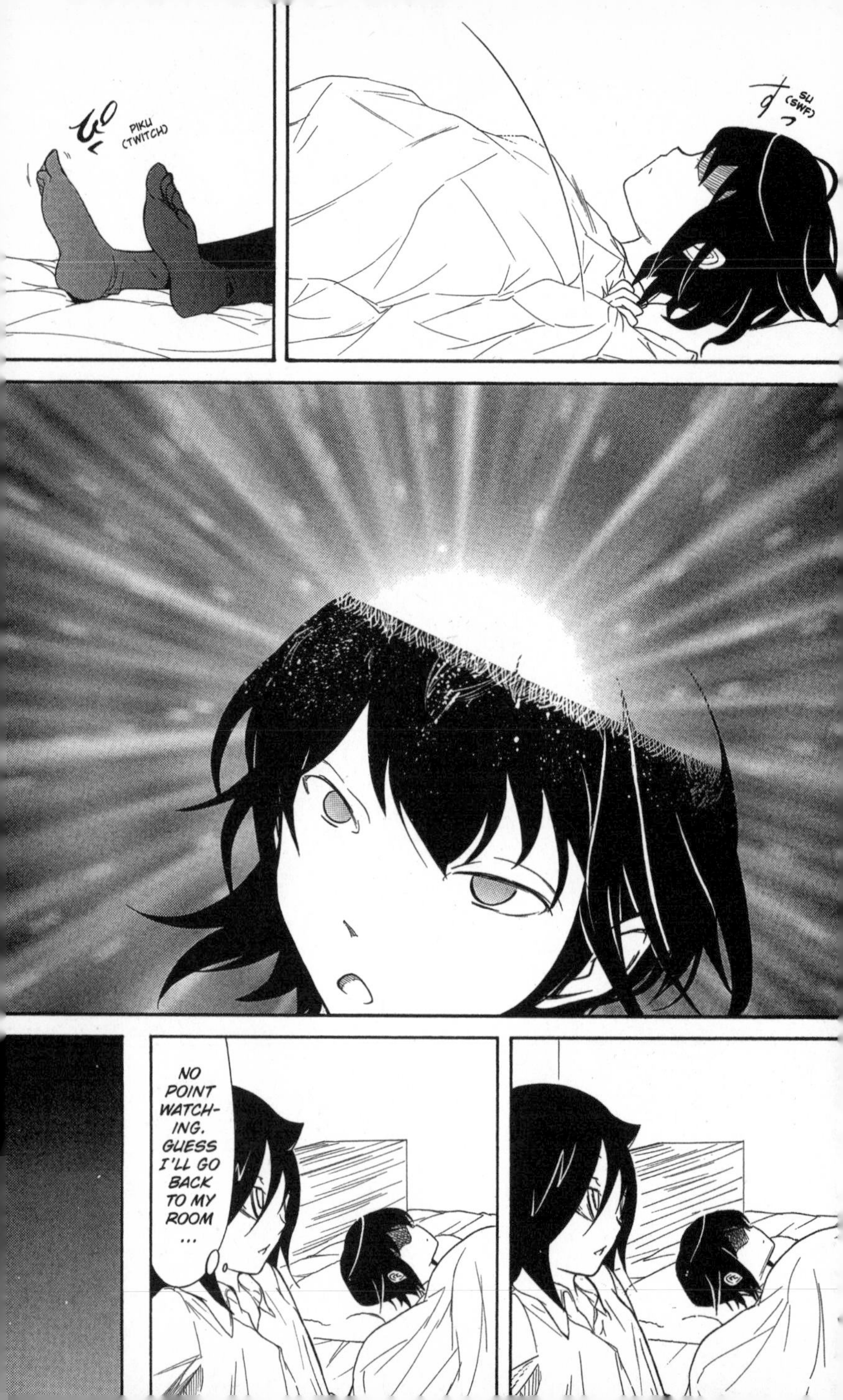
SU (SWF)
PIKU (TWITCH)
NO POINT WATCHING. GUESS I'LL GO BACK TO MY ROOM ...

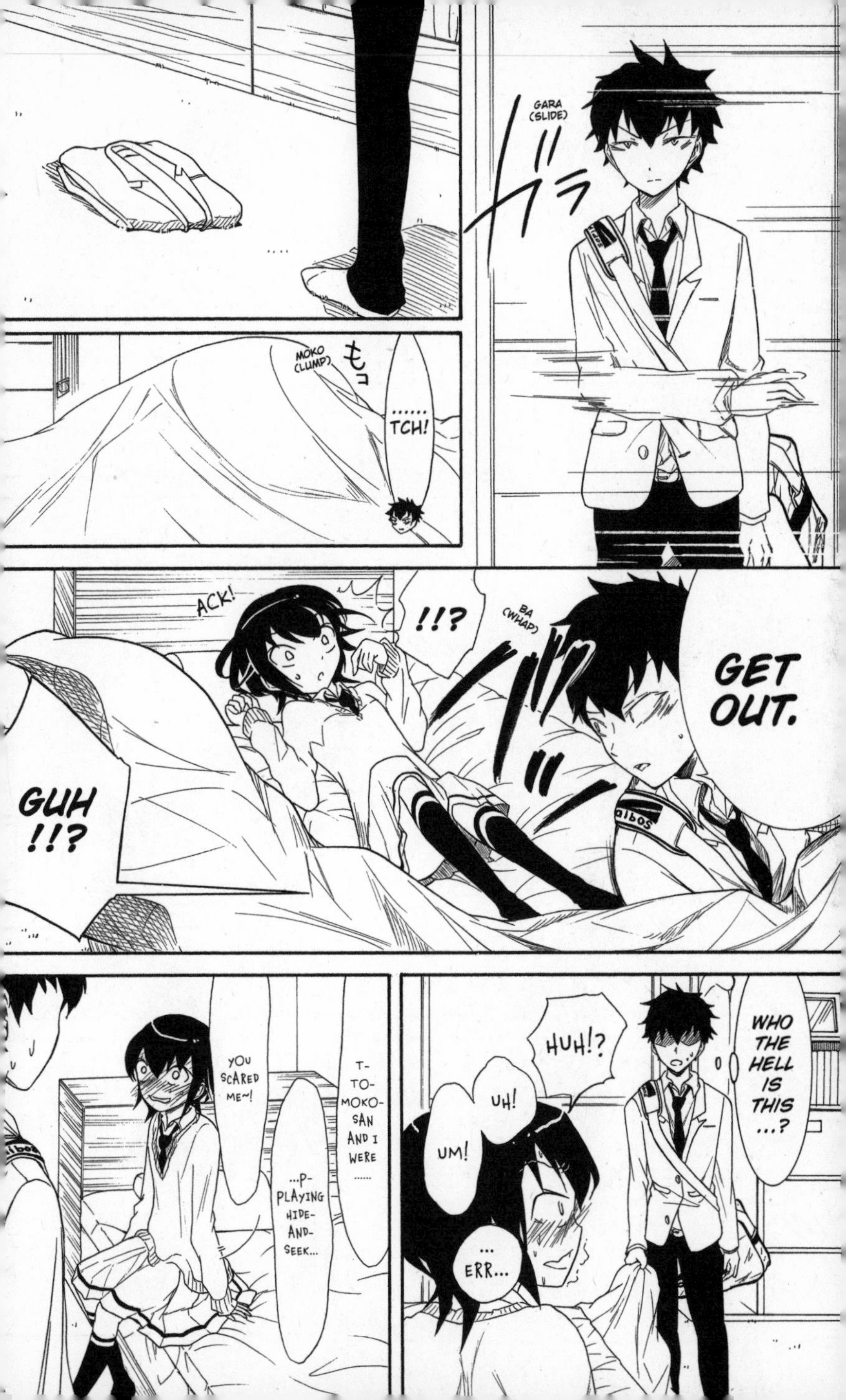
GARA (SLIDE)
MOKO (CLUMP)
......TCH!
GET OUT.
BA (WHAP)
!!?
ACK!
GUH !!?
WHO THE HELL IS THIS ...?
HUH!?
UH!
UM!
... ERR...
T-TO-MOKO-SAN AND I WERE ......
...P-PLAYING HIDE-AND-SEEK...
YOU SCARED ME~!

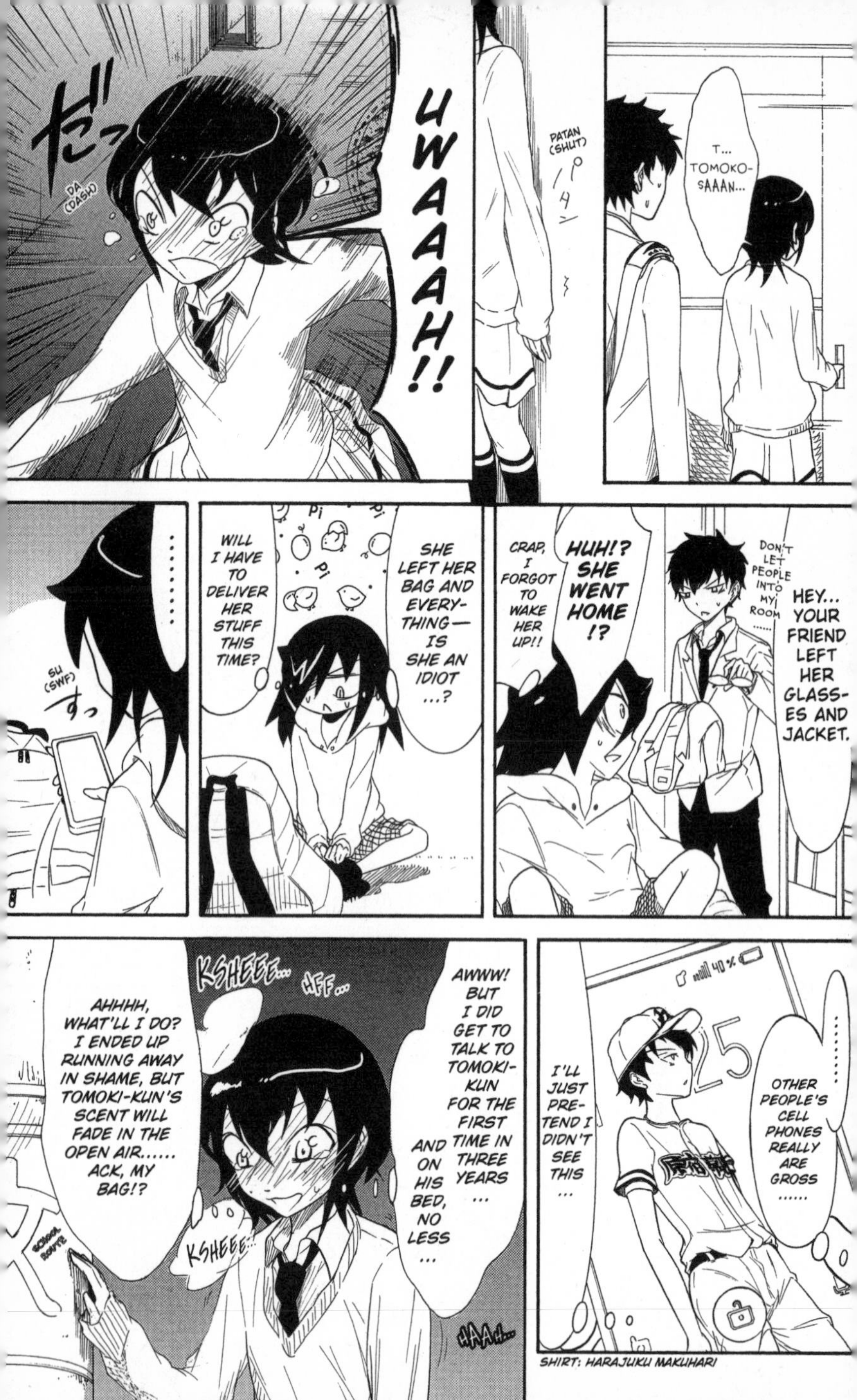
T... TOMOKO-SAAAN...
PATAN (SHUT)
UWAAAAH!!
DA (DASH)
HEY... YOUR FRIEND LEFT HER GLASSES AND JACKET.
DON'T LET PEOPLE INTO MY ROOM ......
HUH!? SHE WENT HOME!?
CRAP, I FORGOT TO WAKE HER UP!!
SHE LEFT HER BAG AND EVERYTHING— IS SHE AN IDIOT ...?
WILL I HAVE TO DELIVER HER STUFF THIS TIME?
Pi
Pi
Pi
......
SU (SWF)
......
OTHER PEOPLE'S CELL PHONES REALLY ARE GROSS ......
40%
25
I'LL JUST PRETEND I DIDN'T SEE THIS ...
AWWW! BUT I DID GET TO TALK TO TOMOKI-KUN FOR THE FIRST TIME IN THREE YEARS ...
AND ON HIS BED, NO LESS ...
KSHEEE... HFF...
AHHHH, WHAT'LL I DO? I ENDED UP RUNNING AWAY IN SHAME, BUT TOMOKI-KUN'S SCENT WILL FADE IN THE OPEN AIR...... ACK, MY BAG!?
KSHEEE...
HAAH...
SCHOOL ROUTE

SHIRT: HARAJUKU MAKUHARI

No Matter How I Look at It, It's You Guys' Fault I'm Not Popular!

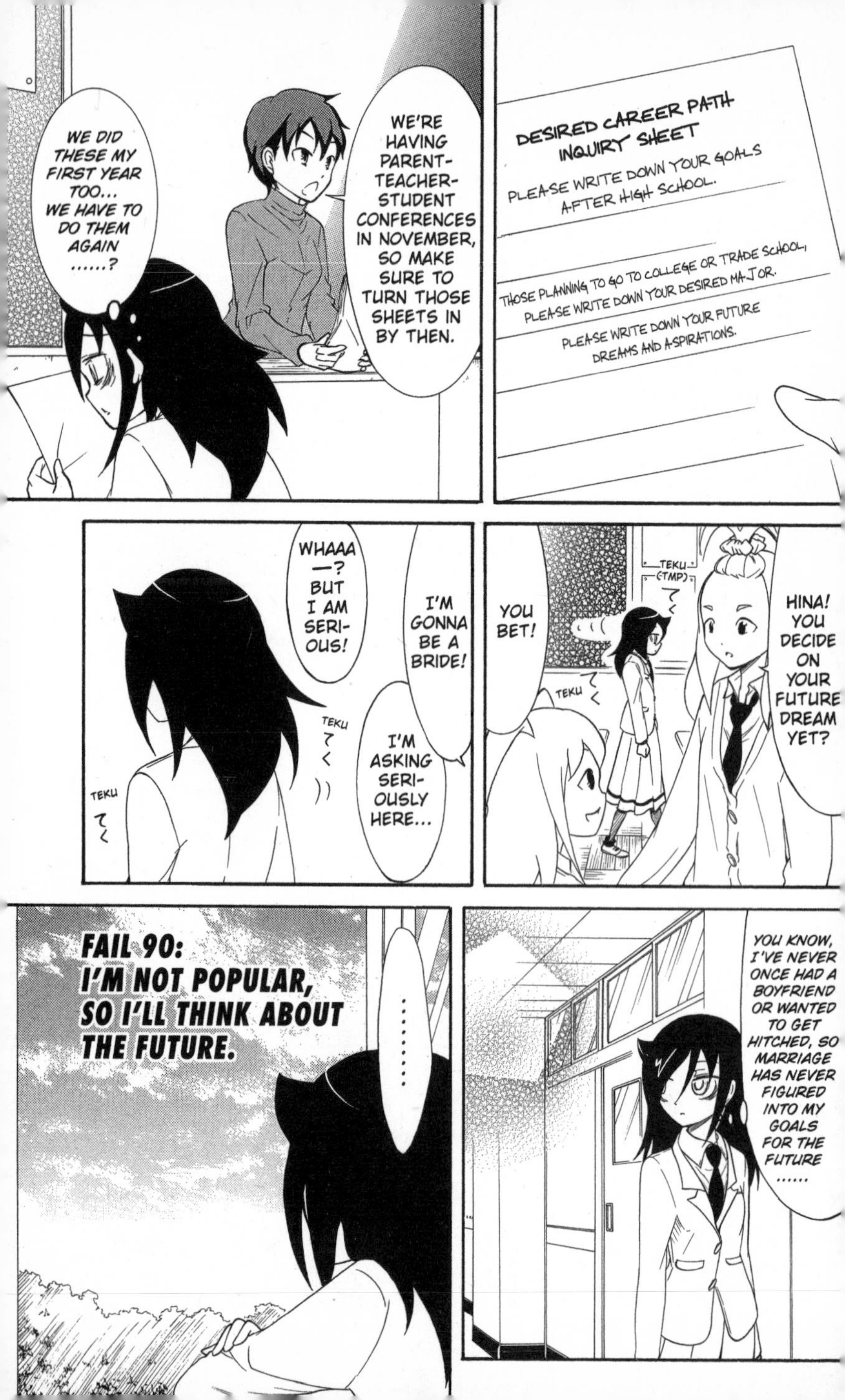
DESIRED CAREER PATH INQUIRY SHEET
PLEASE WRITE DOWN YOUR GOALS AFTER HIGH SCHOOL.
THOSE PLANNING TO GO TO COLLEGE OR TRADE SCHOOL, PLEASE WRITE DOWN YOUR DESIRED MAJOR.
PLEASE WRITE DOWN YOUR FUTURE DREAMS AND ASPIRATIONS.
WE'RE HAVING PARENT-TEACHER-STUDENT CONFERENCES IN NOVEMBER, SO MAKE SURE TO TURN THOSE SHEETS IN BY THEN.
WE DID THESE MY FIRST YEAR TOO... WE HAVE TO DO THEM AGAIN ......?
HINA! YOU DECIDE ON YOUR FUTURE DREAM YET?
YOU BET!
TEKU (TMP)
TEKU
I'M GONNA BE A BRIDE!
I'M ASKING SERIOUSLY HERE...
WHAAA—? BUT I AM SERI-OUS!
TEKU
TEKU
YOU KNOW, I'VE NEVER ONCE HAD A BOYFRIEND OR WANTED TO GET HITCHED, SO MARRIAGE HAS NEVER FIGURED INTO MY GOALS FOR THE FUTURE ......
....
FAIL 90: I'M NOT POPULAR, SO I'LL THINK ABOUT THE FUTURE.

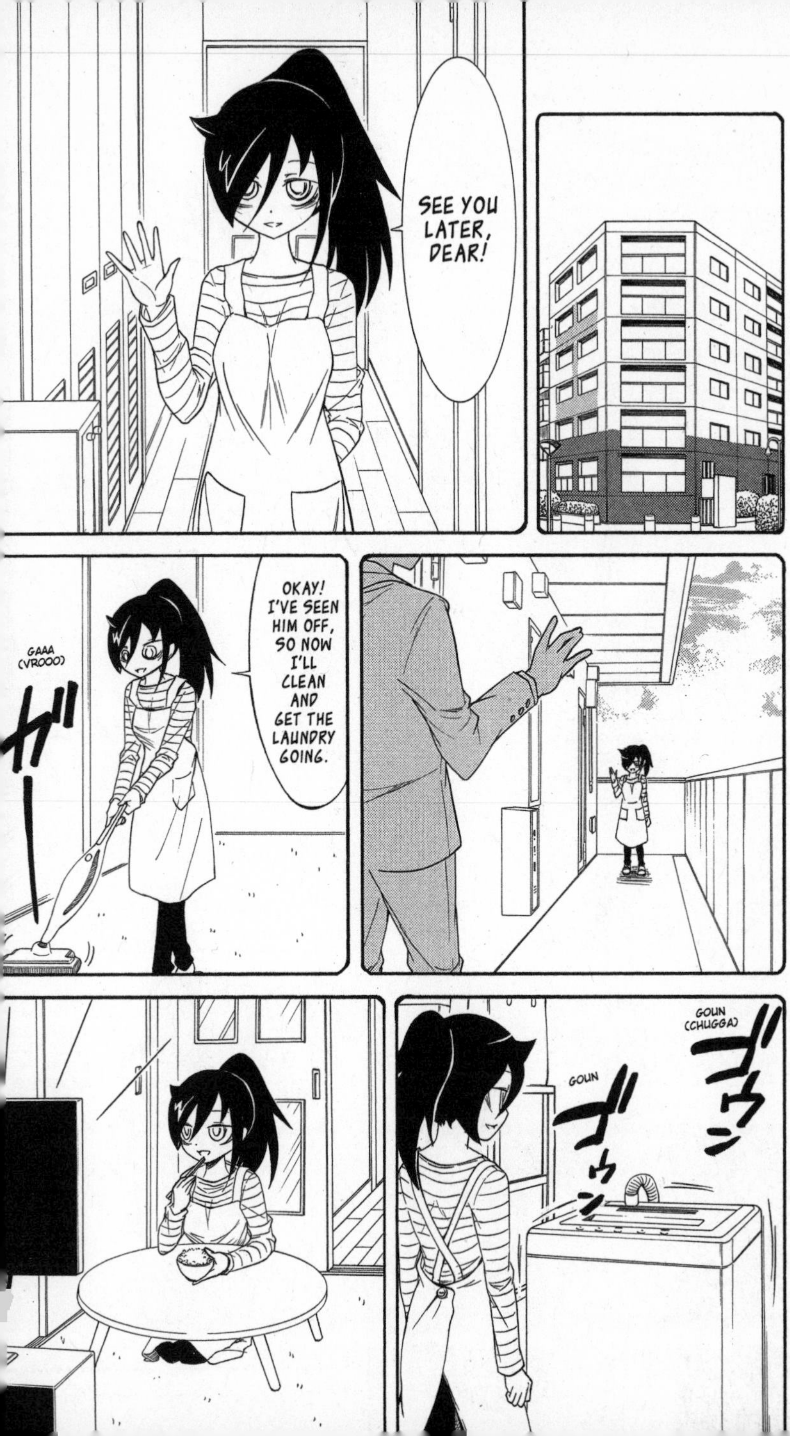
SEE YOU LATER, DEAR!
OKAY! I'VE SEEN HIM OFF, SO NOW I'LL CLEAN AND GET THE LAUNDRY GOING.
GAAA (VROOO)
ガー
GOUN (CHUGGA)
ゴウン
GOUN
ゴウン

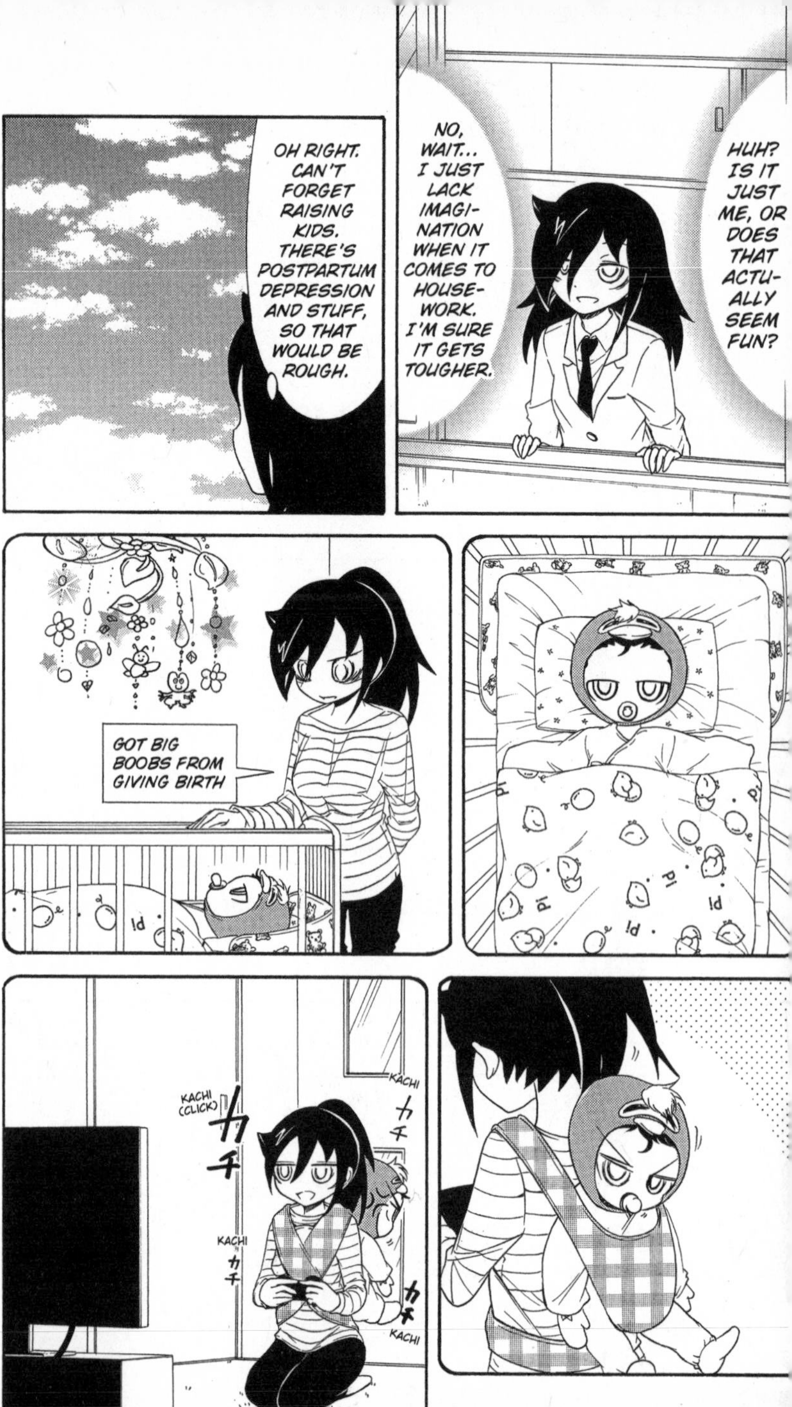
HUH? IS IT JUST ME, OR DOES THAT ACTUALLY SEEM FUN?
NO, WAIT... I JUST LACK IMAGINATION WHEN IT COMES TO HOUSEWORK. I'M SURE IT GETS TOUGHER.
OH RIGHT. CAN'T FORGET RAISING KIDS. THERE'S POSTPARTUM DEPRESSION AND STUFF, SO THAT WOULD BE ROUGH.
GOT BIG BOOBS FROM GIVING BIRTH
KACHI
KACHI (CLICK)
KACHI
KACHI

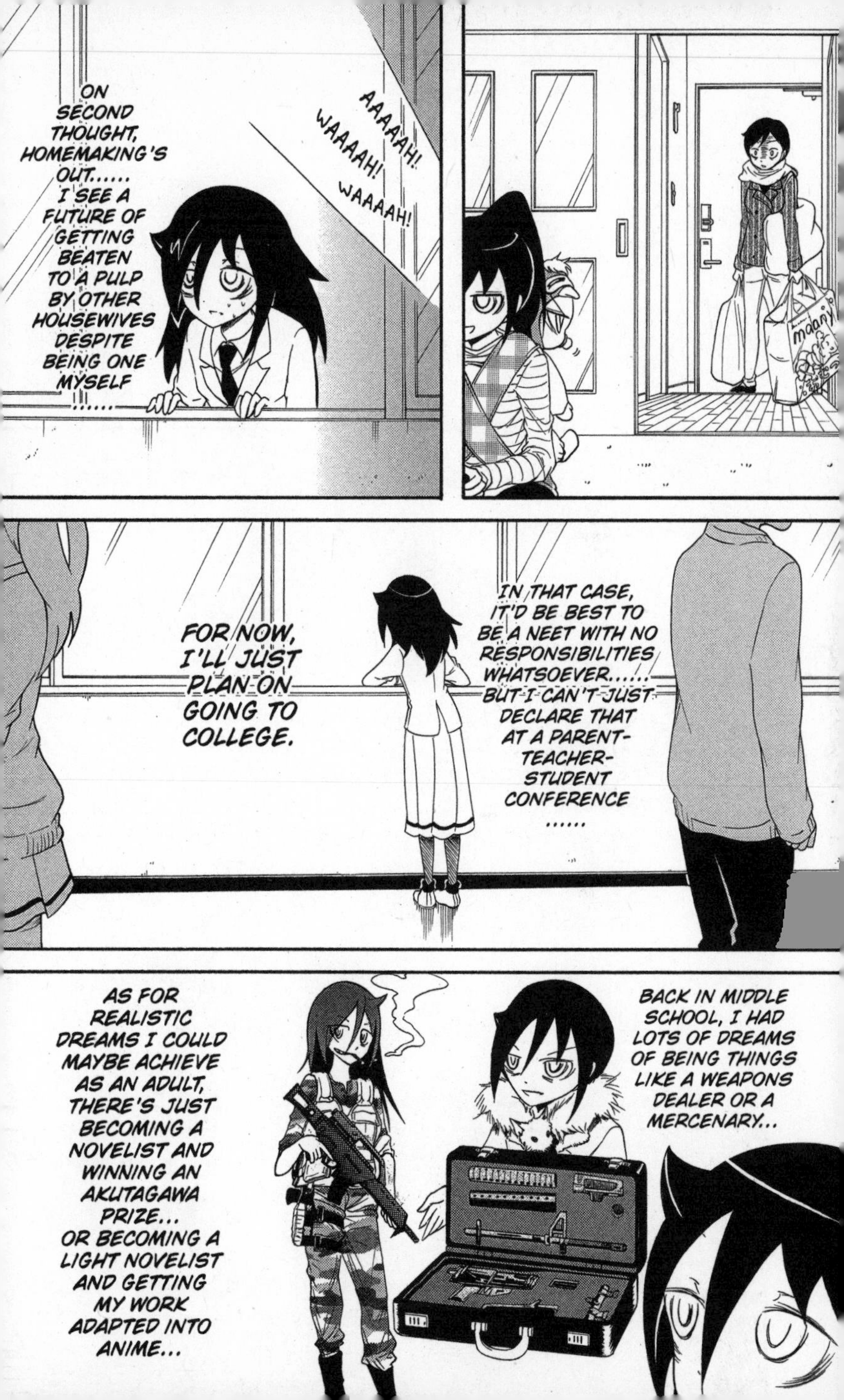
AAAAAH!
WAAAAAH!
WAAAAAH!
ON SECOND THOUGHT, HOMEMAKING'S OUT...... I SEE A FUTURE OF GETTING BEATEN TO A PULP BY OTHER HOUSEWIVES DESPITE BEING ONE MYSELF ......
IN THAT CASE, IT'D BE BEST TO BE A NEET WITH NO RESPONSIBILITIES WHATSOEVER...... BUT I CAN'T JUST DECLARE THAT AT A PARENT-TEACHER-STUDENT CONFERENCE ......
FOR NOW, I'LL JUST PLAN ON GOING TO COLLEGE.
BACK IN MIDDLE SCHOOL, I HAD LOTS OF DREAMS OF BEING THINGS LIKE A WEAPONS DEALER OR A MERCENARY...
AS FOR REALISTIC DREAMS I COULD MAYBE ACHIEVE AS AN ADULT, THERE'S JUST BECOMING A NOVELIST AND WINNING AN AKUTAGAWA PRIZE... OR BECOMING A LIGHT NOVELIST AND GETTING MY WORK ADAPTED INTO ANIME...

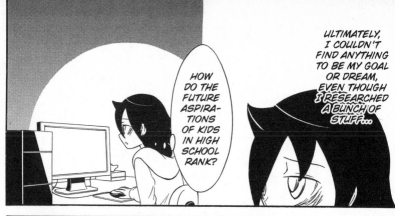

ULTIMATELY, I COULDN'T FIND ANYTHING TO BE MY GOAL OR DREAM, EVEN THOUGH I RESEARCHED A BUNCH OF STUFF...

HOW DO THE FUTURE ASPIRATIONS OF KIDS IN HIGH SCHOOL RANK?

WOW...... I DON'T WANNA DO ANY OF THOSE ...!!

1	Teacher
2	Civil servant
3	Preschool or kindergarten teacher
4	Pharmacist
5	Doctor

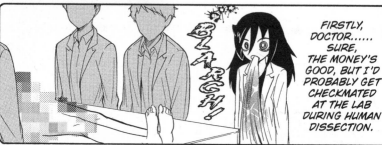

FIRSTLY, DOCTOR...... SURE, THE MONEY'S GOOD, BUT I'D PROBABLY GET CHECKMATED AT THE LAB DURING HUMAN DISSECTION.

BLARGH!

SIGN: TOMOKO-SENSEI

SIGN: HAMADA KIYOSHI / KUROKI

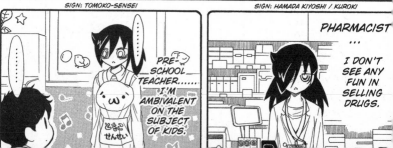

PRE-SCHOOL TEACHER...... I'M AMBIVALENT ON THE SUBJECT OF KIDS.

PHARMACIST ...

I DON'T SEE ANY FUN IN SELLING DRUGS.

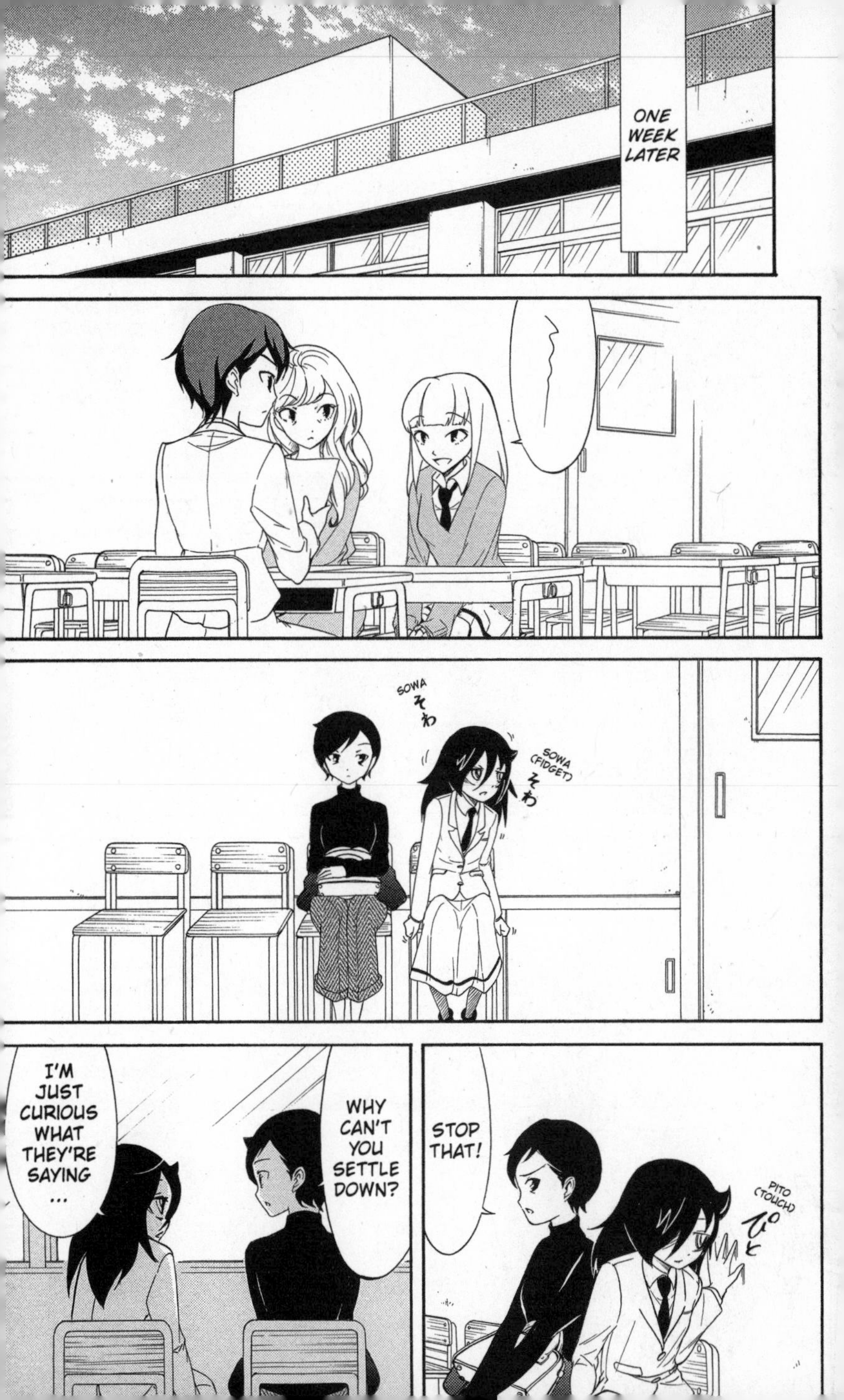
ONE WEEK LATER
SOWA (FIDGET)
そわ
SOWA
そわ
PITO (TOUCH)
ぴと
STOP THAT!
WHY CAN'T YOU SETTLE DOWN?
I'M JUST CURIOUS WHAT THEY'RE SAYING ...

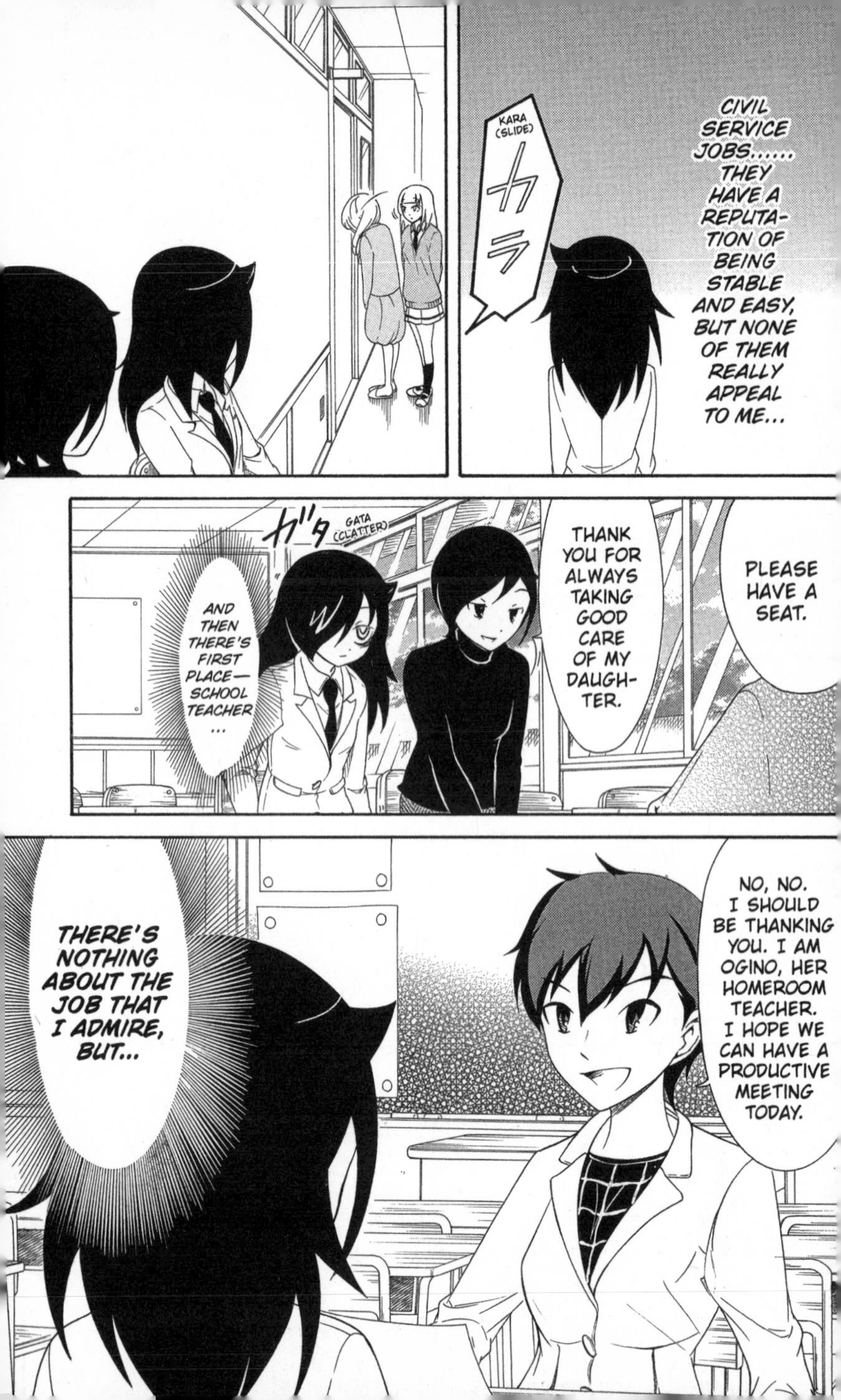
CIVIL SERVICE JOBS...... THEY HAVE A REPUTATION OF BEING STABLE AND EASY, BUT NONE OF THEM REALLY APPEAL TO ME...
カラ
KARA (SLIDE)
PLEASE HAVE A SEAT.
THANK YOU FOR ALWAYS TAKING GOOD CARE OF MY DAUGHTER.
ガタ
GATA (CLATTER)
AND THEN THERE'S FIRST PLACE—SCHOOL TEACHER...
NO, NO. I SHOULD BE THANKING YOU. I AM OGINO, HER HOMEROOM TEACHER. I HOPE WE CAN HAVE A PRODUCTIVE MEETING TODAY.
THERE'S NOTHING ABOUT THE JOB THAT I ADMIRE, BUT...

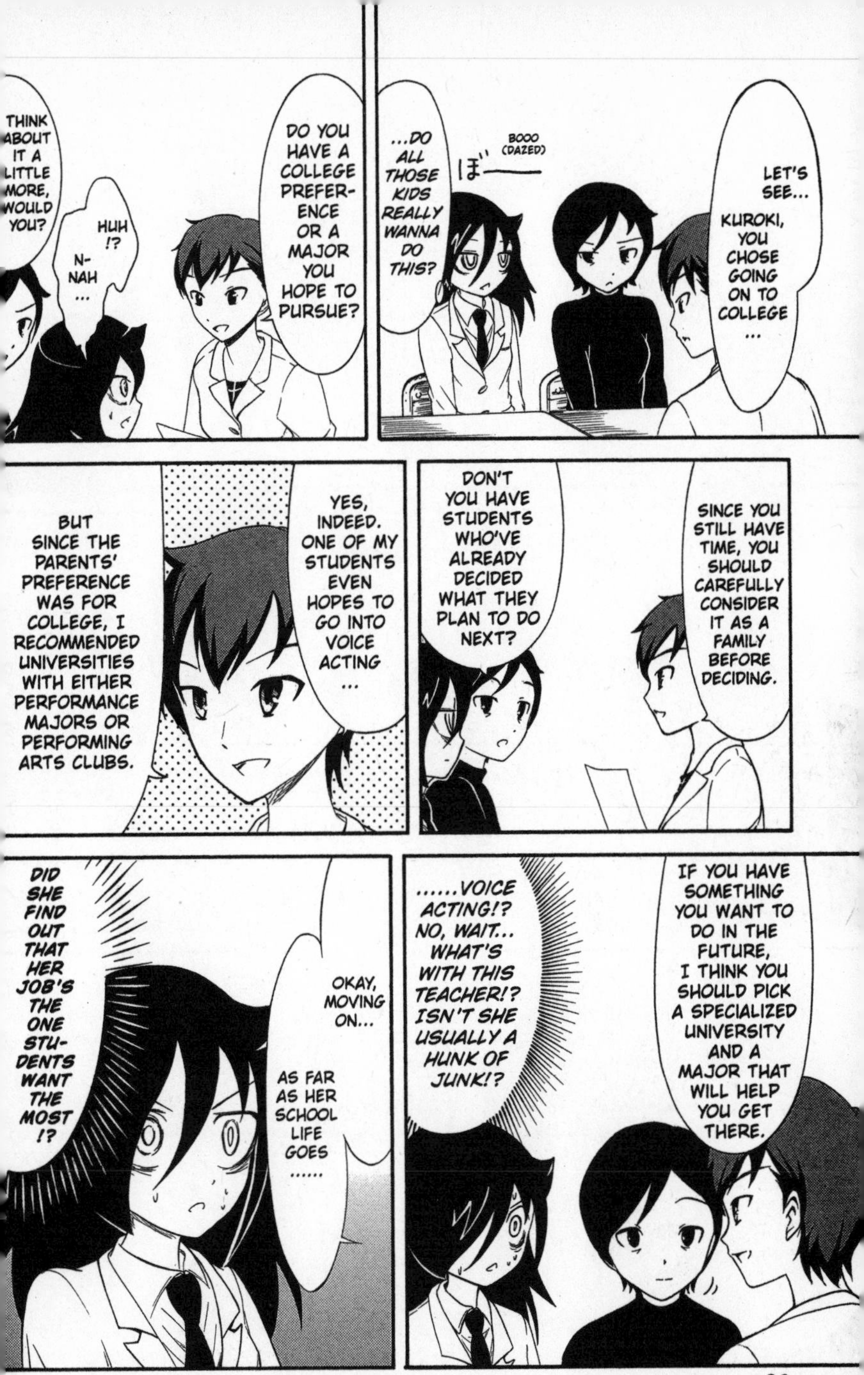
LET'S SEE... KUROKI, YOU CHOSE GOING ON TO COLLEGE...
ぼーー BOOO (DAZED)
...DO ALL THOSE KIDS REALLY WANNA DO THIS?
DO YOU HAVE A COLLEGE PREFER-ENCE OR A MAJOR YOU HOPE TO PURSUE?
HUH!? N-NAH...
THINK ABOUT IT A LITTLE MORE, WOULD YOU?
SINCE YOU STILL HAVE TIME, YOU SHOULD CAREFULLY CONSIDER IT AS A FAMILY BEFORE DECIDING.
DON'T YOU HAVE STUDENTS WHO'VE ALREADY DECIDED WHAT THEY PLAN TO DO NEXT?
YES, INDEED. ONE OF MY STUDENTS EVEN HOPES TO GO INTO VOICE ACTING...
BUT SINCE THE PARENTS' PREFERENCE WAS FOR COLLEGE, I RECOMMENDED UNIVERSITIES WITH EITHER PERFORMANCE MAJORS OR PERFORMING ARTS CLUBS.
IF YOU HAVE SOMETHING YOU WANT TO DO IN THE FUTURE, I THINK YOU SHOULD PICK A SPECIALIZED UNIVERSITY AND A MAJOR THAT WILL HELP YOU GET THERE.
......VOICE ACTING!? NO, WAIT... WHAT'S WITH THIS TEACHER!? ISN'T SHE USUALLY A HUNK OF JUNK!?
OKAY, MOVING ON...
AS FAR AS HER SCHOOL LIFE GOES......
DID SHE FIND OUT THAT HER JOB'S THE ONE STU-DENTS WANT THE MOST!?

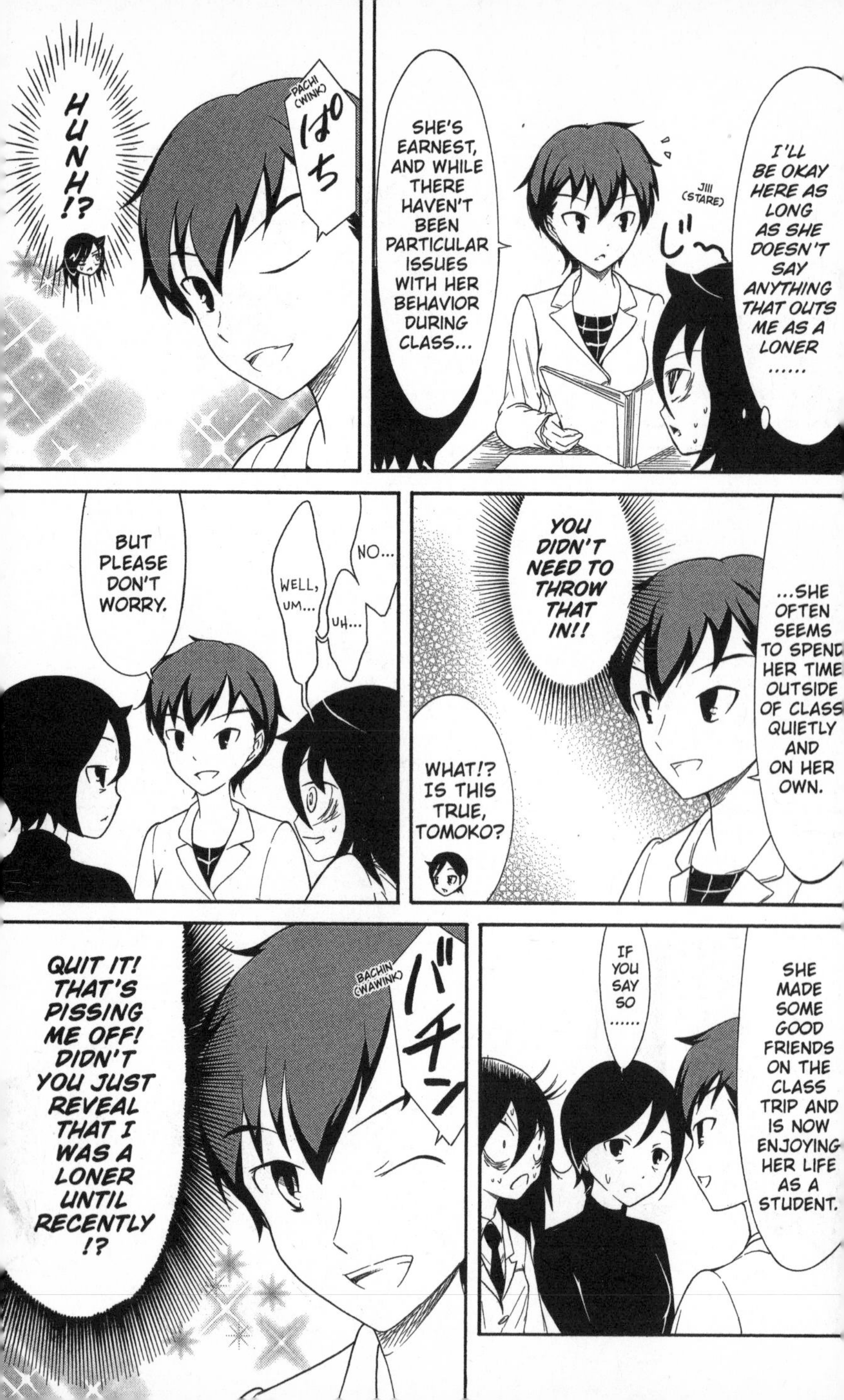
I'LL BE OKAY HERE AS LONG AS SHE DOESN'T SAY ANYTHING THAT OUTS ME AS A LONER ......
JIII (STARE)
じ〜
SHE'S EARNEST, AND WHILE THERE HAVEN'T BEEN PARTICULAR ISSUES WITH HER BEHAVIOR DURING CLASS...
PACHI (WINK)
ぱち
HUNH!?
...SHE OFTEN SEEMS TO SPEND HER TIME OUTSIDE OF CLASS QUIETLY AND ON HER OWN.
YOU DIDN'T NEED TO THROW THAT IN!!
WHAT!? IS THIS TRUE, TOMOKO?
NO...
UH...
WELL, UM...
BUT PLEASE DON'T WORRY.
SHE MADE SOME GOOD FRIENDS ON THE CLASS TRIP AND IS NOW ENJOYING HER LIFE AS A STUDENT.
IF YOU SAY SO ......
BACHIN (WAWINK)
バチーン
QUIT IT! THAT'S PISSING ME OFF! DIDN'T YOU JUST REVEAL THAT I WAS A LONER UNTIL RECENTLY!?

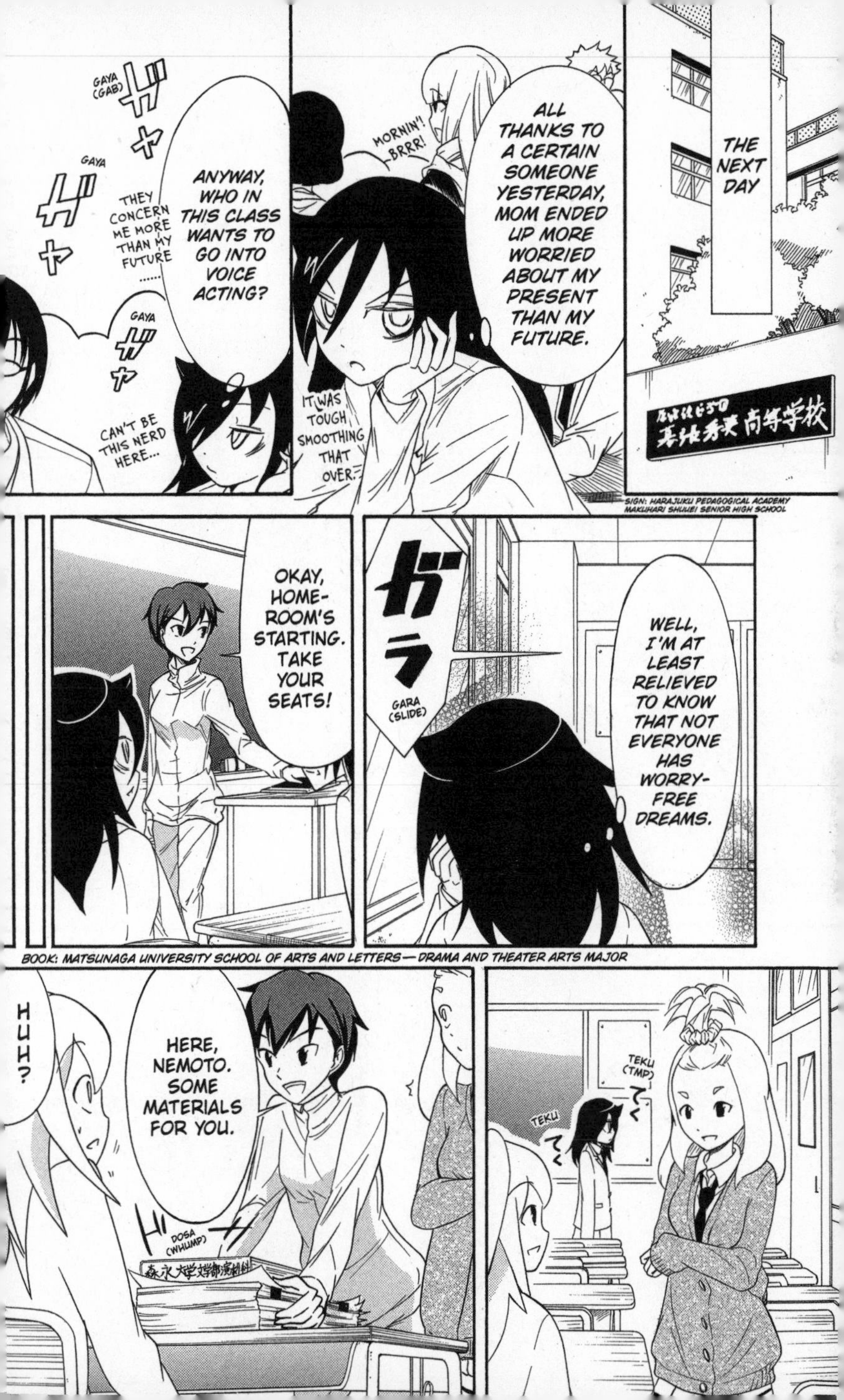
THE NEXT DAY
MORNIN'! BRRR!
ALL THANKS TO A CERTAIN SOMEONE YESTERDAY, MOM ENDED UP MORE WORRIED ABOUT MY PRESENT THAN MY FUTURE.
IT WAS TOUGH SMOOTHING THAT OVER.
ANYWAY, WHO IN THIS CLASS WANTS TO GO INTO VOICE ACTING?
GAYA (GAB)
GAYA
THEY CONCERN ME MORE THAN MY FUTURE ......
GAYA
CAN'T BE THIS NERD HERE...
SIGN: HARAJUKU PEDAGOGICAL ACADEMY MAKUHARI SHUUEI SENIOR HIGH SCHOOL
GARA (SLIDE)
WELL, I'M AT LEAST RELIEVED TO KNOW THAT NOT EVERYONE HAS WORRY-FREE DREAMS.
OKAY, HOME-ROOM'S STARTING. TAKE YOUR SEATS!
BOOK: MATSUNAGA UNIVERSITY SCHOOL OF ARTS AND LETTERS—DRAMA AND THEATER ARTS MAJOR
TEKU (TMP)
TEKU
HERE, NEMOTO. SOME MATERIALS FOR YOU.
DOSA (WHUMP)
HUH?

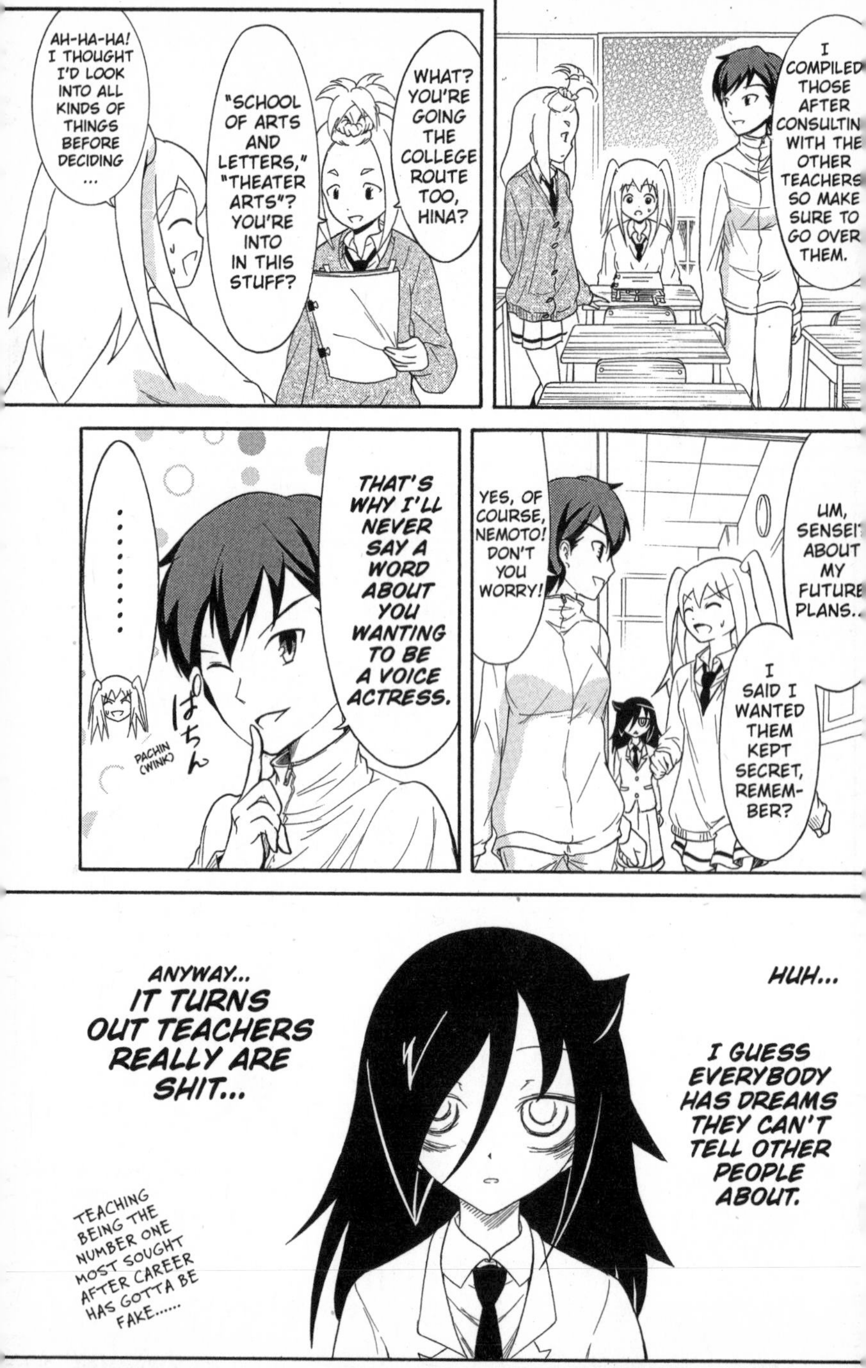
I COMPILED THOSE AFTER CONSULTIN WITH THE OTHER TEACHERS SO MAKE SURE TO GO OVER THEM.
WHAT? YOU'RE GOING THE COLLEGE ROUTE TOO, HINA?
"SCHOOL OF ARTS AND LETTERS," "THEATER ARTS"? YOU'RE INTO IN THIS STUFF?
AH-HA-HA! I THOUGHT I'D LOOK INTO ALL KINDS OF THINGS BEFORE DECIDING ...
UM, SENSEI ABOUT MY FUTURE PLANS...
YES, OF COURSE, NEMOTO! DON'T YOU WORRY!
I SAID I WANTED THEM KEPT SECRET, REMEMBER?
THAT'S WHY I'LL NEVER SAY A WORD ABOUT YOU WANTING TO BE A VOICE ACTRESS.
ぱちん
PACHIN (WINK)
....
HUH...
I GUESS EVERYBODY HAS DREAMS THEY CAN'T TELL OTHER PEOPLE ABOUT.
ANYWAY... IT TURNS OUT TEACHERS REALLY ARE SHIT...
TEACHING BEING THE NUMBER ONE MOST SOUGHT AFTER CAREER HAS GOTTA BE FAKE......

No Matter How I Look at It, It's You Guys' Fault I'm Not Popular!

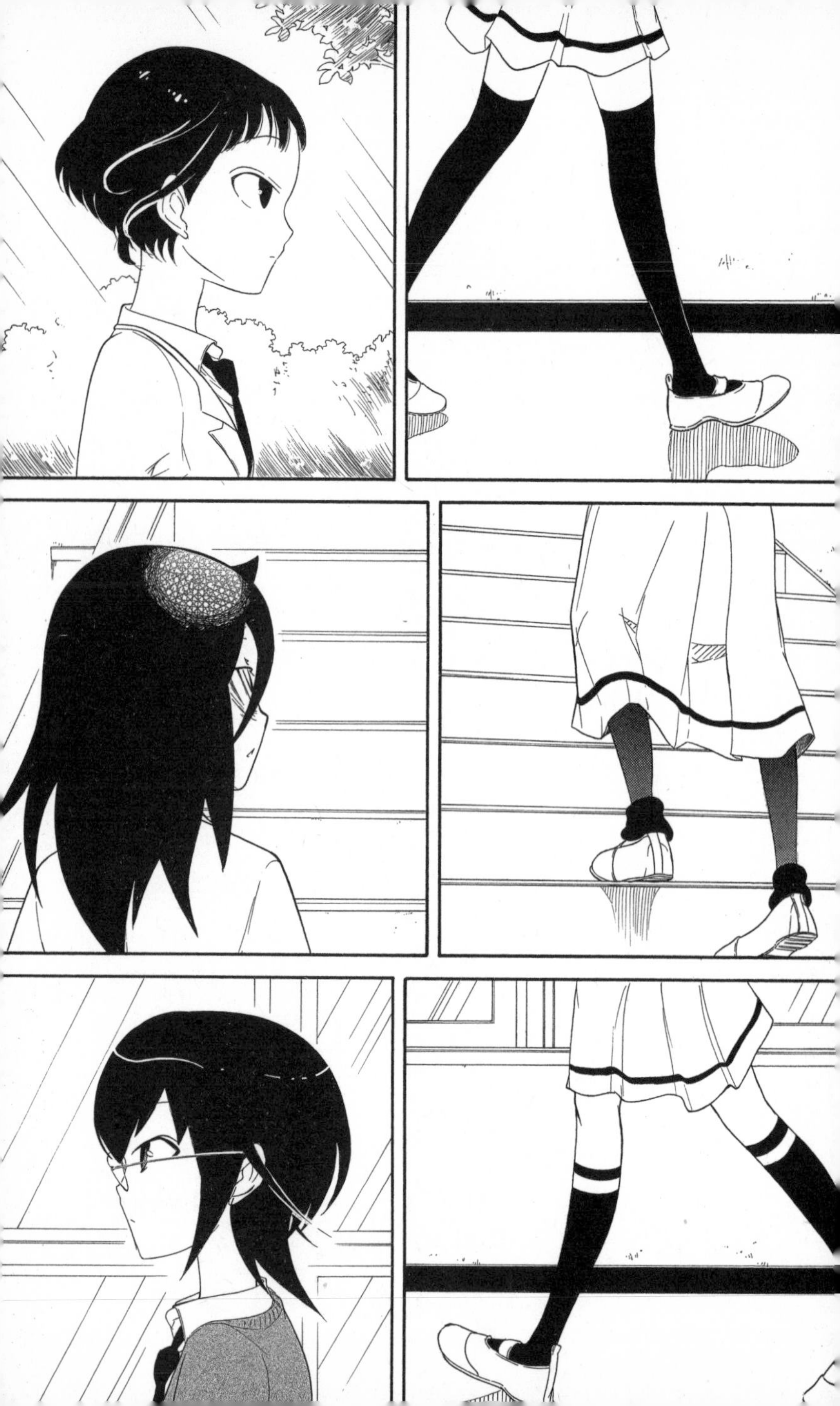

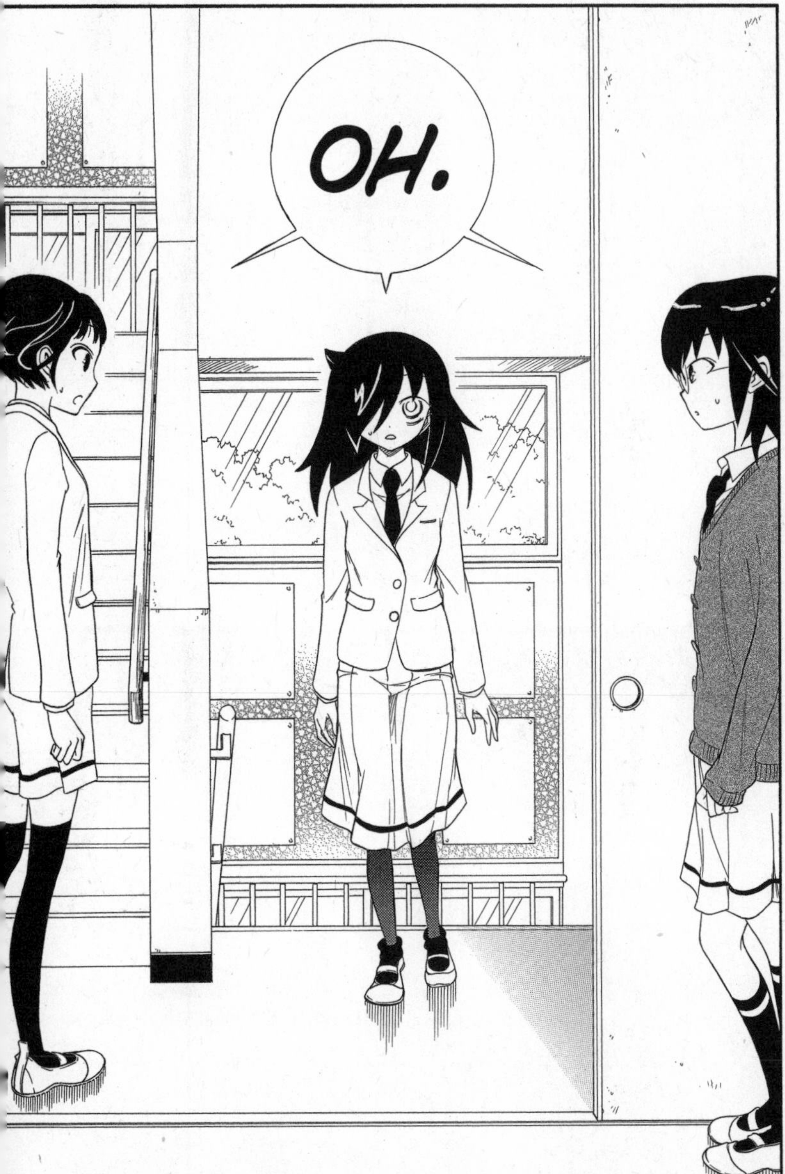
OH.

FAIL 91: I'M NOT POPULAR, SO I'LL HAVE A CHANCE ENCOUNTER.

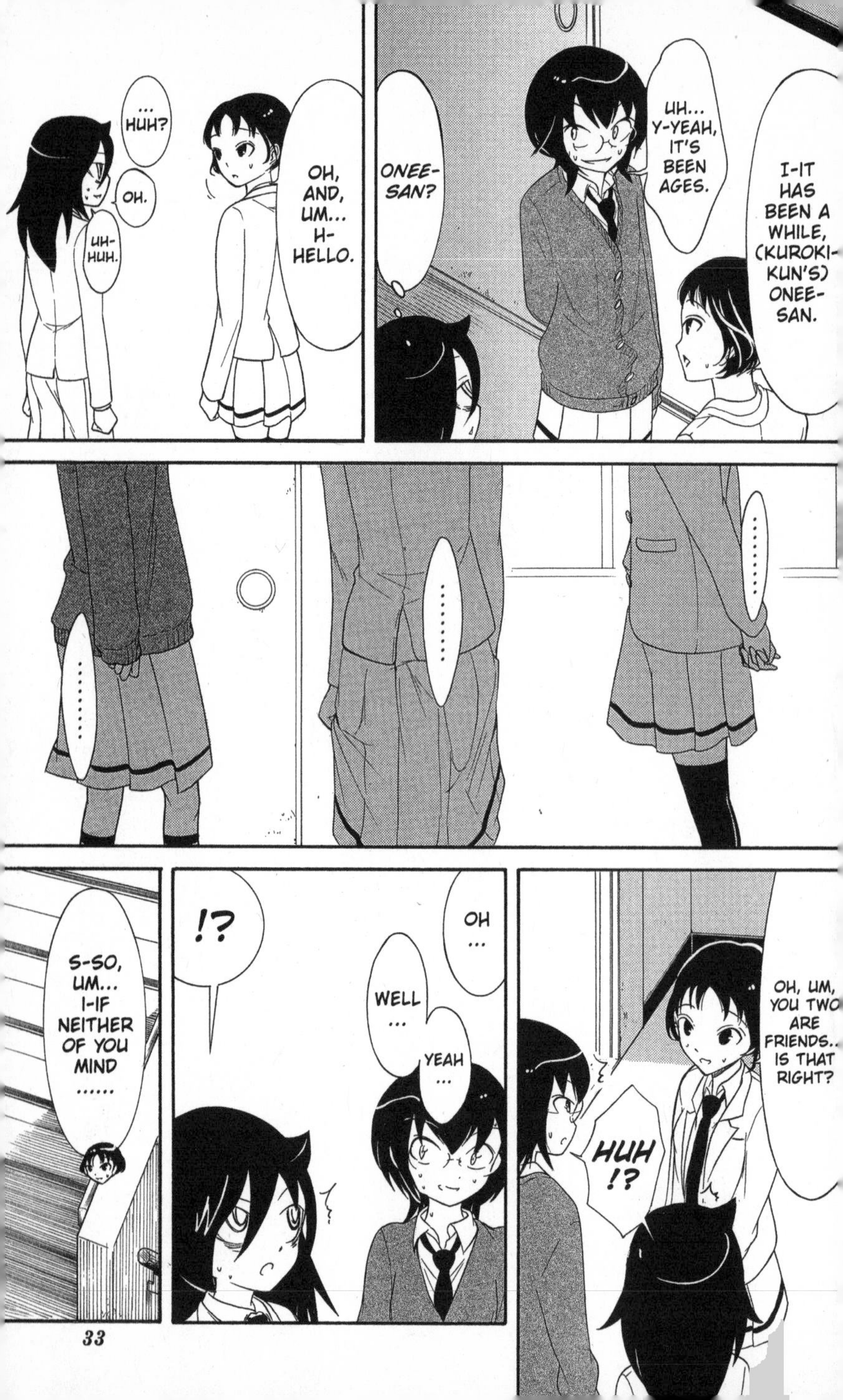

I-IT HAS BEEN A WHILE, (KUROKI-KUN'S) ONEE-SAN.
UH... Y-YEAH, IT'S BEEN AGES.
ONEE-SAN?
OH, AND, UM... H-HELLO.
... HUH?
OH.
UH-HUH.
......
......
......
OH, UM, YOU TWO ARE FRIENDS.. IS THAT RIGHT?
HUH !?
OH ...
WELL ...
YEAH ...
!?
S-SO, UM... I-IF NEITHER OF YOU MIND ......

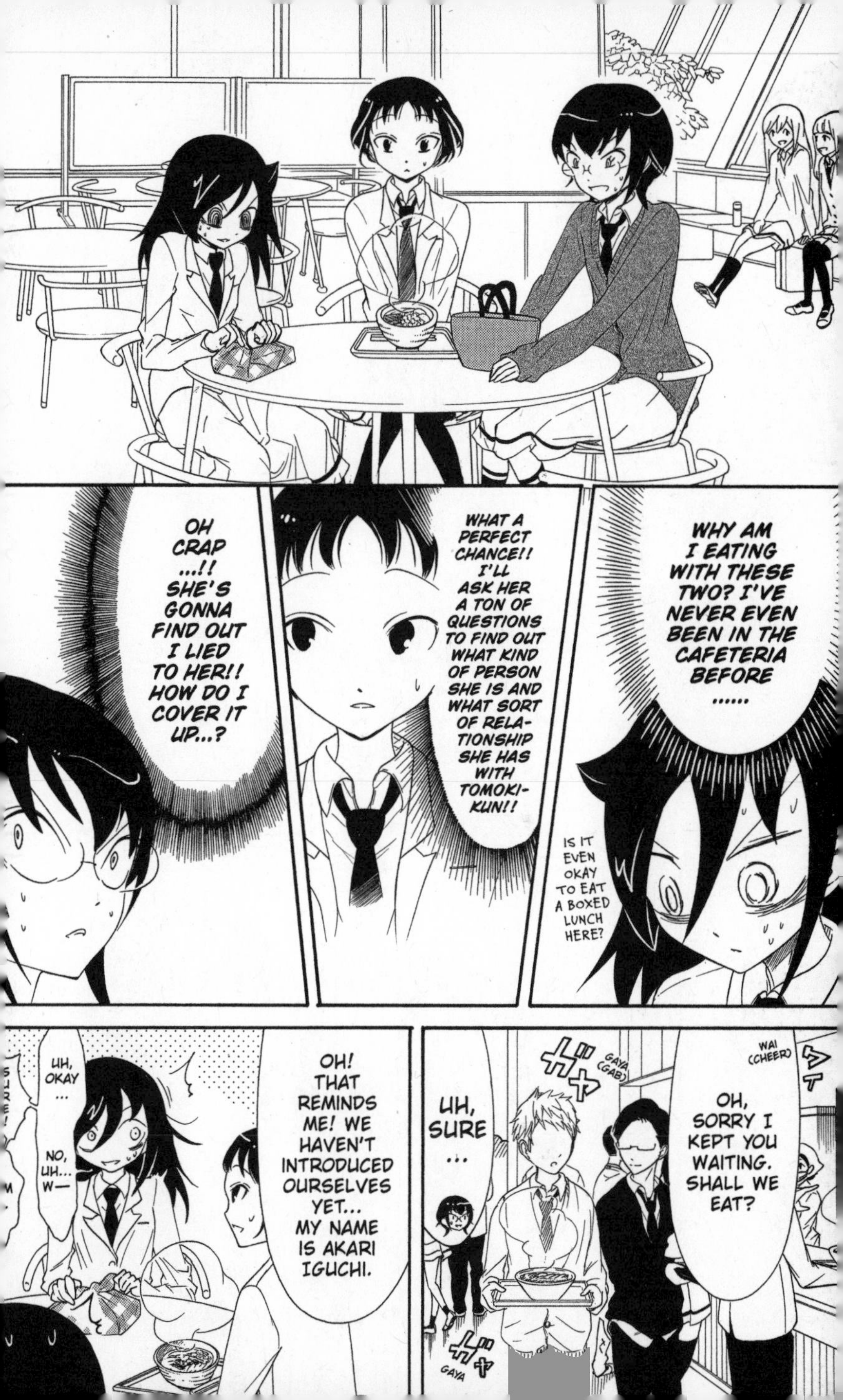
WHY AM I EATING WITH THESE TWO? I'VE NEVER EVEN BEEN IN THE CAFETERIA BEFORE ......
IS IT EVEN OKAY TO EAT A BOXED LUNCH HERE?
WHAT A PERFECT CHANCE!! I'LL ASK HER A TON OF QUESTIONS TO FIND OUT WHAT KIND OF PERSON SHE IS AND WHAT SORT OF RELATIONSHIP SHE HAS WITH TOMOKI-KUN!!
OH CRAP ...!! SHE'S GONNA FIND OUT I LIED TO HER!! HOW DO I COVER IT UP...?
WAI (CHEER)
OH, SORRY I KEPT YOU WAITING. SHALL WE EAT?
GAYA (GAB)
UH, SURE ...
GAYA
OH! THAT REMINDS ME! WE HAVEN'T INTRODUCED OURSELVES YET... MY NAME IS AKARI IGUCHI.
UH, OKAY ...
NO, UH... W—

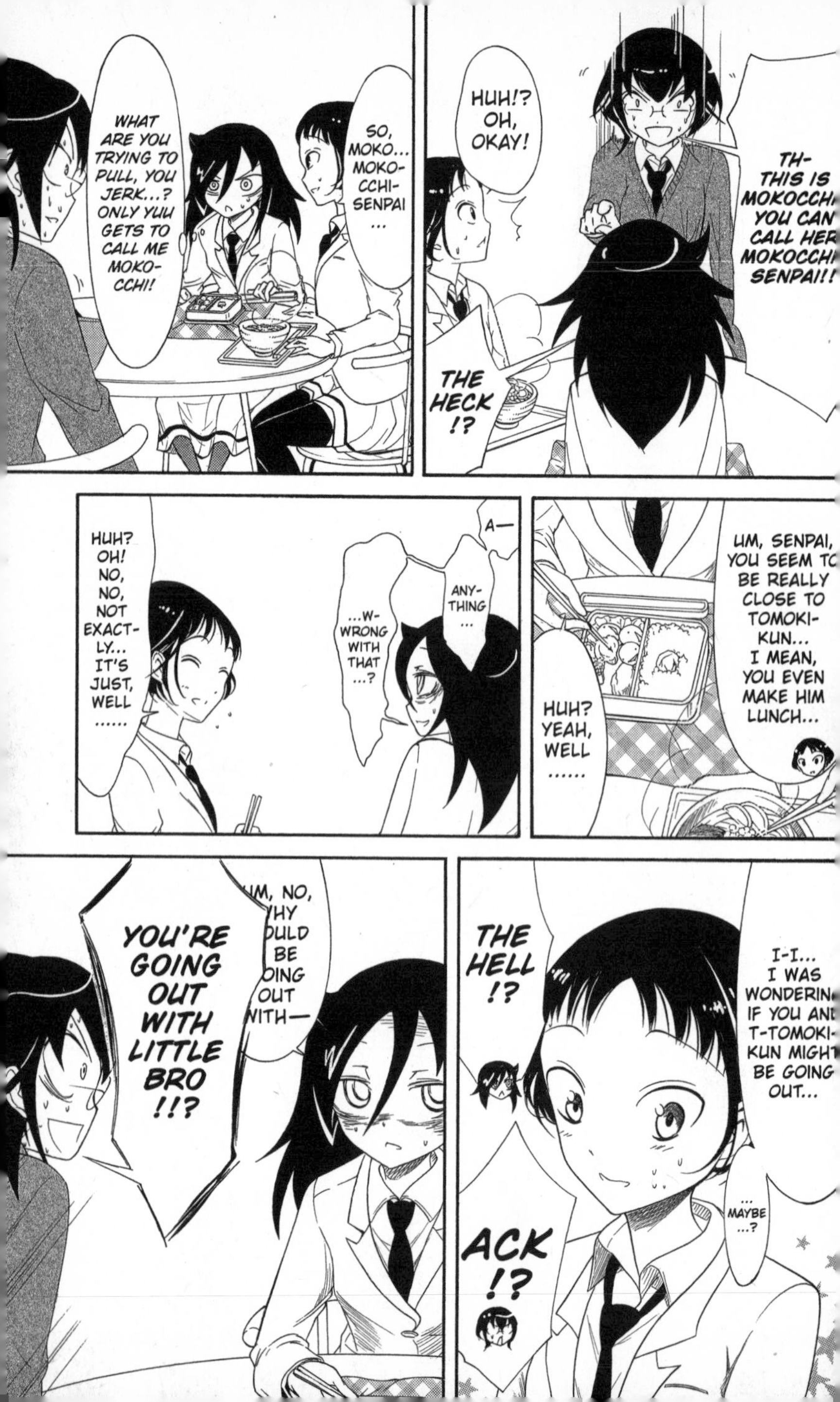
TH- THIS IS MOKOCCH YOU CAN CALL HER MOKOCCHI SENPAI!!
THE HECK!?
HUH!? OH, OKAY!
SO, MOKO... MOKOCCHI-SENPAI...
WHAT ARE YOU TRYING TO PULL, YOU JERK...? ONLY YUU GETS TO CALL ME MOKOCCHI!
UM, SENPAI, YOU SEEM TO BE REALLY CLOSE TO TOMOKI-KUN... I MEAN, YOU EVEN MAKE HIM LUNCH...
HUH? YEAH, WELL ......
A—
ANY-THING...
...W-WRONG WITH THAT...?
HUH? OH! NO, NO, NOT EXACTLY... IT'S JUST, WELL ......
I-I... I WAS WONDERIN IF YOU AN T-TOMOKI-KUN MIGH BE GOING OUT...
...MAYBE...?
THE HELL!?
ACK!?
M, NO, HY OULD BE OING OUT ITH—
YOU'RE GOING OUT WITH LITTLE BRO!!?

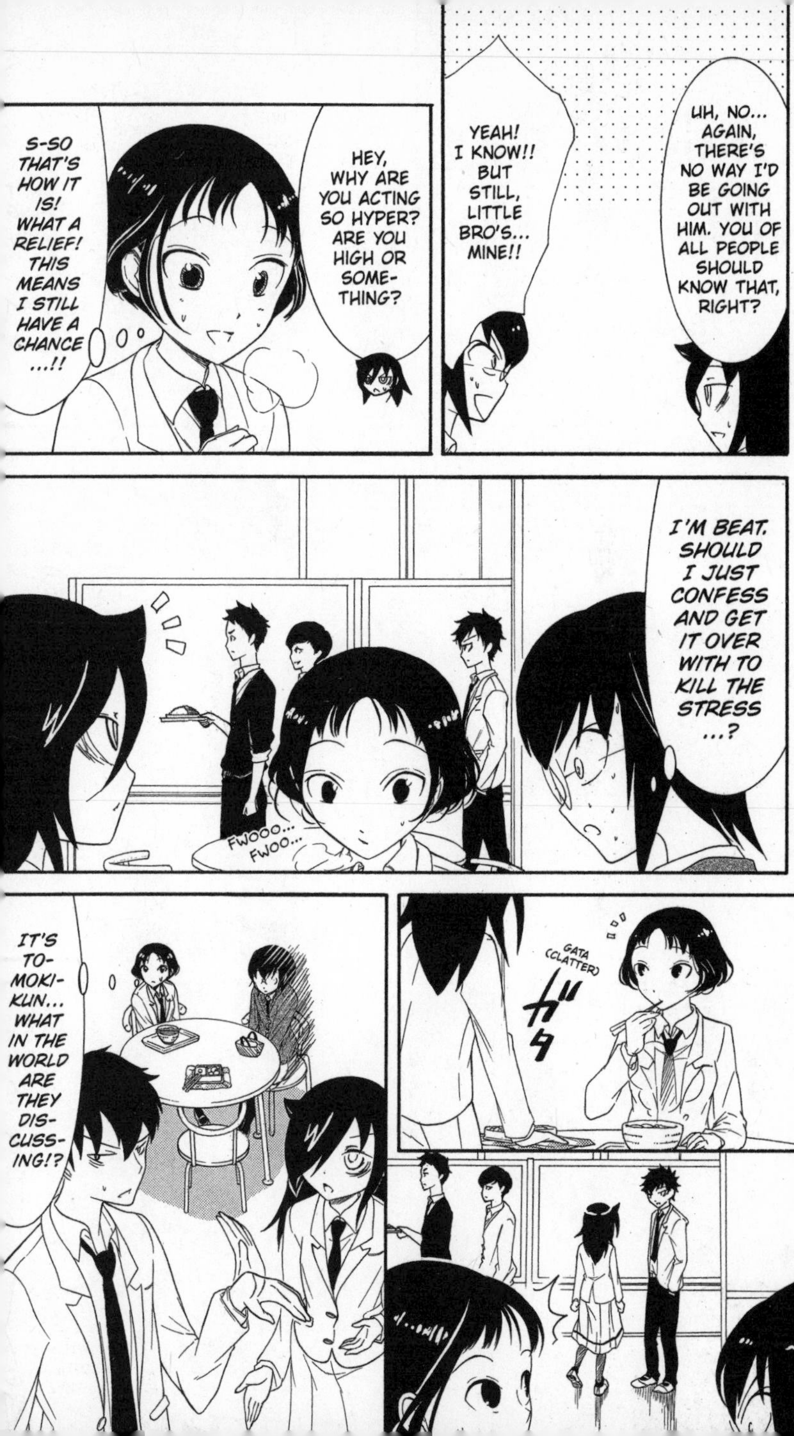
UH, NO... AGAIN, THERE'S NO WAY I'D BE GOING OUT WITH HIM. YOU OF ALL PEOPLE SHOULD KNOW THAT, RIGHT?
YEAH! I KNOW!! BUT STILL, LITTLE BRO'S... MINE!!
HEY, WHY ARE YOU ACTING SO HYPER? ARE YOU HIGH OR SOME-THING?
S-SO THAT'S HOW IT IS! WHAT A RELIEF! THIS MEANS I STILL HAVE A CHANCE ...!!
I'M BEAT. SHOULD I JUST CONFESS AND GET IT OVER WITH TO KILL THE STRESS ...?
FWOOO... FWOO...
GATA (CLATTER)
ガタ
IT'S TO-MOKI-KUN... WHAT IN THE WORLD ARE THEY DIS-CUSS-ING!?

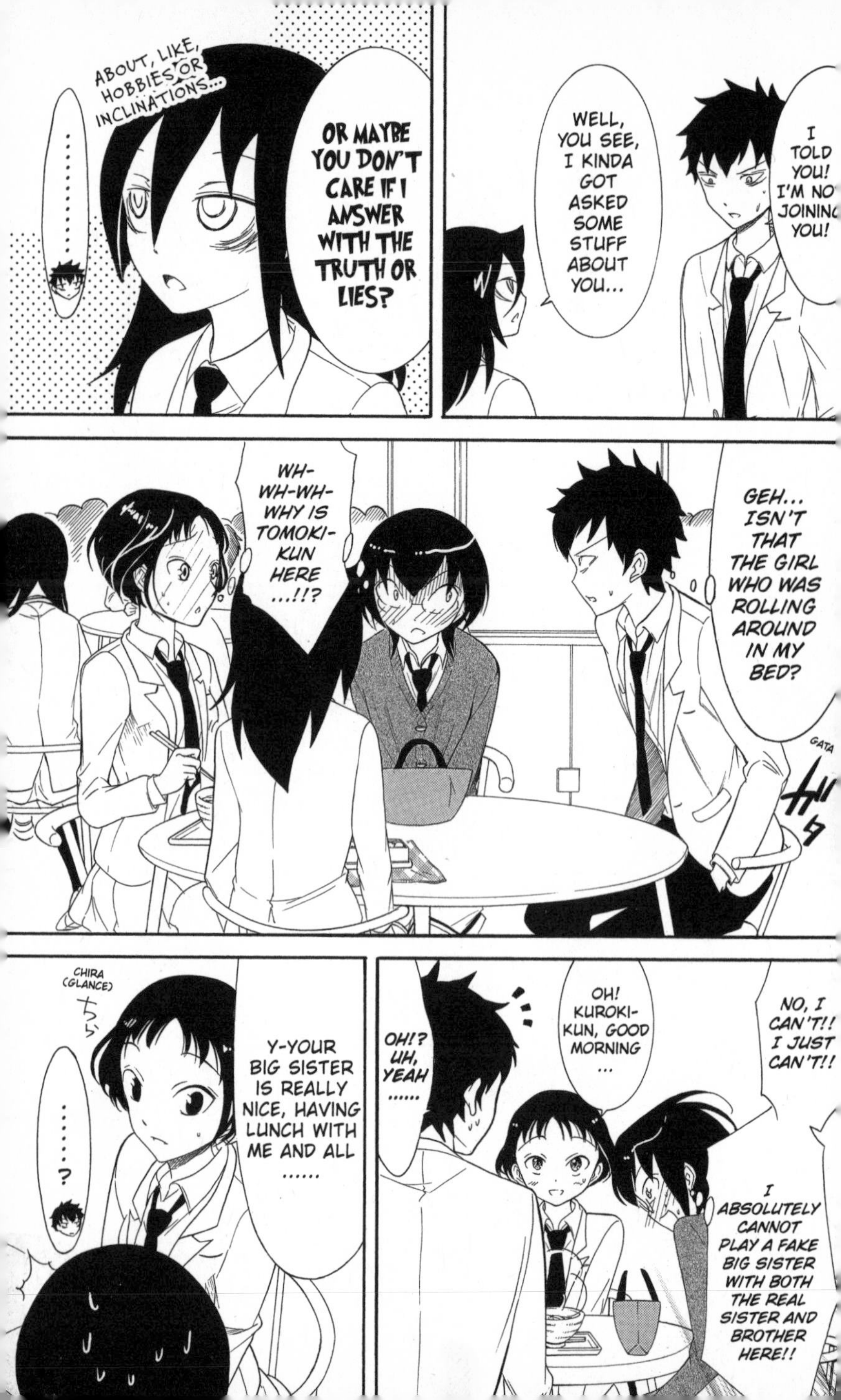

I TOLD YOU! I'M NO JOININ YOU!
WELL, YOU SEE, I KINDA GOT ASKED SOME STUFF ABOUT YOU...
OR MAYBE YOU DON'T CARE IF I ANSWER WITH THE TRUTH OR LIES?
ABOUT, LIKE, HOBBIES OR INCLINATIONS...
......
GEH... ISN'T THAT THE GIRL WHO WAS ROLLING AROUND IN MY BED?
GATA
WH-WH-WH-WHY IS TOMOKI-KUN HERE ...!!?
NO, I CAN'T!! I JUST CAN'T!!
OH! KUROKI-KUN, GOOD MORNING ...
OH!? UH, YEAH ......
I ABSOLUTELY CANNOT PLAY A FAKE BIG SISTER WITH BOTH THE REAL SISTER AND BROTHER HERE!!
CHIRA (GLANCE)
Y-YOUR BIG SISTER IS REALLY NICE, HAVING LUNCH WITH ME AND ALL ......
......?

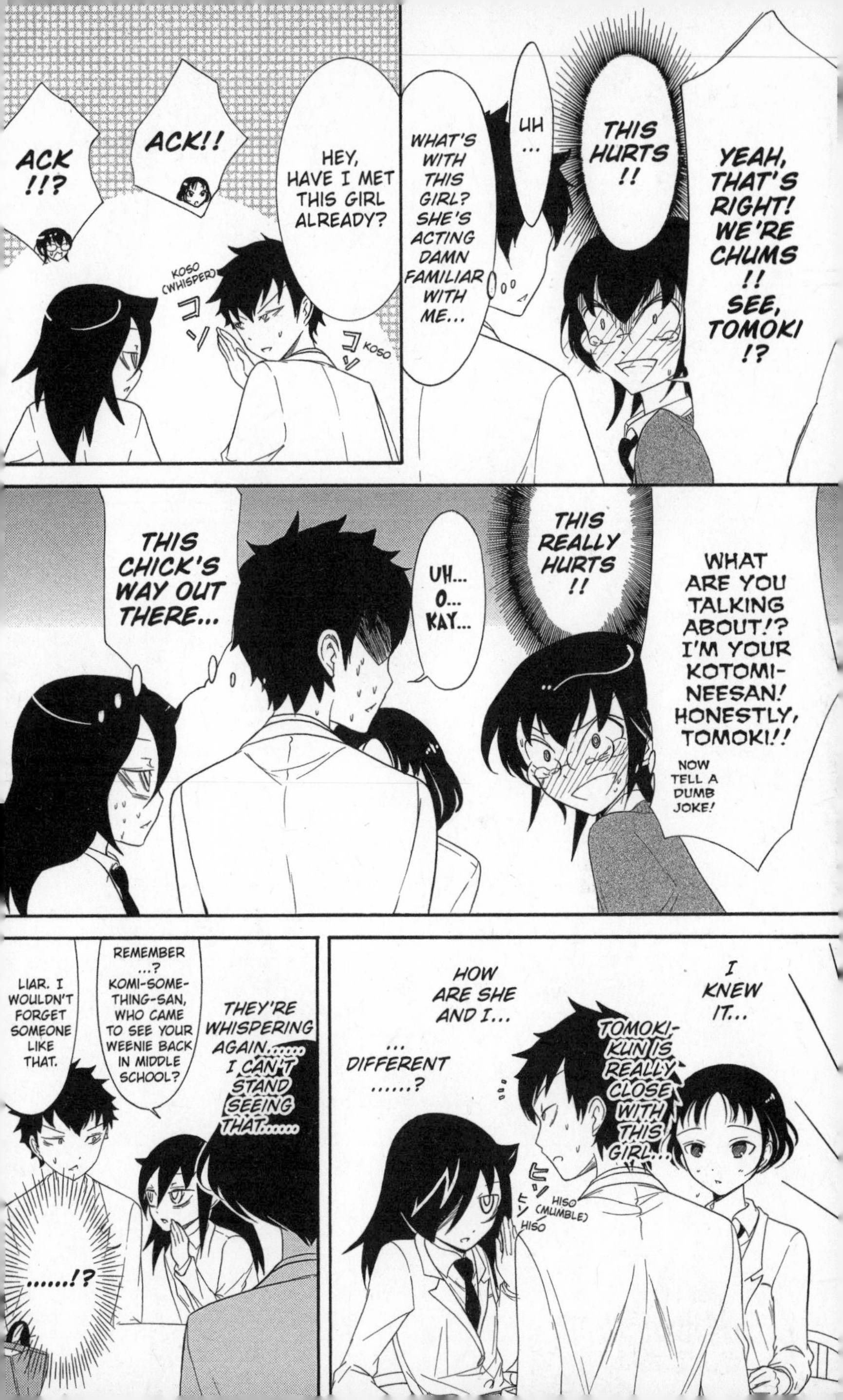
YEAH, THAT'S RIGHT! WE'RE CHUMS!! SEE, TOMOKI!?
THIS HURTS!!
UH...
WHAT'S WITH THIS GIRL? SHE'S ACTING DAMN FAMILIAR WITH ME...
HEY, HAVE I MET THIS GIRL ALREADY?
ACK!!
ACK!!?
KOSO (WHISPER)
KOSO
WHAT ARE YOU TALKING ABOUT!? I'M YOUR KOTOMI-NEESAN! HONESTLY, TOMOKI!!
NOW TELL A DUMB JOKE!
THIS REALLY HURTS!!
UH... O... KAY...
THIS CHICK'S WAY OUT THERE...
I KNEW IT...
TOMOKI-KUN IS REALLY CLOSE WITH THIS GIRL...
HOW ARE SHE AND I...
... DIFFERENT ......?
HISO (MUMBLE)
HISO
THEY'RE WHISPERING AGAIN...... I CAN'T STAND SEEING THAT......
REMEMBER...? KOMI-SOME-THING-SAN, WHO CAME TO SEE YOUR WEENIE BACK IN MIDDLE SCHOOL?
LIAR. I WOULDN'T FORGET SOMEONE LIKE THAT.
......!?

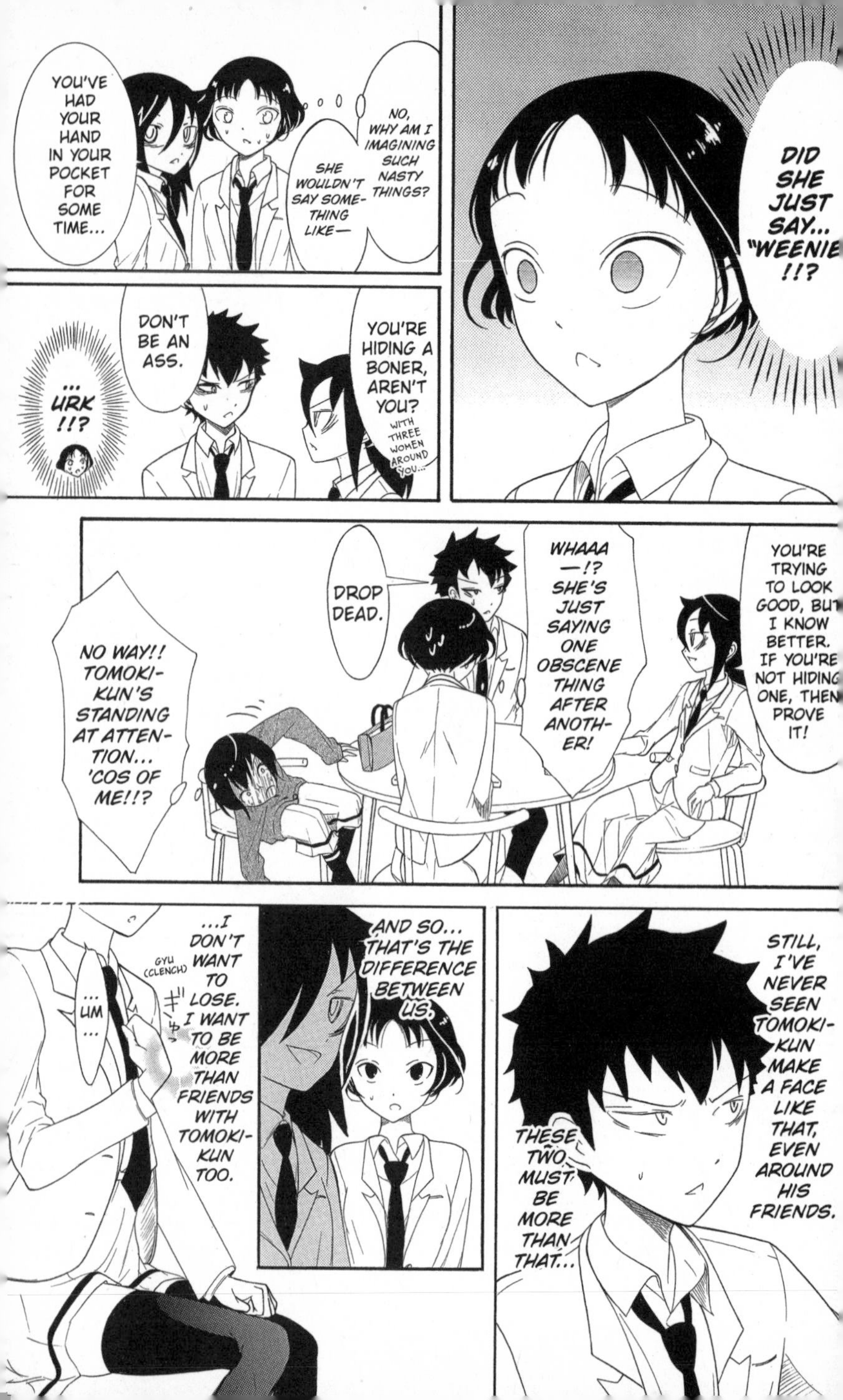
DID SHE JUST SAY... "WEENIE!!?
NO, WHY AM I IMAGINING SUCH NASTY THINGS?
SHE WOULDN'T SAY SOMETHING LIKE—
YOU'VE HAD YOUR HAND IN YOUR POCKET FOR SOME TIME...
YOU'RE HIDING A BONER, AREN'T YOU?
WITH THREE WOMEN AROUND YOU...
DON'T BE AN ASS.
...ÜRK!!?
YOU'RE TRYING TO LOOK GOOD, BUT I KNOW BETTER. IF YOU'RE NOT HIDING ONE, THEN PROVE IT!
WHAAA—!? SHE'S JUST SAYING ONE OBSCENE THING AFTER ANOTHER!
DROP DEAD.
NO WAY!! TOMOKI-KUN'S STANDING AT ATTENTION... 'COS OF ME!!?
STILL, I'VE NEVER SEEN TOMOKI-KUN MAKE A FACE LIKE THAT, EVEN AROUND HIS FRIENDS.
THESE TWO MUST BE MORE THAN THAT...
AND SO... THAT'S THE DIFFERENCE BETWEEN US.
...I DON'T WANT TO LOSE. I WANT TO BE MORE THAN FRIENDS WITH TOMOKI-KUN TOO.
GYU (CLENCH)
...UM...

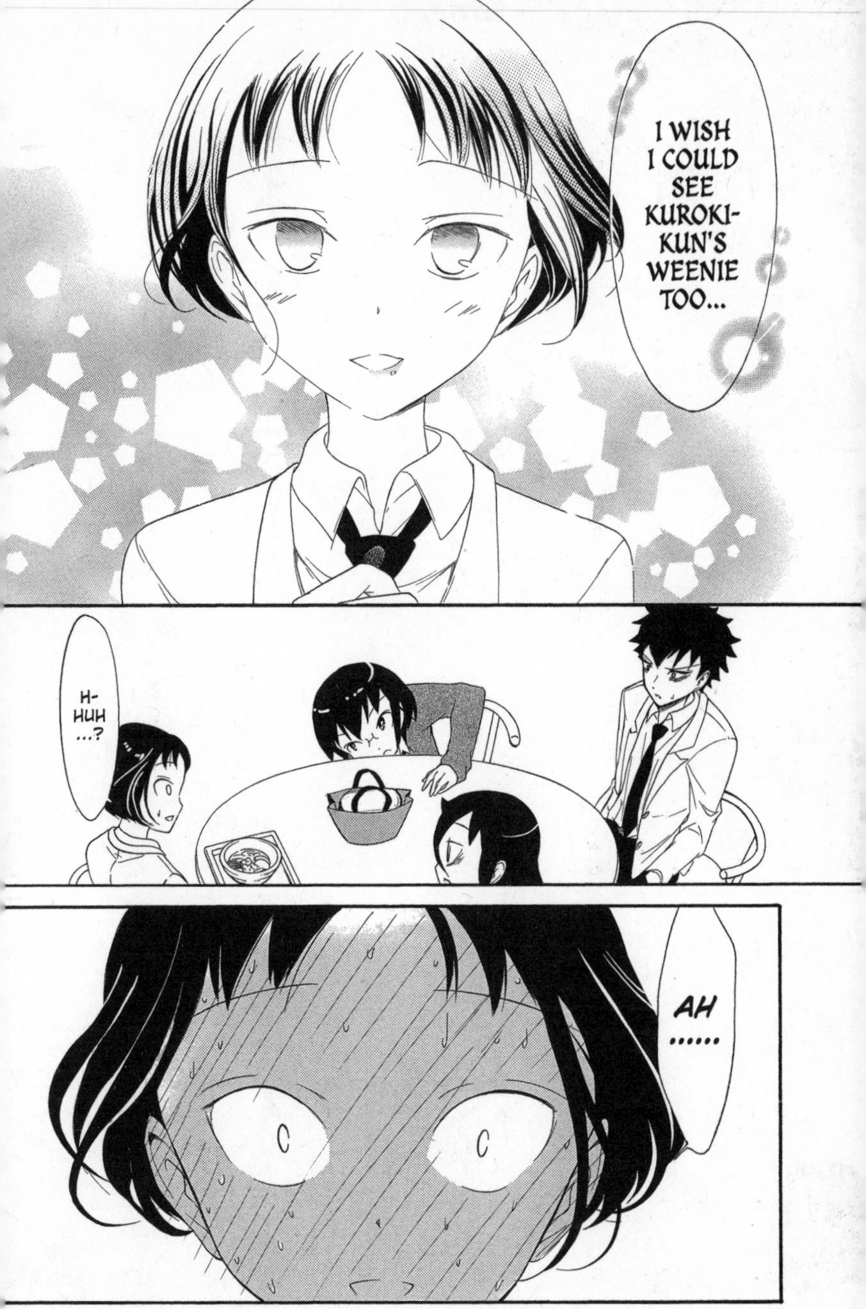
I WISH I COULD SEE KUROKI-KUN'S WEENIE TOO...
H-HUH ...?
AH ......

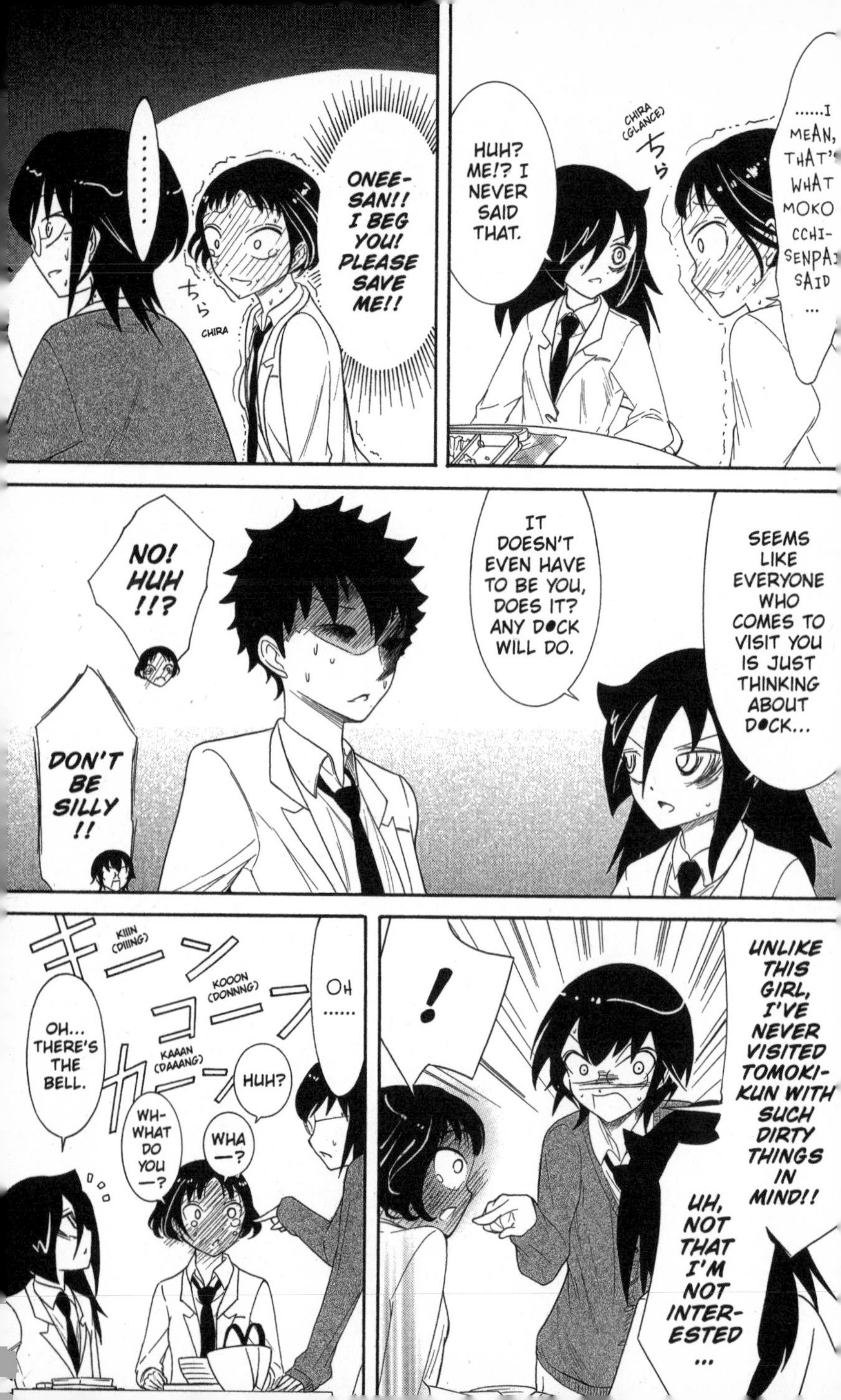
......I MEAN, THAT'S WHAT MOKOCCHI-SENPAI SAID...
CHIRA (GLANCE)
HUH? ME!? I NEVER SAID THAT.
ONEE-SAN!! I BEG YOU! PLEASE SAVE ME!!
......
CHIRA
SEEMS LIKE EVERYONE WHO COMES TO VISIT YOU IS JUST THINKING ABOUT D●CK...
IT DOESN'T EVEN HAVE TO BE YOU, DOES IT? ANY D●CK WILL DO.
NO! HUH!!?
DON'T BE SILLY!!
UNLIKE THIS GIRL, I'VE NEVER VISITED TOMOKI-KUN WITH SUCH DIRTY THINGS IN MIND!!
!
UH, NOT THAT I'M NOT INTERESTED...
OH ......
KOOON (DONNNG)
KIIN (DIIING)
HUH?
KAAAN (DAAANG)
OH... THERE'S THE BELL.
WHA—?
WH-WHAT DO YOU—?

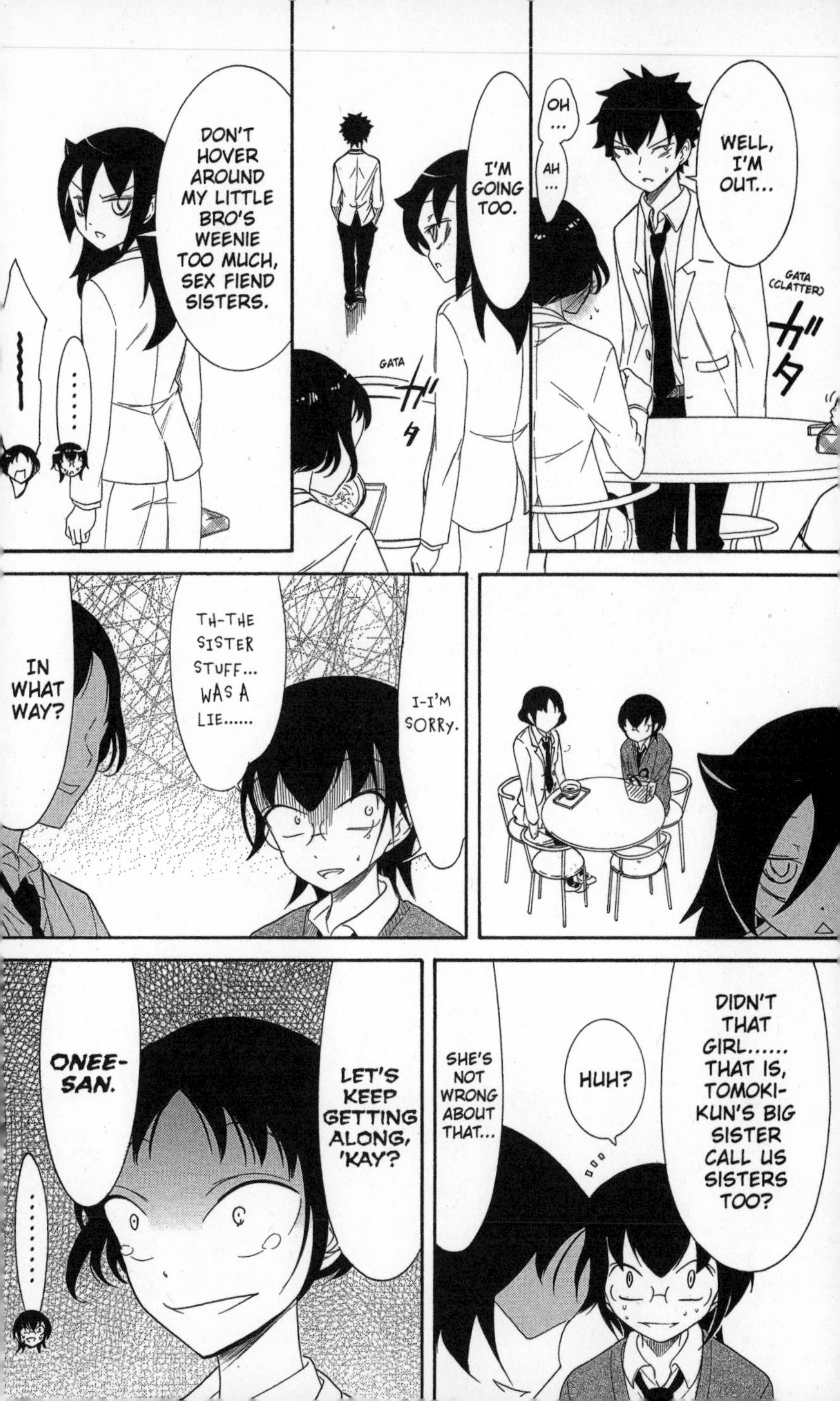
WELL, I'M OUT...
GATA (CLATTER)
OH ...
AH ...
I'M GOING TOO.
GATA
DON'T HOVER AROUND MY LITTLE BRO'S WEENIE TOO MUCH, SEX FIEND SISTERS.
......
I-I'M SORRY.
TH-THE SISTER STUFF... WAS A LIE......
IN WHAT WAY?
DIDN'T THAT GIRL...... THAT IS, TOMOKI-KUN'S BIG SISTER CALL US SISTERS TOO?
HUH?
SHE'S NOT WRONG ABOUT THAT...
LET'S KEEP GETTING ALONG, 'KAY?
ONEE-SAN.
......!

No Matter How I Look at It, It's You Guys' Fault I'm Not Popular!

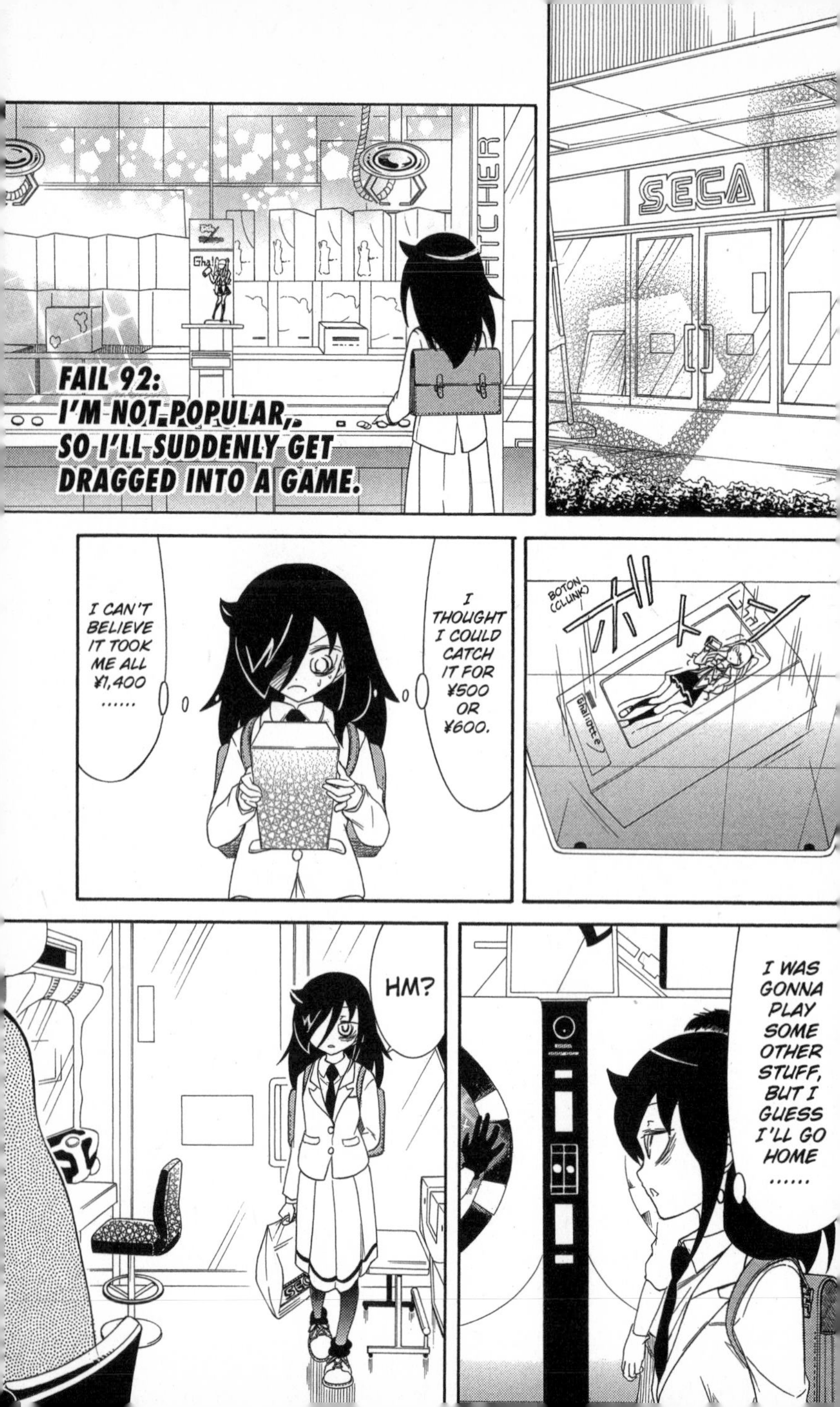
SECA
FAIL 92:
I'M NOT POPULAR,
SO I'LL SUDDENLY GET
DRAGGED INTO A GAME.
BOTON (CLUNK)
I THOUGHT I COULD CATCH IT FOR ¥500 OR ¥600.
I CAN'T BELIEVE IT TOOK ME ALL ¥1,400 ......
I WAS GONNA PLAY SOME OTHER STUFF, BUT I GUESS I'LL GO HOME ......
HM?

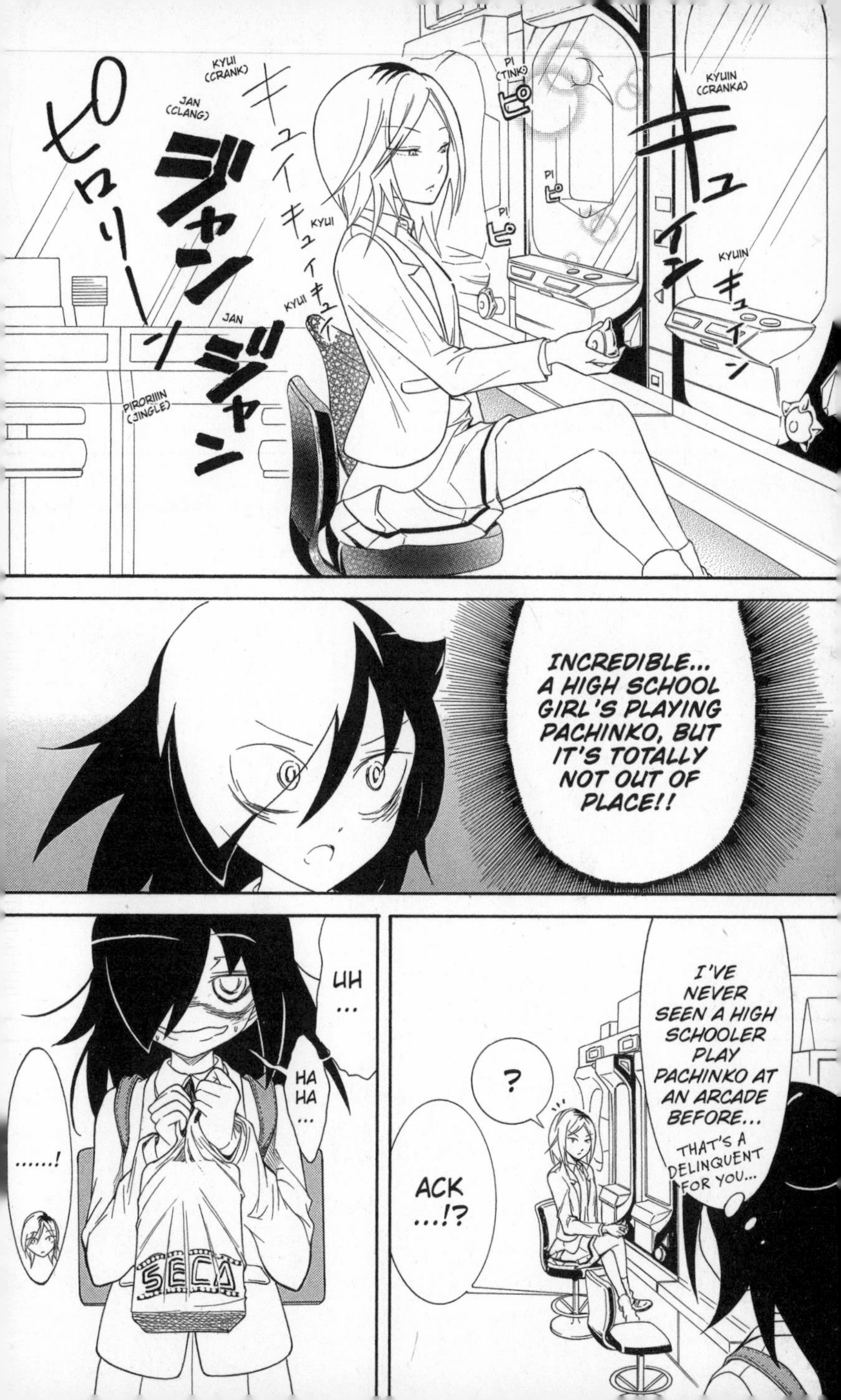
KYUIN (CRANKA)
キュイーン
KYUIN
キュイーン
PI (TINK)
ピ
PI
ピ
PI
ピ
KYUI (CRANK)
KYUI
KYUI
キュイーキュイキュイ
JAN (CLANG)
ジャン
JAN
ジャン
PIRORIIIN (JINGLE)
ピロリーン
INCREDIBLE... A HIGH SCHOOL GIRL'S PLAYING PACHINKO, BUT IT'S TOTALLY NOT OUT OF PLACE!!
I'VE NEVER SEEN A HIGH SCHOOLER PLAY PACHINKO AT AN ARCADE BEFORE...
THAT'S A DELINQUENT FOR YOU...
?
ACK ...!?
UH ...
HA HA ...
......!
SEGA

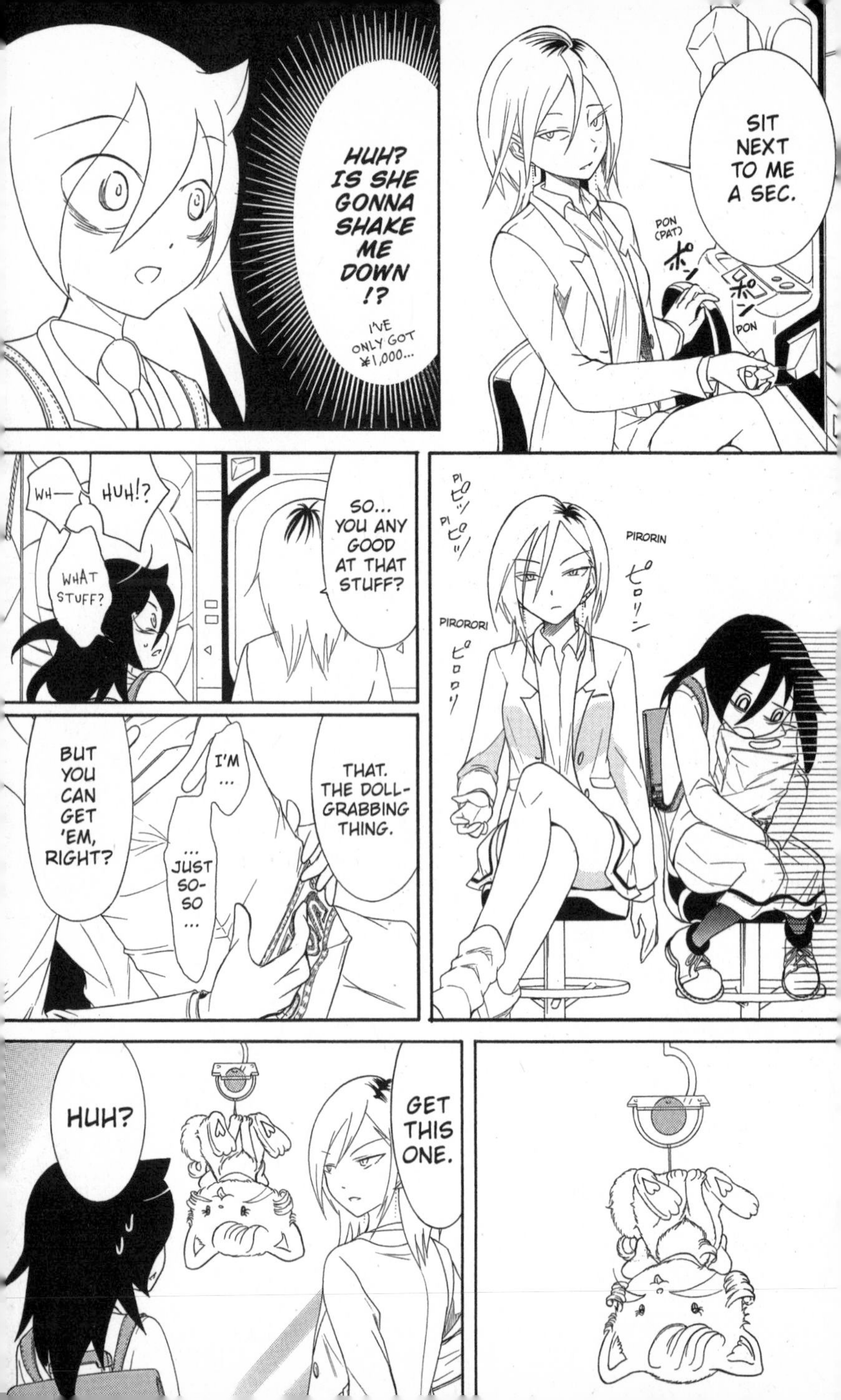
SIT NEXT TO ME A SEC.
PON (PAT)
ポン
ポン
PON
HUH? IS SHE GONNA SHAKE ME DOWN!?
I'VE ONLY GOT ¥1,000...
PI
ピッ
PI
ピッ
PIRORIN
ピロリン
PIRORORI
ピロロリ
SO... YOU ANY GOOD AT THAT STUFF?
WH— HUH!?
WHAT STUFF?
THAT. THE DOLL-GRABBING THING.
I'M...
...JUST SO-SO...
BUT YOU CAN GET 'EM, RIGHT?
GET THIS ONE.
HUH?

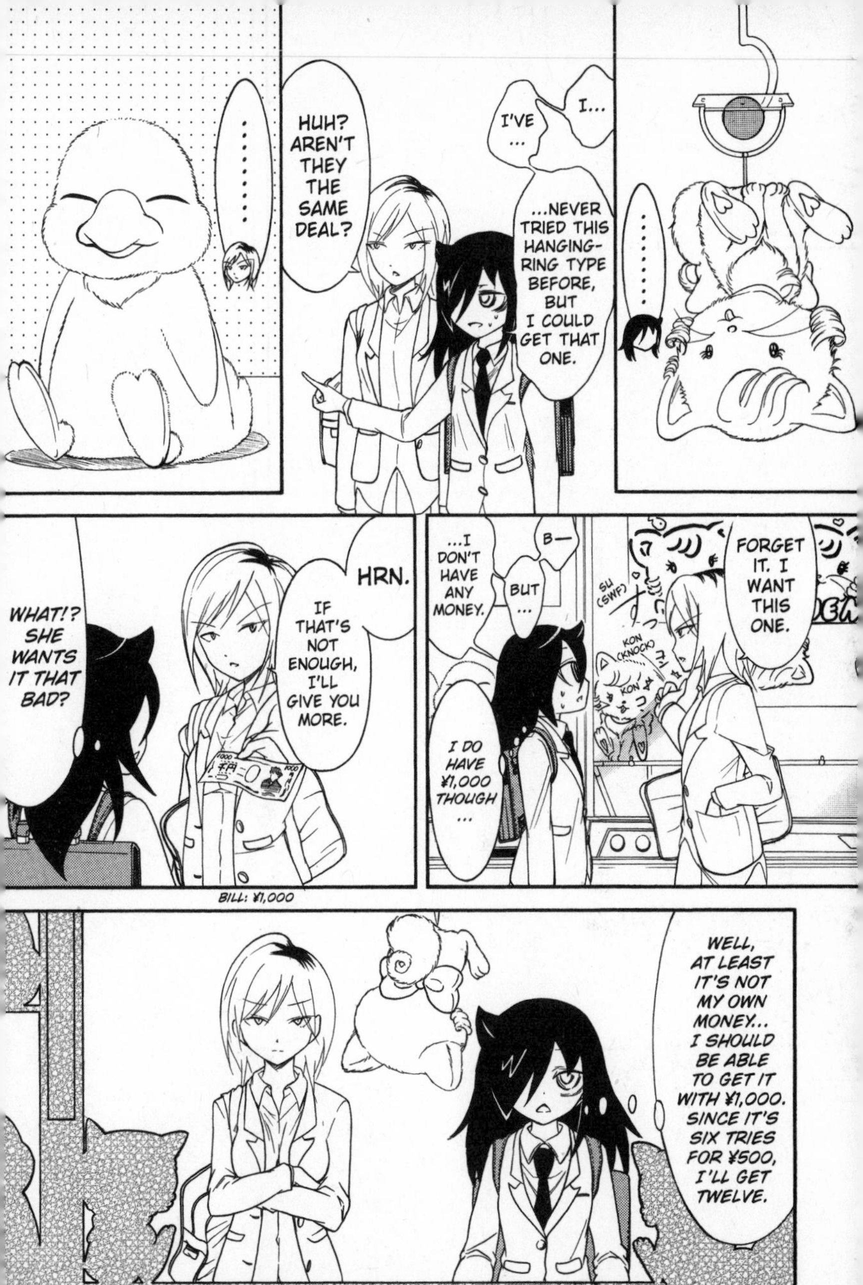
......
I...
I'VE ...
...NEVER TRIED THIS HANGING-RING TYPE BEFORE, BUT I COULD GET THAT ONE.
HUH? AREN'T THEY THE SAME DEAL?
......
FORGET IT. I WANT THIS ONE.
SU (SWF)
KON (KNOCK)
KON
B—
BUT ...
...I DON'T HAVE ANY MONEY.
I DO HAVE ¥1,000 THOUGH ...
HRN.
IF THAT'S NOT ENOUGH, I'LL GIVE YOU MORE.
WHAT!? SHE WANTS IT THAT BAD?
BILL: ¥1,000
WELL, AT LEAST IT'S NOT MY OWN MONEY... I SHOULD BE ABLE TO GET IT WITH ¥1,000. SINCE IT'S SIX TRIES FOR ¥500, I'LL GET TWELVE.

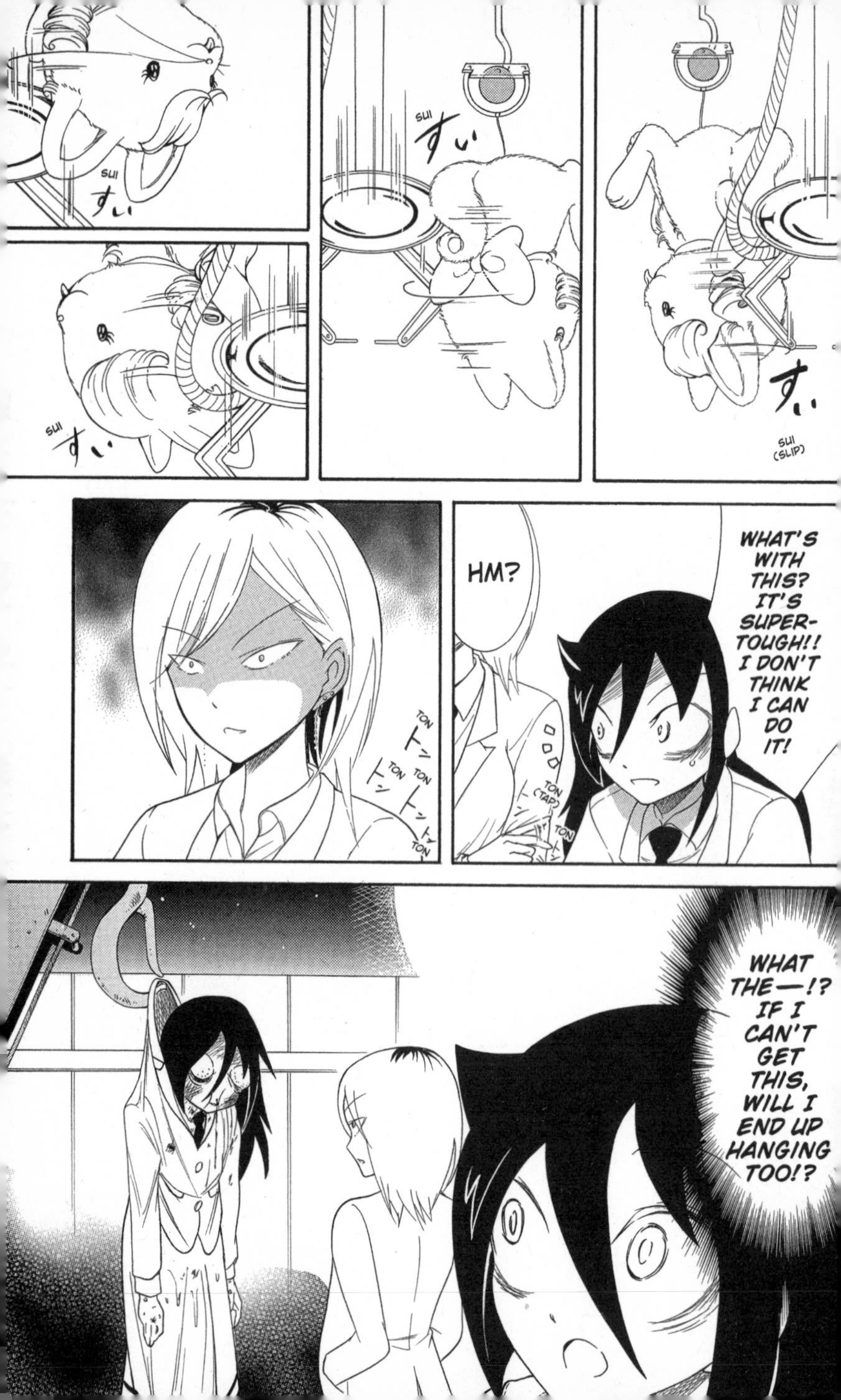

すい
SUI (SLIP)
SUI
すい
SUI
すい
SUI
すい
WHAT'S WITH THIS? IT'S SUPER-TOUGH!! I DON'T THINK I CAN DO IT!
HM?
TON (TAP)
TON
TON
TON
TON
TON
WHAT THE—!? IF I CAN'T GET THIS, WILL I END UP HANGING TOO!?

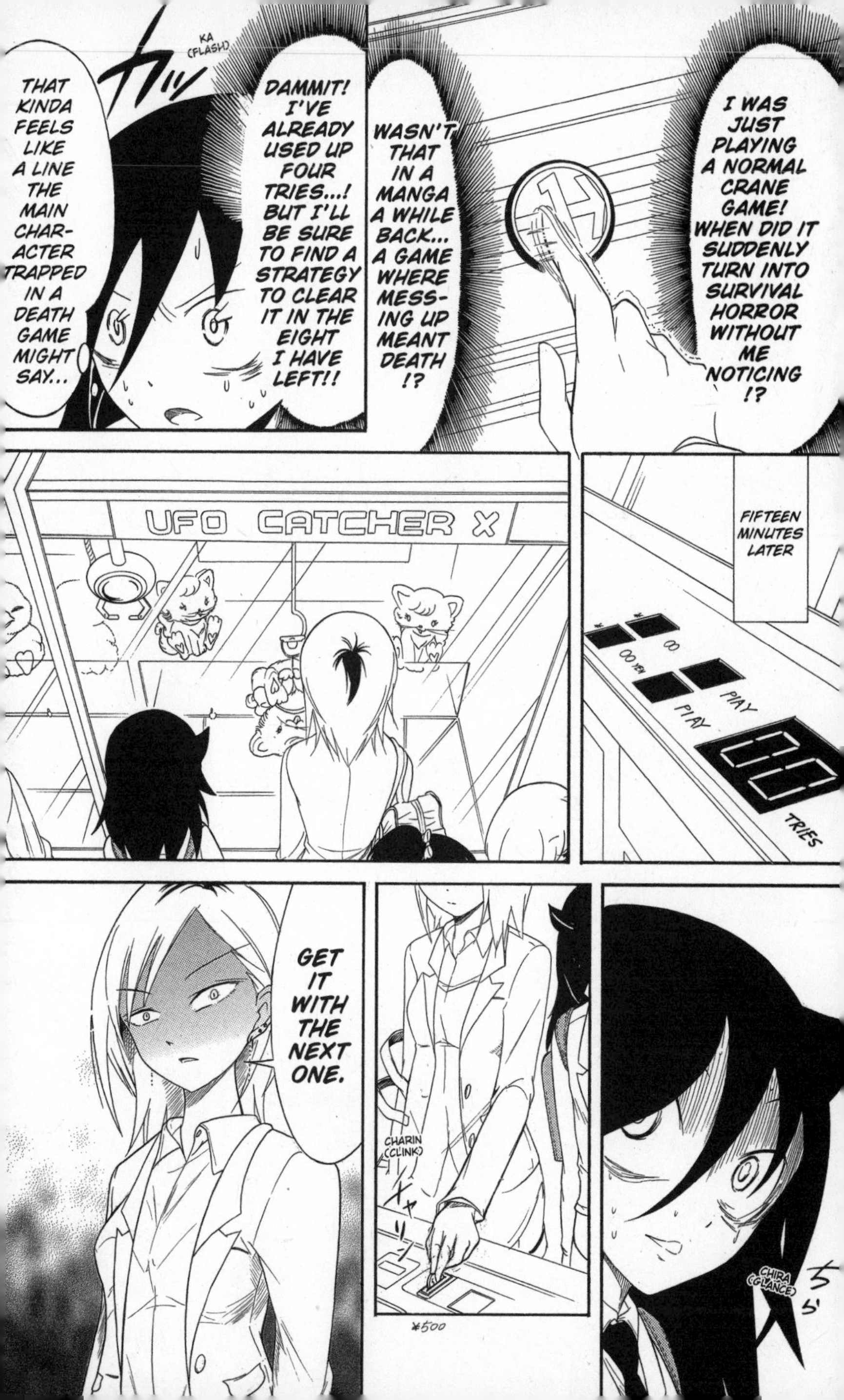
I WAS JUST PLAYING A NORMAL CRANE GAME! WHEN DID IT SUDDENLY TURN INTO SURVIVAL HORROR WITHOUT ME NOTICING !?
WASN'T THAT IN A MANGA A WHILE BACK... A GAME WHERE MESSING UP MEANT DEATH !?
DAMMIT! I'VE ALREADY USED UP FOUR TRIES...! BUT I'LL BE SURE TO FIND A STRATEGY TO CLEAR IT IN THE EIGHT I HAVE LEFT!!
KA (FLASH)
THAT KINDA FEELS LIKE A LINE THE MAIN CHARACTER TRAPPED IN A DEATH GAME MIGHT SAY...
FIFTEEN MINUTES LATER
PLAY
PLAY
TRIES
UFO CATCHER X
CHIRA (GLANCE)
CHARIN (CLINK)
¥500
GET IT WITH THE NEXT ONE.

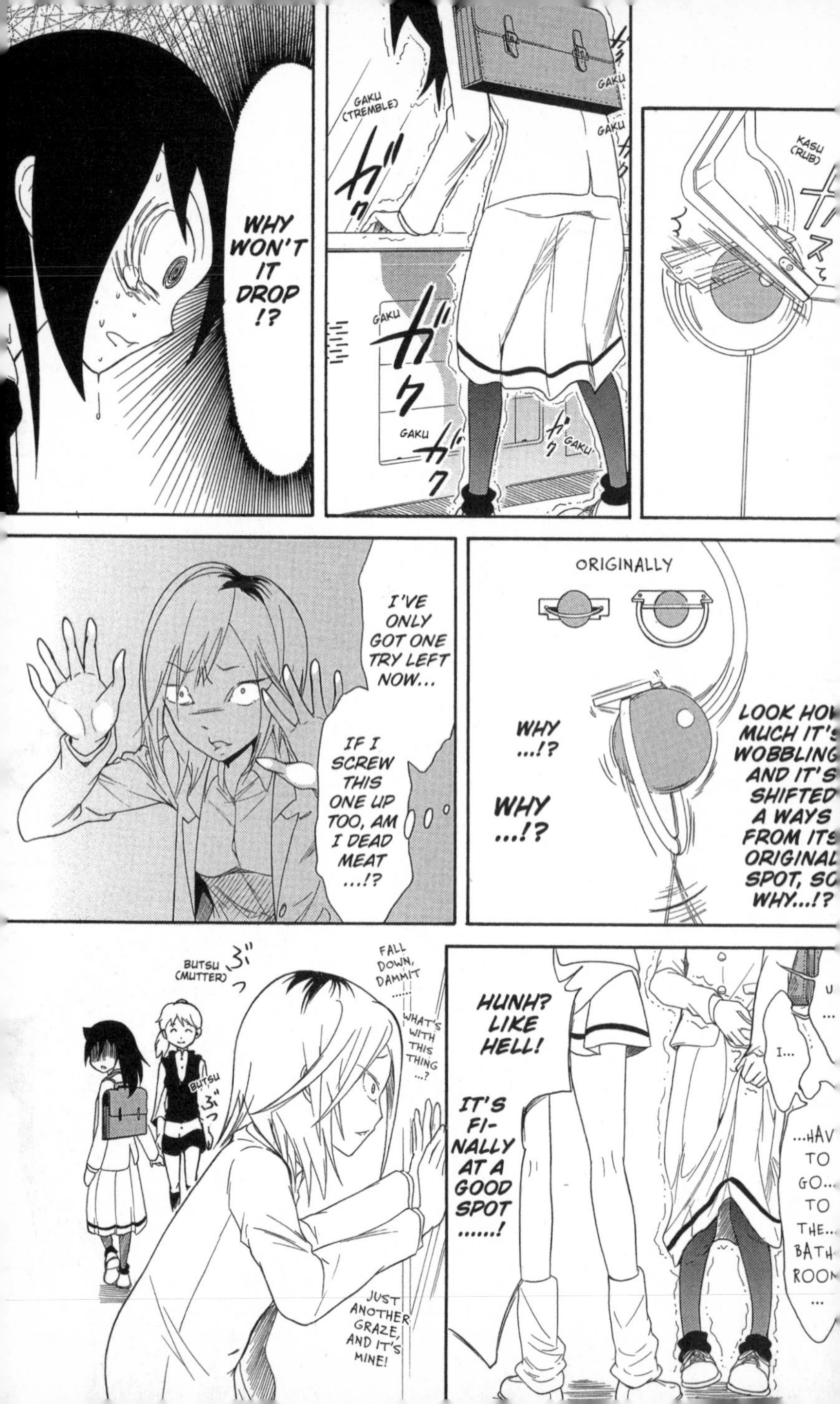
KASU (RUB)
カスッ
GAKU
GAKU
GAKU (TREMBLE)
ガク
GAKU
ガク
GAKU
ガク
GAKU
ガク
WHY WON'T IT DROP!?
ORIGINALLY
LOOK HOW MUCH IT'S WOBBLING AND IT'S SHIFTED A WAYS FROM ITS ORIGINAL SPOT, SO WHY...!?
WHY...!?
WHY...!?
I'VE ONLY GOT ONE TRY LEFT NOW...
IF I SCREW THIS ONE UP TOO, AM I DEAD MEAT...!?
U...
I...
...HAVE TO GO... TO THE... BATHROOM...
HUNH? LIKE HELL!
IT'S FINALLY AT A GOOD SPOT......!
FALL DOWN, DAMMIT......
WHAT'S WITH THIS THING...?
BUTSU (MUTTER) ぶつ
BUTSU ぶつ
JUST ANOTHER GRAZE, AND IT'S MINE!

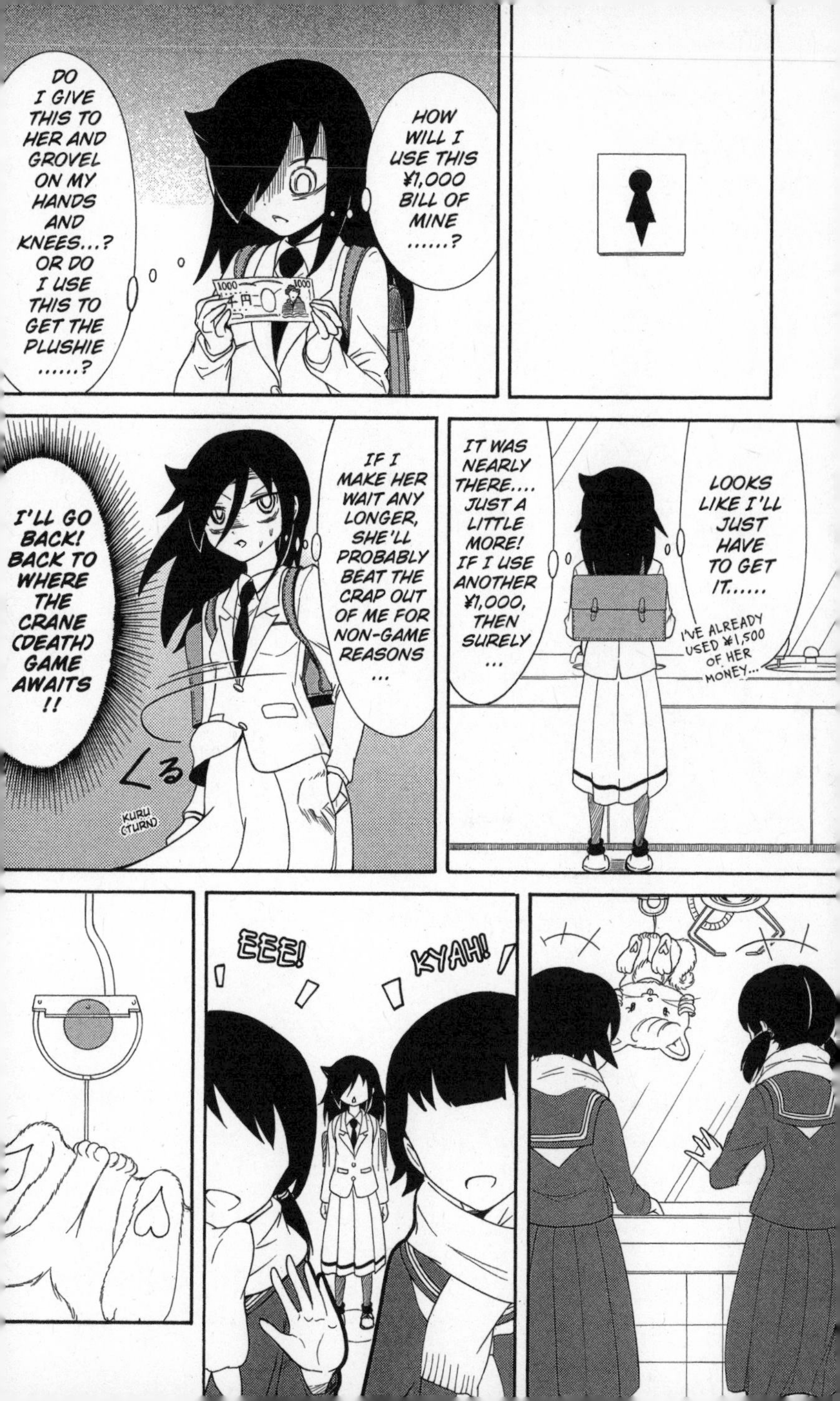
HOW WILL I USE THIS ¥1,000 BILL OF MINE ......?
DO I GIVE THIS TO HER AND GROVEL ON MY HANDS AND KNEES...? OR DO I USE THIS TO GET THE PLUSHIE ......?
LOOKS LIKE I'LL JUST HAVE TO GET IT......
IT WAS NEARLY THERE.... JUST A LITTLE MORE! IF I USE ANOTHER ¥1,000, THEN SURELY ...
I'VE ALREADY USED ¥1,500 OF HER MONEY...
IF I MAKE HER WAIT ANY LONGER, SHE'LL PROBABLY BEAT THE CRAP OUT OF ME FOR NON-GAME REASONS ...
I'LL GO BACK! BACK TO WHERE THE CRANE (DEATH) GAME AWAITS !!
くる
KURU (TURN)
KYAH!
EEE!

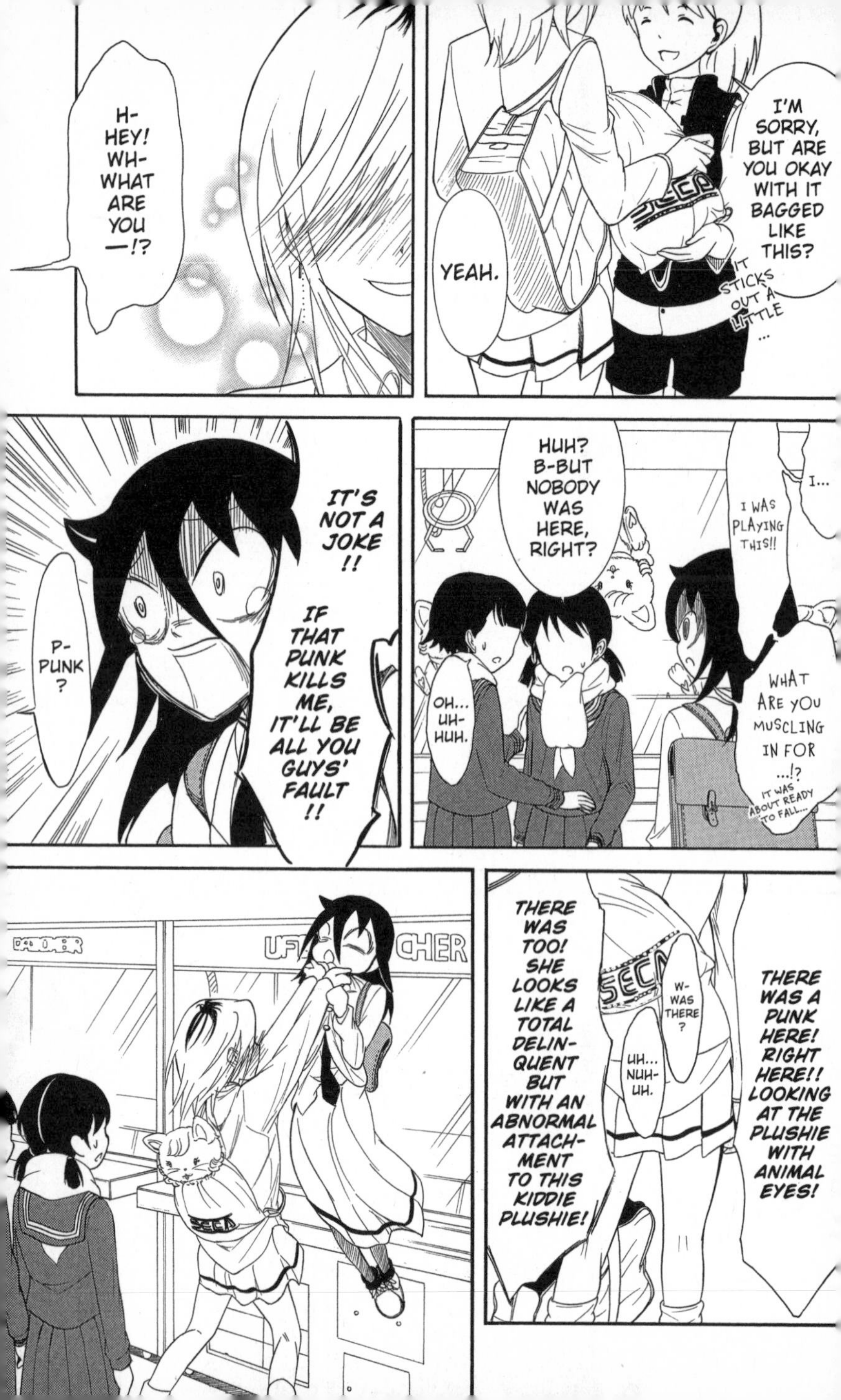

I'M SORRY, BUT ARE YOU OKAY WITH IT BAGGED LIKE THIS?
IT STICKS OUT A LITTLE...
YEAH.
H-HEY! WH-WHAT ARE YOU—!?
I...
I WAS PLAYING THIS!!
HUH? B-BUT NOBODY WAS HERE, RIGHT?
WHAT ARE YOU MUSCLING IN FOR...!?
IT WAS ABOUT READY TO FALL...
OH... UH-HUH.
IT'S NOT A JOKE!!
IF THAT PUNK KILLS ME, IT'LL BE ALL YOU GUYS' FAULT!!
P-PUNK?
THERE WAS A PUNK HERE! RIGHT HERE!! LOOKING AT THE PLUSHIE WITH ANIMAL EYES!
W-WAS THERE?
UH... NUH-UH.
THERE WAS TOO! SHE LOOKS LIKE A TOTAL DELINQUENT BUT WITH AN ABNORMAL ATTACHMENT TO THIS KIDDIE PLUSHIE!

No Matter How I Look at It, It's You Guys' Fault I'm Not Popular!

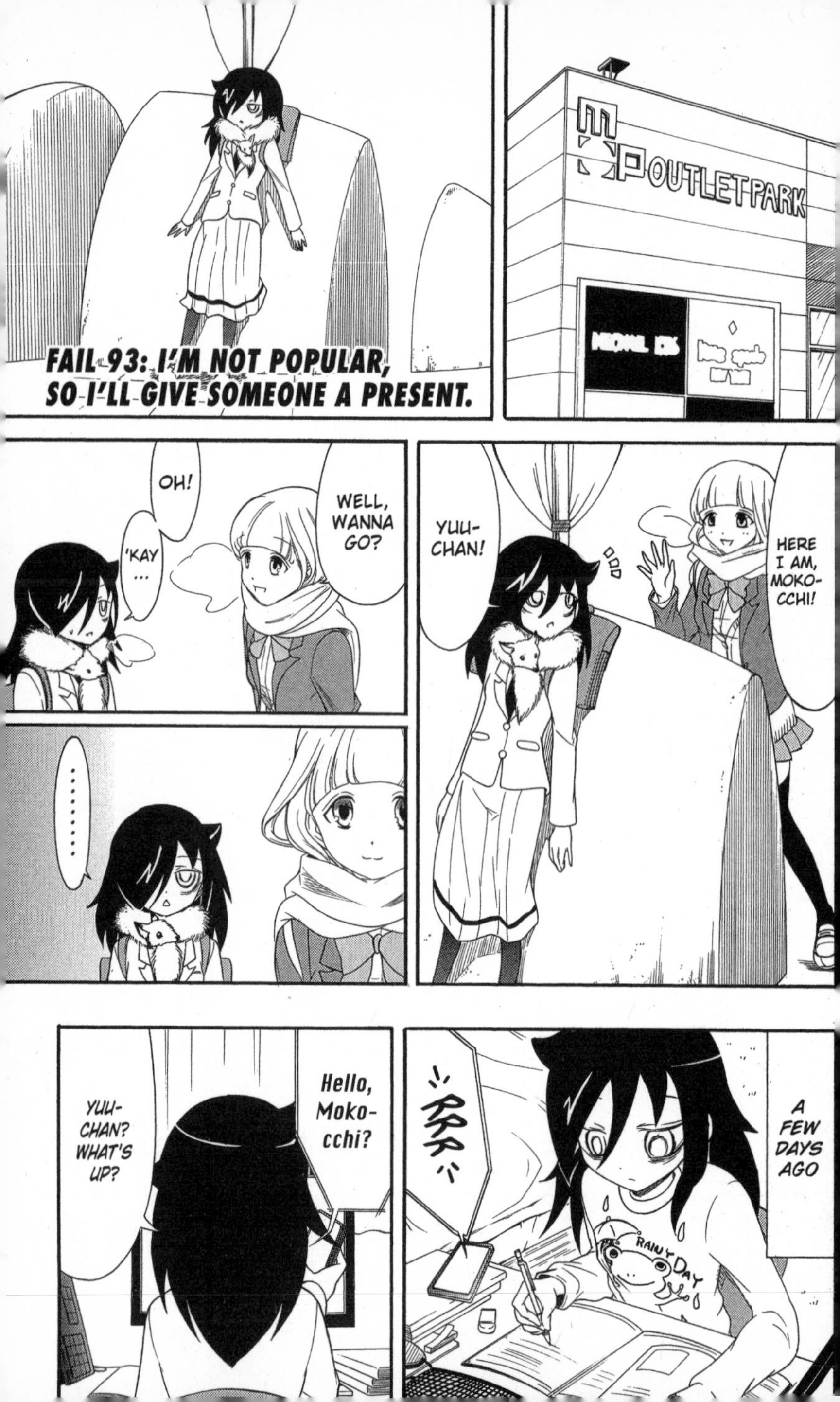

OUTLETPARK
FAIL 93: I'M NOT POPULAR, SO I'LL GIVE SOMEONE A PRESENT.
HERE I AM, MOKOCCHI!
YUU-CHAN!
WELL, WANNA GO?
OH!
'KAY ...
....
A FEW DAYS AGO
RRR
RAINY DAY
Hello, Moko-cchi?
YUU-CHAN? WHAT'S UP?

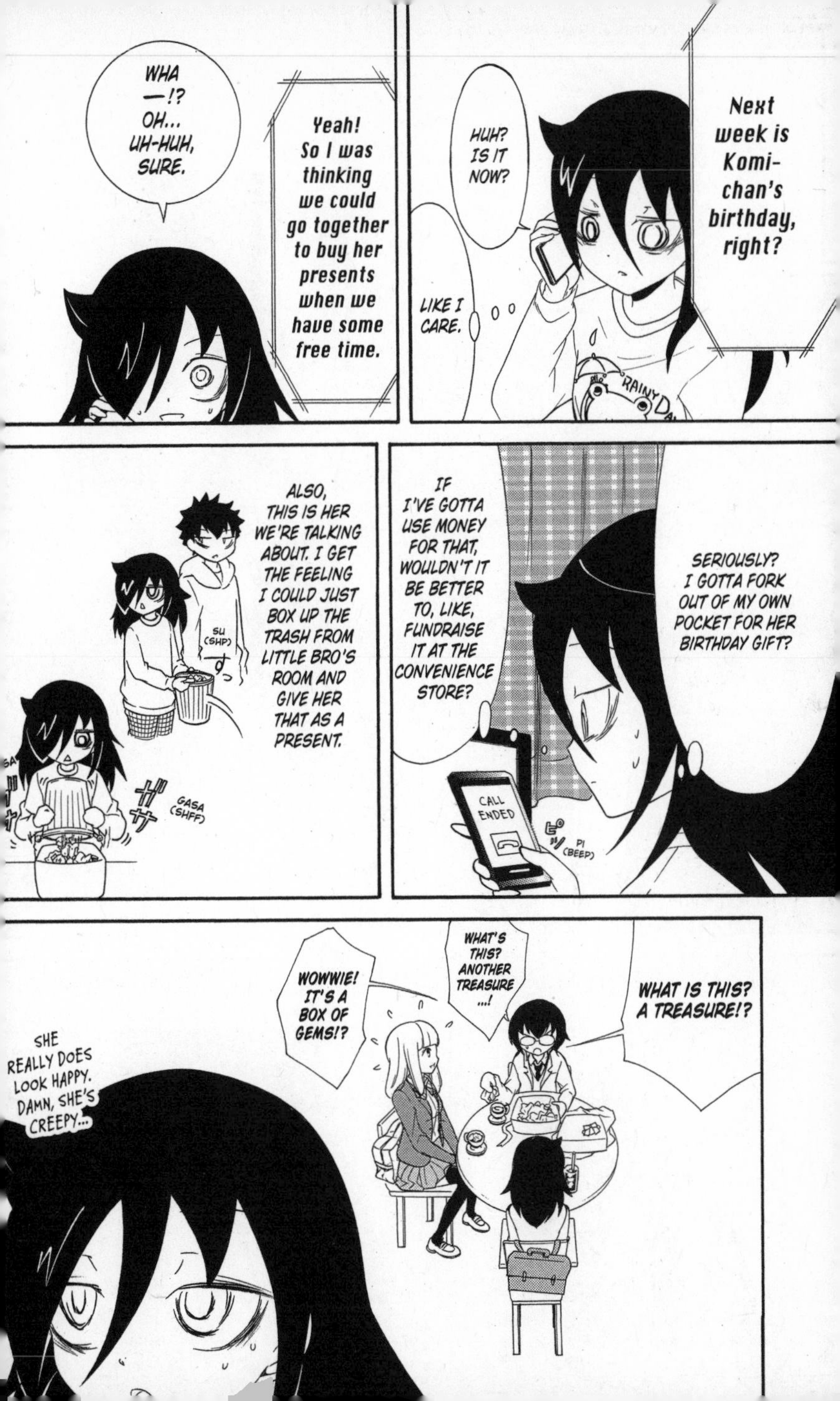
Next week is Komi-chan's birthday, right?
HUH? IS IT NOW?
LIKE I CARE.
Yeah! So I was thinking we could go together to buy her presents when we have some free time.
WHA—!? OH... UH-HUH, SURE.
SERIOUSLY? I GOTTA FORK OUT OF MY OWN POCKET FOR HER BIRTHDAY GIFT?
IF I'VE GOTTA USE MONEY FOR THAT, WOULDN'T IT BE BETTER TO, LIKE, FUNDRAISE IT AT THE CONVENIENCE STORE?
CALL ENDED
PI (BEEP)
ALSO, THIS IS HER WE'RE TALKING ABOUT. I GET THE FEELING I COULD JUST BOX UP THE TRASH FROM LITTLE BRO'S ROOM AND GIVE HER THAT AS A PRESENT.
SU (SHP)
GASA (SHFF)
WHAT IS THIS? A TREASURE!?
WHAT'S THIS? ANOTHER TREASURE...!
WOWWIE! IT'S A BOX OF GEMS!?
SHE REALLY DOES LOOK HAPPY. DAMN, SHE'S CREEPY...

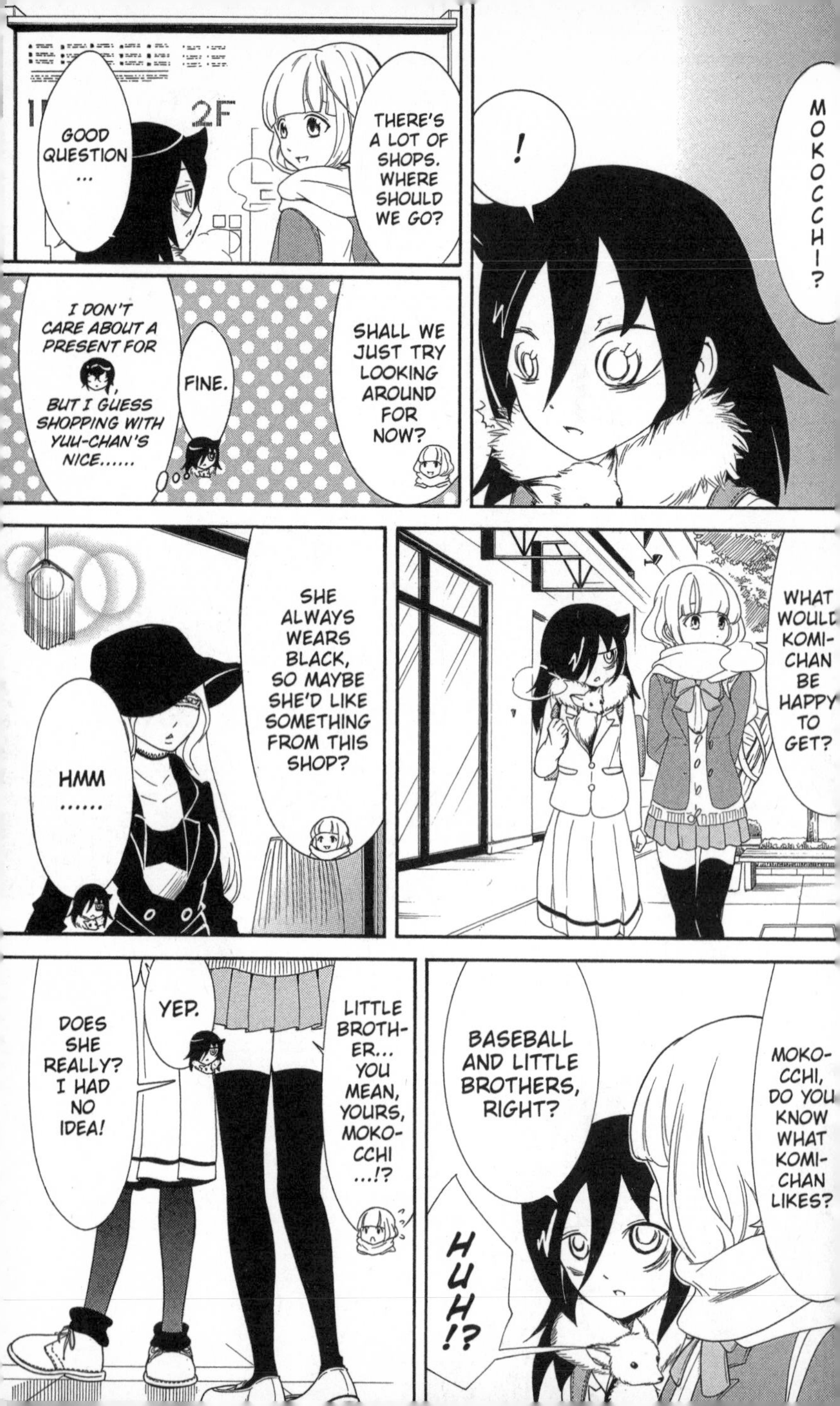
MOKOCCHI?
!
THERE'S A LOT OF SHOPS. WHERE SHOULD WE GO?
GOOD QUESTION ...
SHALL WE JUST TRY LOOKING AROUND FOR NOW?
FINE.
I DON'T CARE ABOUT A PRESENT FOR
BUT I GUESS SHOPPING WITH YUU-CHAN'S NICE......
WHAT WOULD KOMI-CHAN BE HAPPY TO GET?
SHE ALWAYS WEARS BLACK, SO MAYBE SHE'D LIKE SOMETHING FROM THIS SHOP?
HMM ......
MOKO-CCHI, DO YOU KNOW WHAT KOMI-CHAN LIKES?
BASEBALL AND LITTLE BROTHERS, RIGHT?
HUH!?
LITTLE BROTH-ER... YOU MEAN, YOURS, MOKO-CCHI ...!?
YEP.
DOES SHE REALLY? I HAD NO IDEA!

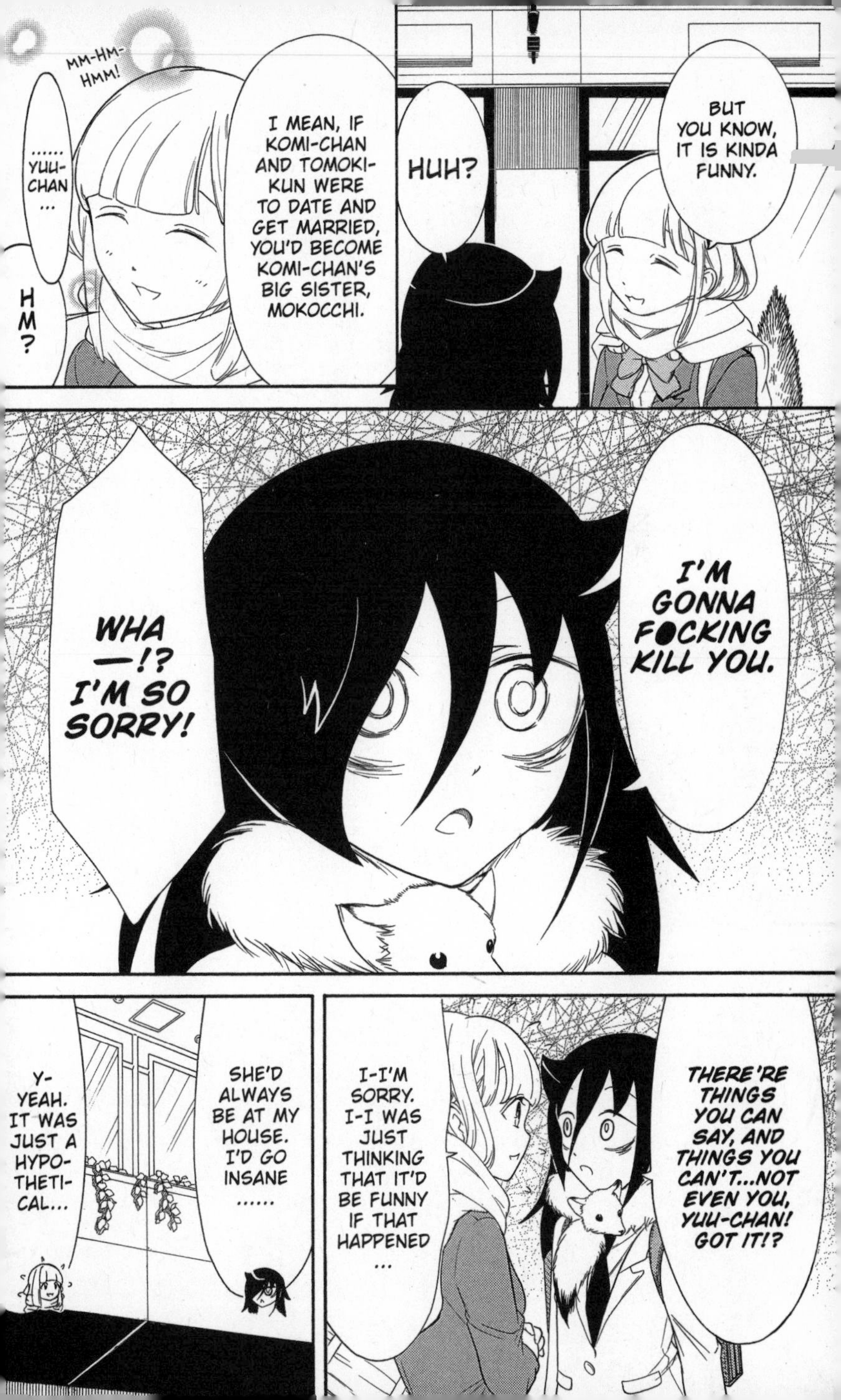
BUT YOU KNOW, IT IS KINDA FUNNY.
HUH?
I MEAN, IF KOMI-CHAN AND TOMOKI-KUN WERE TO DATE AND GET MARRIED, YOU'D BECOME KOMI-CHAN'S BIG SISTER, MOKOCCHI.
MM-HM-HMM!
......YUU-CHAN...
HM?
I'M GONNA F●CKING KILL YOU.
WHA—!? I'M SO SORRY!
THERE'RE THINGS YOU CAN SAY, AND THINGS YOU CAN'T...NOT EVEN YOU, YUU-CHAN! GOT IT!?
I-I'M SORRY. I-I WAS JUST THINKING THAT IT'D BE FUNNY IF THAT HAPPENED...
SHE'D ALWAYS BE AT MY HOUSE. I'D GO INSANE......
Y-YEAH. IT WAS JUST A HYPO-THETI-CAL...

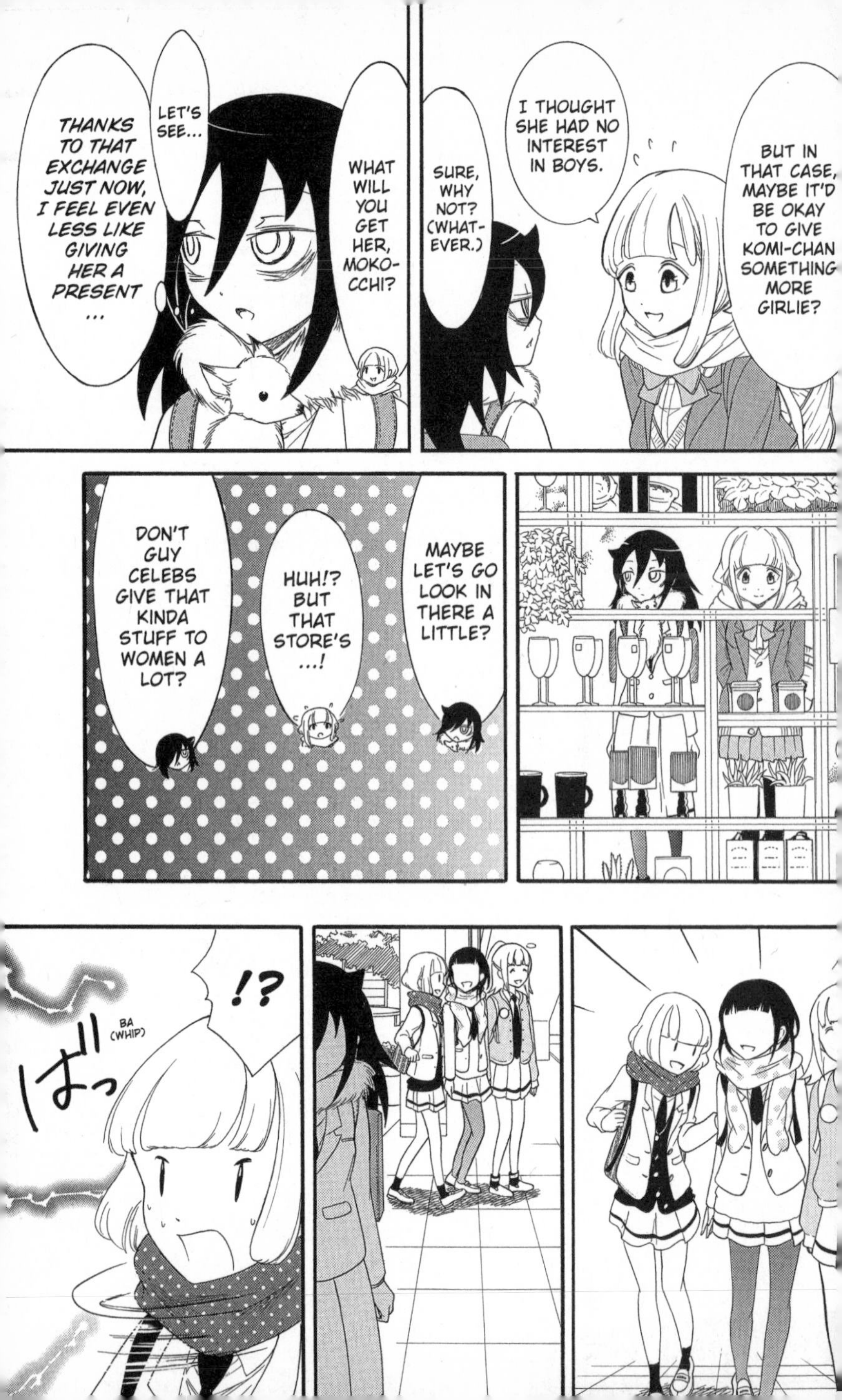
BUT IN THAT CASE, MAYBE IT'D BE OKAY TO GIVE KOMI-CHAN SOMETHING MORE GIRLIE?
I THOUGHT SHE HAD NO INTEREST IN BOYS.
SURE, WHY NOT? (WHATEVER.)
WHAT WILL YOU GET HER, MOKOCCHI?
LET'S SEE...
THANKS TO THAT EXCHANGE JUST NOW, I FEEL EVEN LESS LIKE GIVING HER A PRESENT...
MAYBE LET'S GO LOOK IN THERE A LITTLE?
HUH!? BUT THAT STORE'S...!
DON'T GUY CELEBS GIVE THAT KINDA STUFF TO WOMEN A LOT?
!?
ばっ
BA (WHIP)

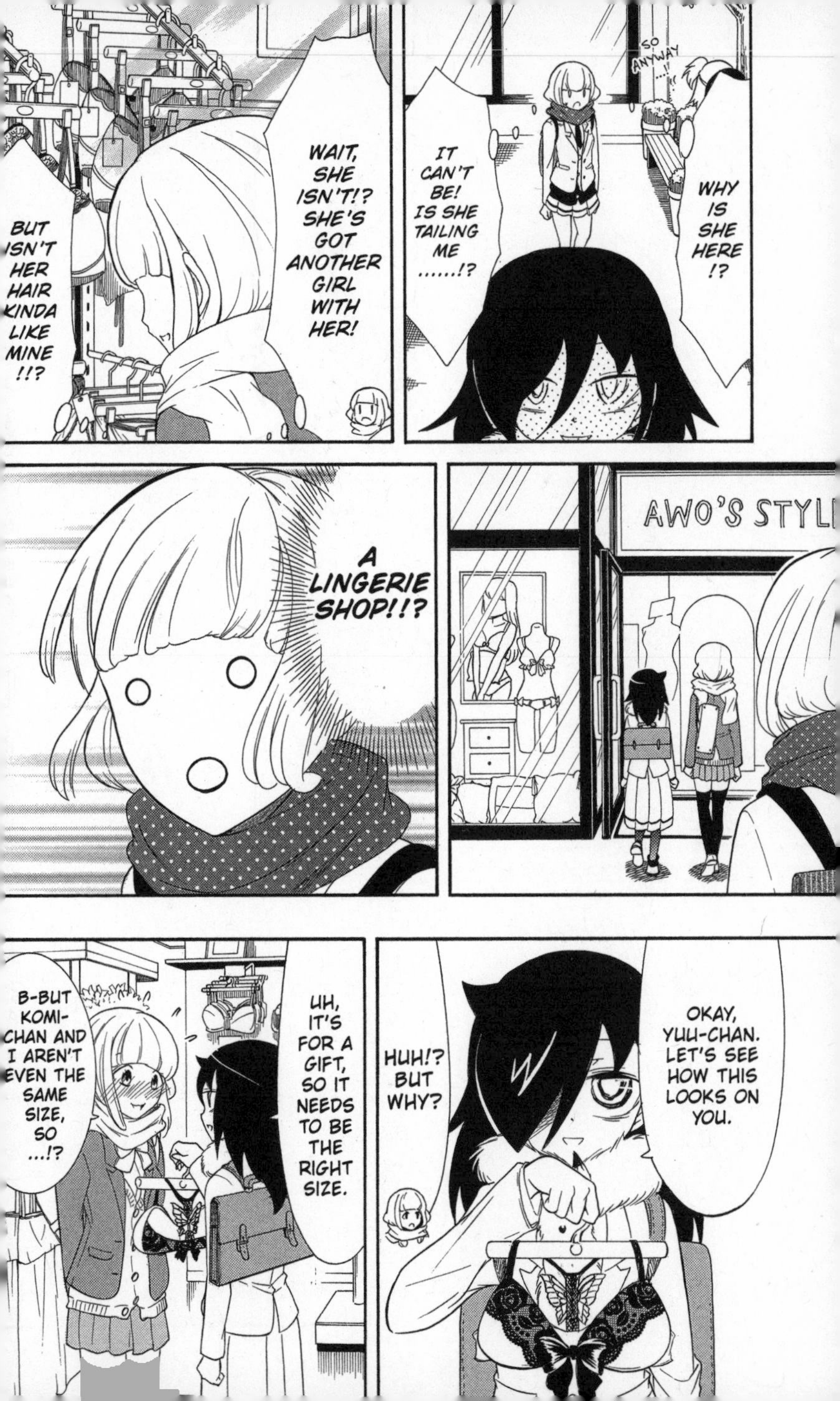
SO ANYWAY ....!!
WHY IS SHE HERE !?
IT CAN'T BE! IS SHE TAILING ME ......!?
WAIT, SHE ISN'T!? SHE'S GOT ANOTHER GIRL WITH HER!
BUT ISN'T HER HAIR KINDA LIKE MINE !!?
AWO'S STYL
A LINGERIE SHOP!!?
OKAY, YUU-CHAN. LET'S SEE HOW THIS LOOKS ON YOU.
HUH!? BUT WHY?
UH, IT'S FOR A GIFT, SO IT NEEDS TO BE THE RIGHT SIZE.
B-BUT KOMI-CHAN AND I AREN'T EVEN THE SAME SIZE, SO ...!?

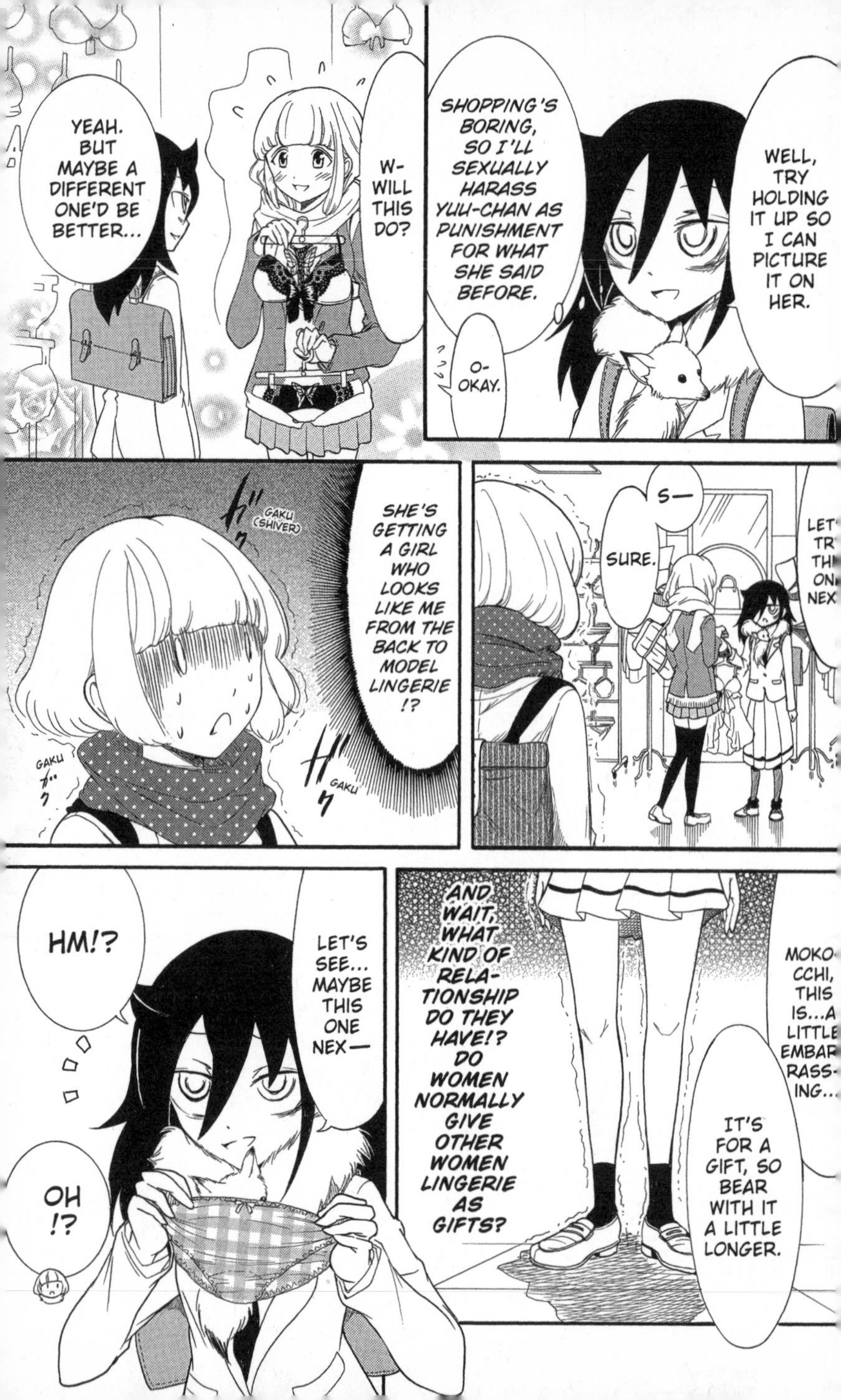

WELL, TRY HOLDING IT UP SO I CAN PICTURE IT ON HER.
SHOPPING'S BORING, SO I'LL SEXUALLY HARASS YUU-CHAN AS PUNISHMENT FOR WHAT SHE SAID BEFORE.
O-OKAY.
W-WILL THIS DO?
YEAH. BUT MAYBE A DIFFERENT ONE'D BE BETTER...
LET' TR THI ON NEX
S—
SURE.
SHE'S GETTING A GIRL WHO LOOKS LIKE ME FROM THE BACK TO MODEL LINGERIE !?
GAKU (SHIVER)
GAKU
GAKU
MOKOCCHI, THIS IS...A LITTLE EMBARRASSING...
IT'S FOR A GIFT, SO BEAR WITH IT A LITTLE LONGER.
AND WAIT, WHAT KIND OF RELATIONSHIP DO THEY HAVE!? DO WOMEN NORMALLY GIVE OTHER WOMEN LINGERIE AS GIFTS?
LET'S SEE... MAYBE THIS ONE NEX—
HM!?
OH !?

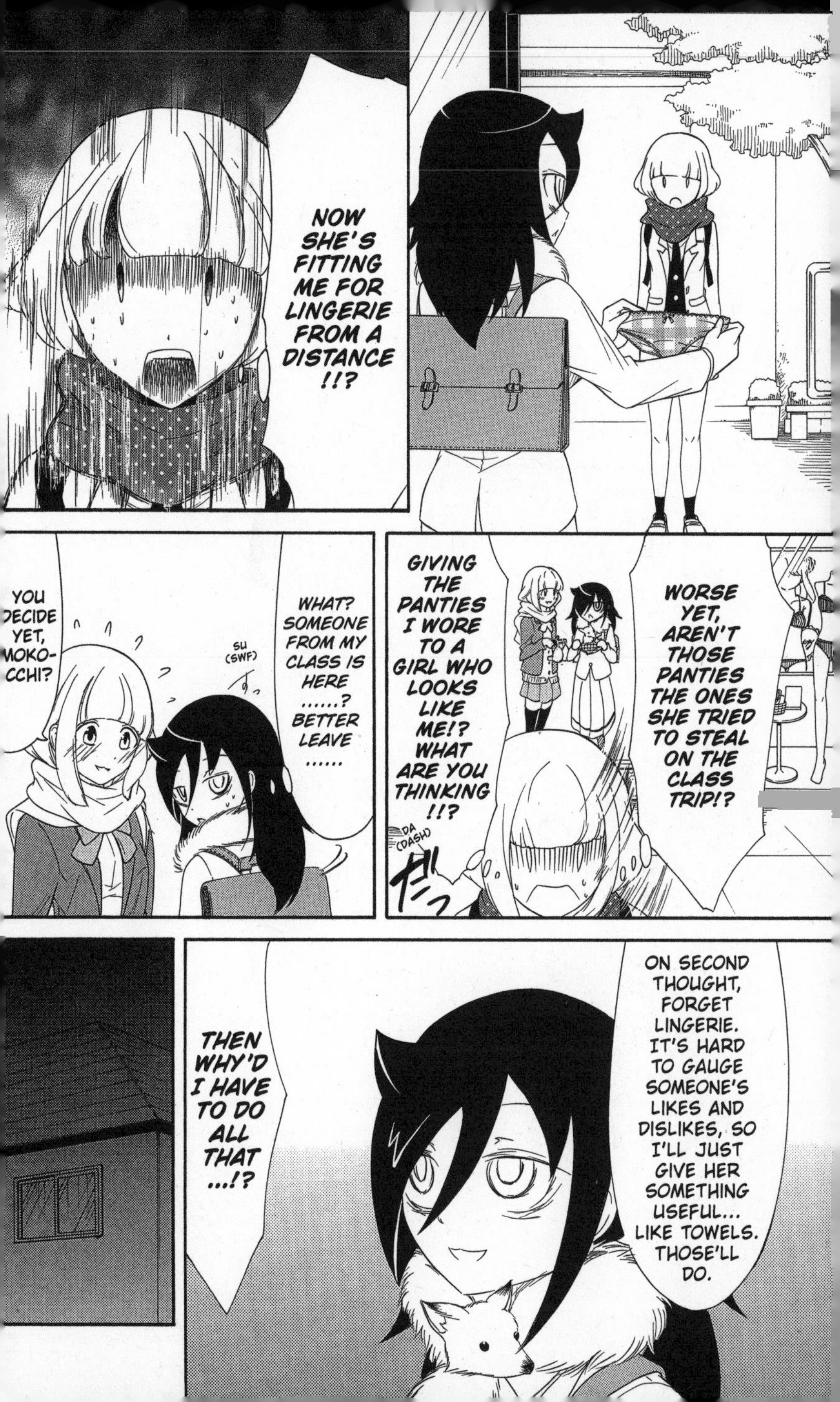
NOW SHE'S FITTING ME FOR LINGERIE FROM A DISTANCE!!?
WORSE YET, AREN'T THOSE PANTIES THE ONES SHE TRIED TO STEAL ON THE CLASS TRIP!?
GIVING THE PANTIES I WORE TO A GIRL WHO LOOKS LIKE ME!? WHAT ARE YOU THINKING!!?
DA (DASH)
WHAT? SOMEONE FROM MY CLASS IS HERE ......? BETTER LEAVE ......
SU (SWF)
YOU DECIDE YET, MOKO-CCHI?
ON SECOND THOUGHT, FORGET LINGERIE. IT'S HARD TO GAUGE SOMEONE'S LIKES AND DISLIKES, SO I'LL JUST GIVE HER SOMETHING USEFUL... LIKE TOWELS. THOSE'LL DO.
THEN WHY'D I HAVE TO DO ALL THAT...!?

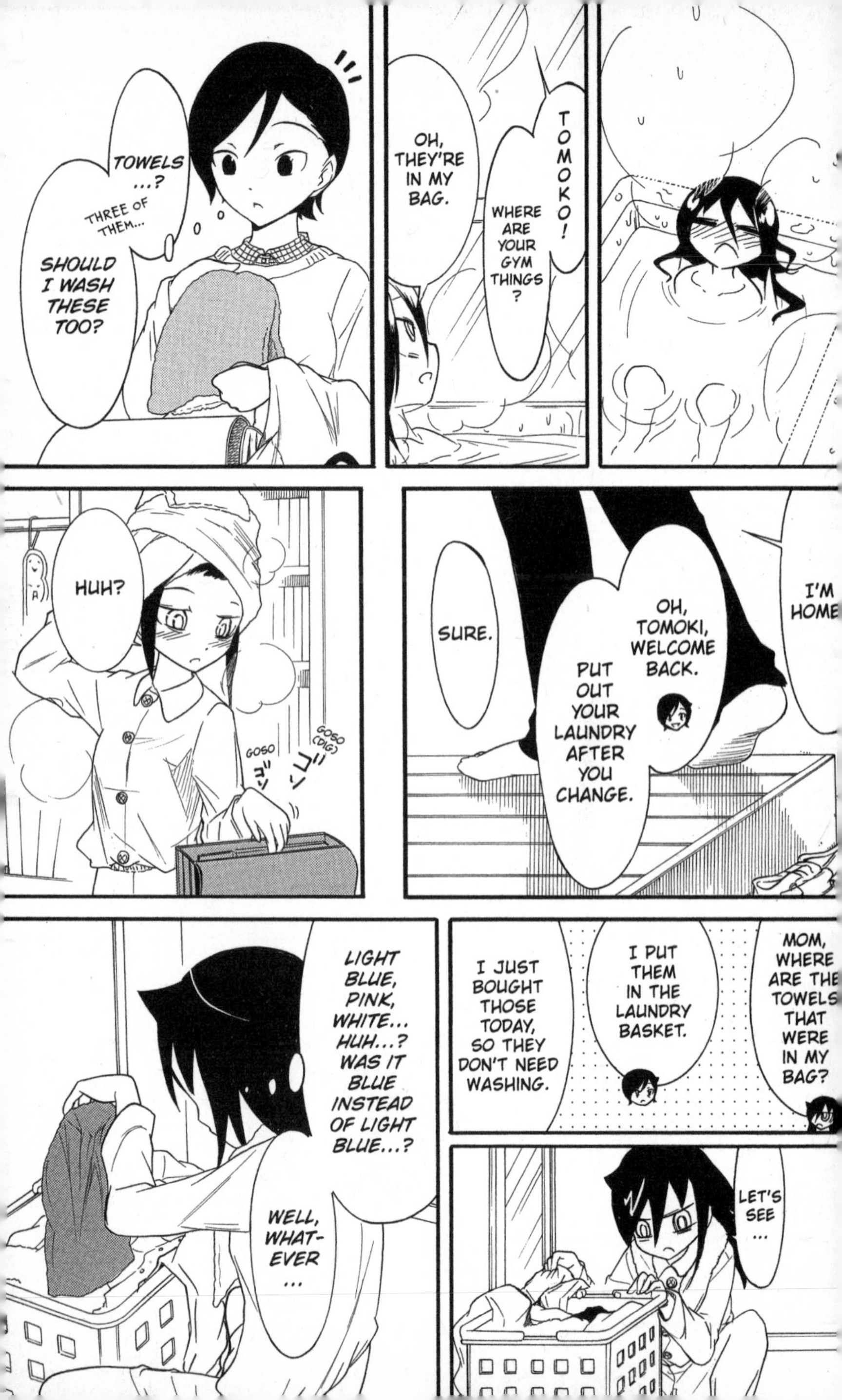
TOMOKO! WHERE ARE YOUR GYM THINGS?
OH, THEY'RE IN MY BAG.
TOWELS ...?
THREE OF THEM...
SHOULD I WASH THESE TOO?
I'M HOME
OH, TOMOKI, WELCOME BACK.
PUT OUT YOUR LAUNDRY AFTER YOU CHANGE.
SURE.
HUH?
GOSO (DIG)
GOSO
MOM, WHERE ARE THE TOWELS THAT WERE IN MY BAG?
I PUT THEM IN THE LAUNDRY BASKET.
I JUST BOUGHT THOSE TODAY, SO THEY DON'T NEED WASHING.
LET'S SEE ...
LIGHT BLUE, PINK, WHITE... HUH...? WAS IT BLUE INSTEAD OF LIGHT BLUE...?
WELL, WHATEVER ...

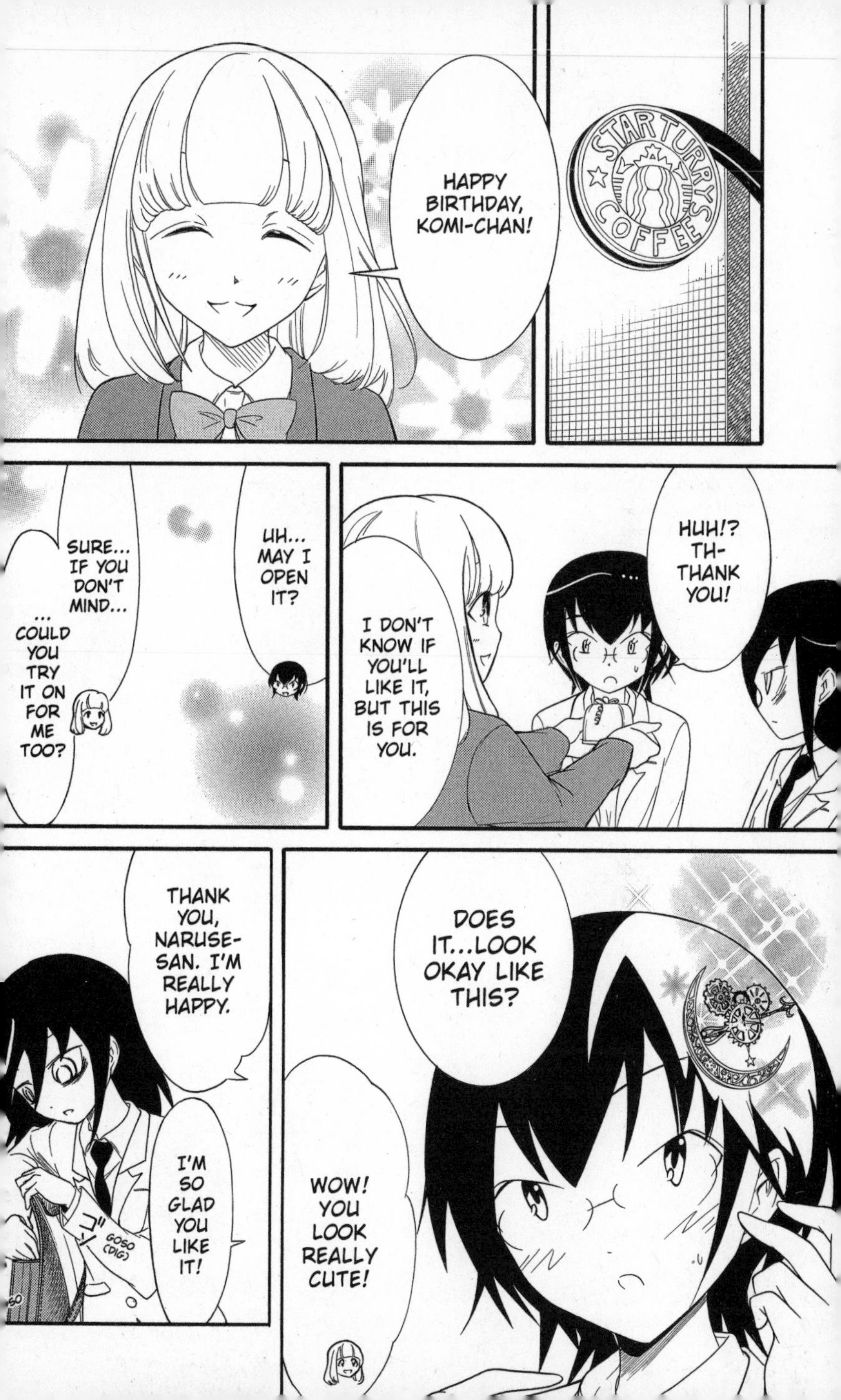
STARTURRY COFFEE
HAPPY BIRTHDAY, KOMI-CHAN!
HUH!? TH-THANK YOU!
I DON'T KNOW IF YOU'LL LIKE IT, BUT THIS IS FOR YOU.
UH... MAY I OPEN IT?
SURE... IF YOU DON'T MIND...
...COULD YOU TRY IT ON FOR ME TOO?
DOES IT...LOOK OKAY LIKE THIS?
WOW! YOU LOOK REALLY CUTE!
THANK YOU, NARUSE-SAN. I'M REALLY HAPPY.
I'M SO GLAD YOU LIKE IT!
ゴソ
GOSO (DIG)

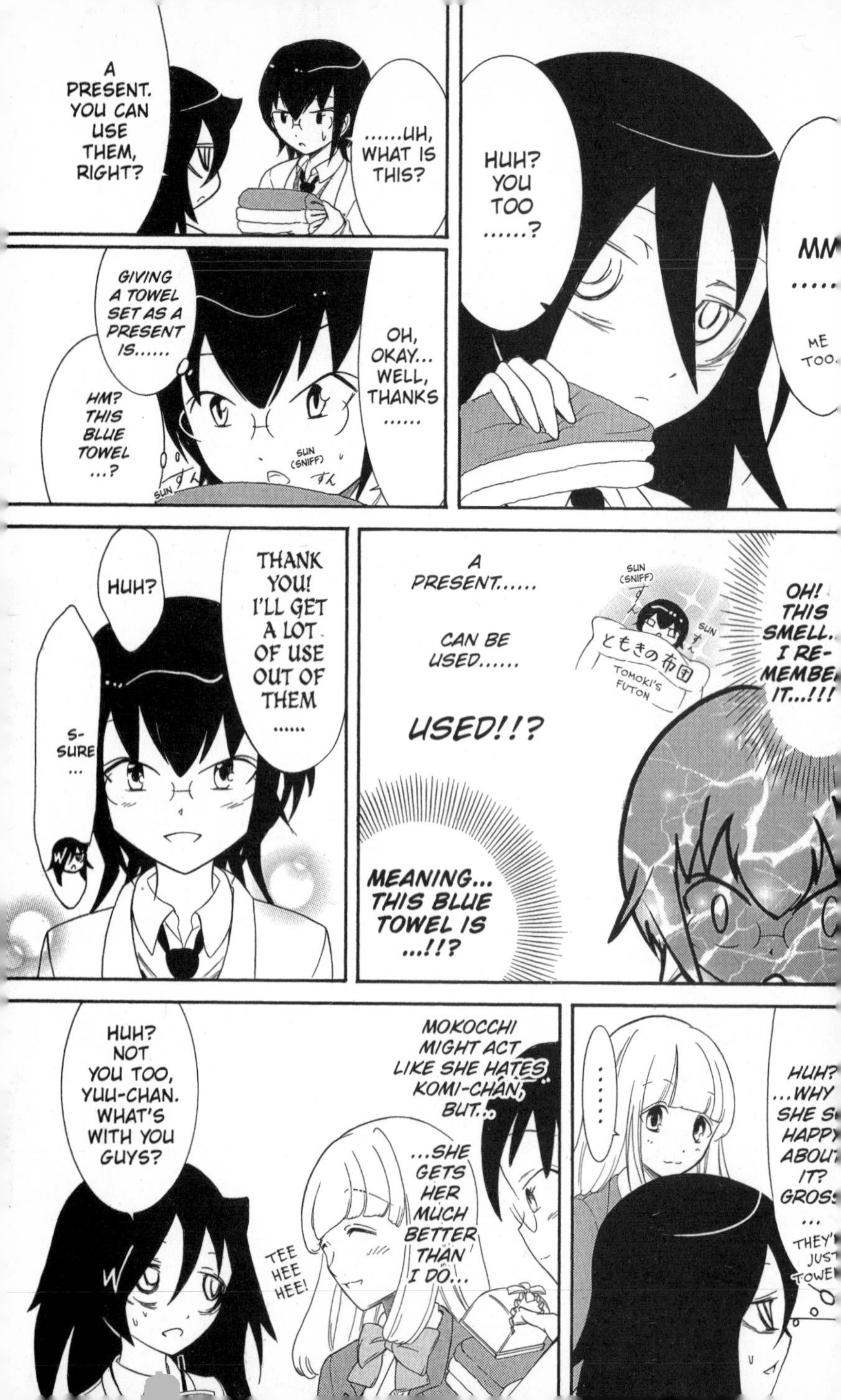
MN ......
ME TOO.
HUH? YOU TOO ......?
......UH, WHAT IS THIS?
A PRESENT. YOU CAN USE THEM, RIGHT?
OH, OKAY... WELL, THANKS ......
GIVING A TOWEL SET AS A PRESENT IS......
SUN (SNIFF)
HM? THIS BLUE TOWEL ...?
SUN
OH! THIS SMELL.. I RE- MEMBE IT...!!!
SUN (SNIFF)
SUN
ともきの布団
TOMOKI'S FUTON
A PRESENT......
CAN BE USED......
USED!!?
MEANING... THIS BLUE TOWEL IS ...!!?
THANK YOU! I'LL GET A LOT OF USE OUT OF THEM ......
HUH?
S-SURE ...
HUH? ...WHY SHE S HAPPY ABOUT IT? GROSS ...
......
THEY' JUST TOWE
MOKOCCHI MIGHT ACT LIKE SHE HATES KOMI-CHAN, BUT...
...SHE GETS HER MUCH BETTER THAN I DO...
TEE HEE HEE!
HUH? NOT YOU TOO, YUU-CHAN. WHAT'S WITH YOU GUYS?

No Matter How I Look at It, It's You Guys' Fault I'm Not Popular!

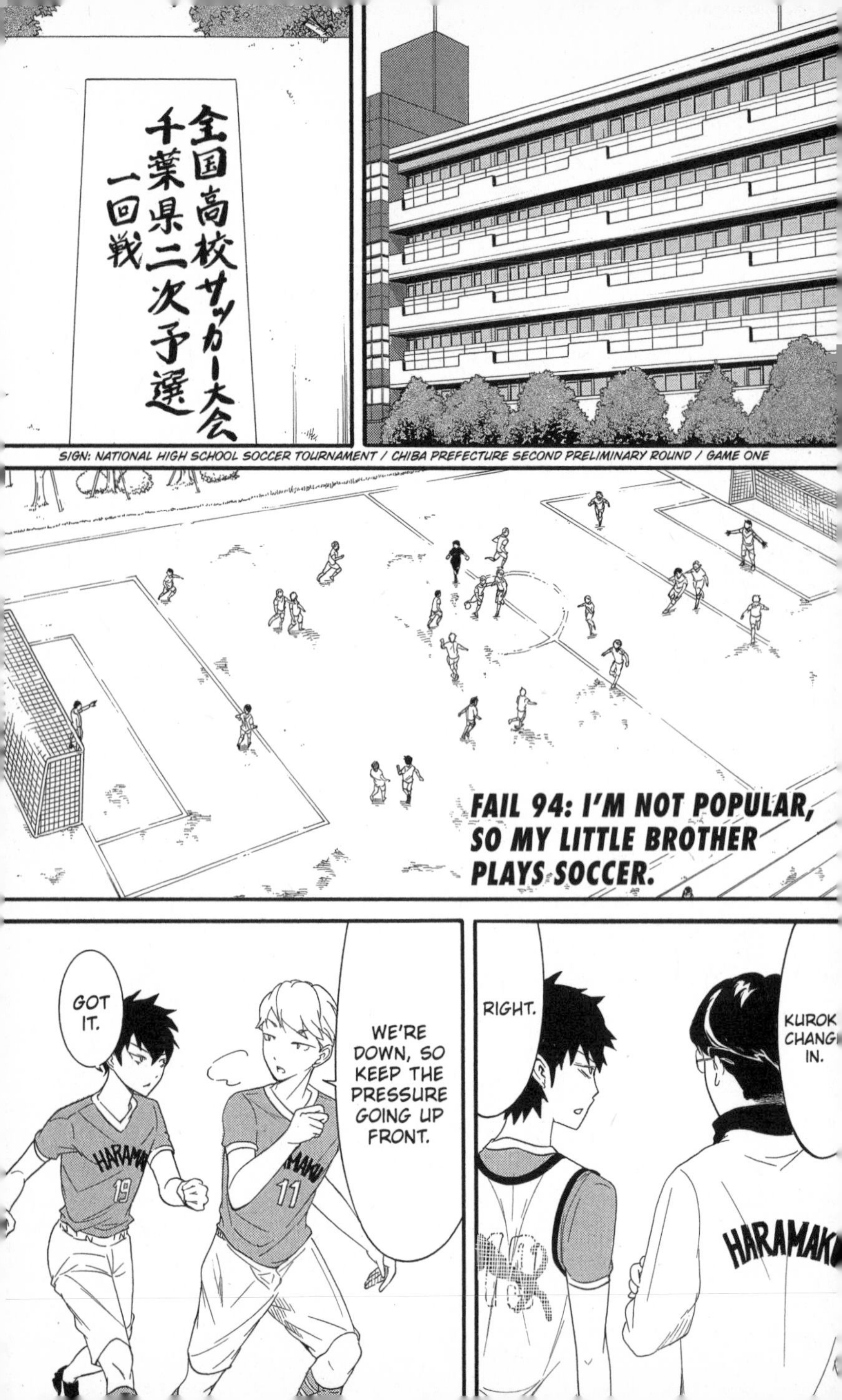
全国高校サッカー大会
千葉県二次予選
一回戦
SIGN: NATIONAL HIGH SCHOOL SOCCER TOURNAMENT / CHIBA PREFECTURE SECOND PRELIMINARY ROUND / GAME ONE
FAIL 94: I'M NOT POPULAR, SO MY LITTLE BROTHER PLAYS SOCCER.
KUROK CHANG IN.
RIGHT.
WE'RE DOWN, SO KEEP THE PRESSURE GOING UP FRONT.
GOT IT.

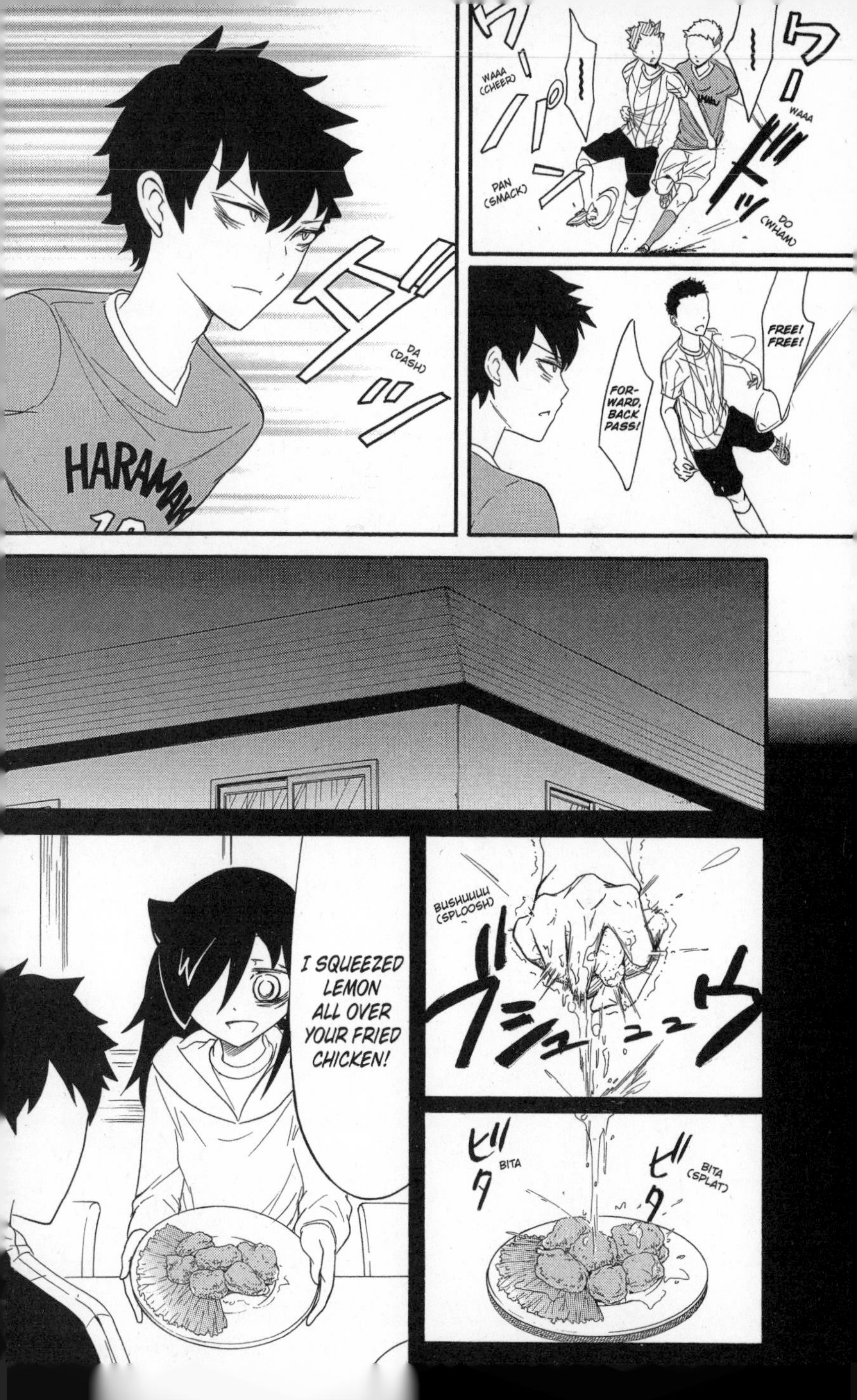
WAAA
WAAA (CHEER)
PAN (SMACK)
DO (WHAM)
FREE! FREE!
FOR-WARD, BACK PASS!
DA (DASH)
BUSHUUUU (SPLOOSH)
BITA (SPLAT)
BITA
I SQUEEZED LEMON ALL OVER YOUR FRIED CHICKEN!

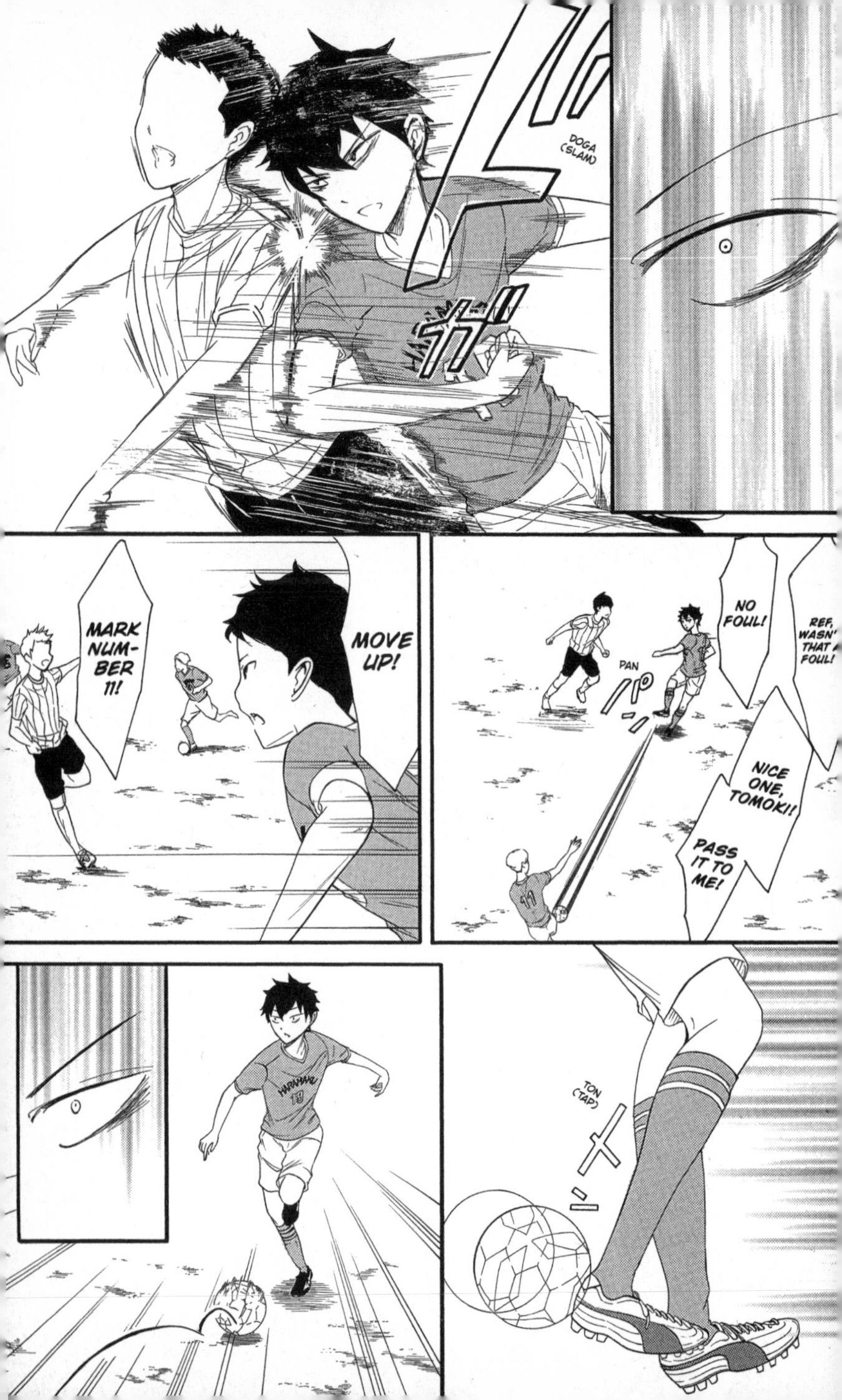
DOGA (SLAM)
REF, WASN' THAT FOUL!
NO FOUL!
PAN
NICE ONE, TOMOKI!!
PASS IT TO ME!
MOVE UP!
MARK NUM-BER 11!
TON (TAP)

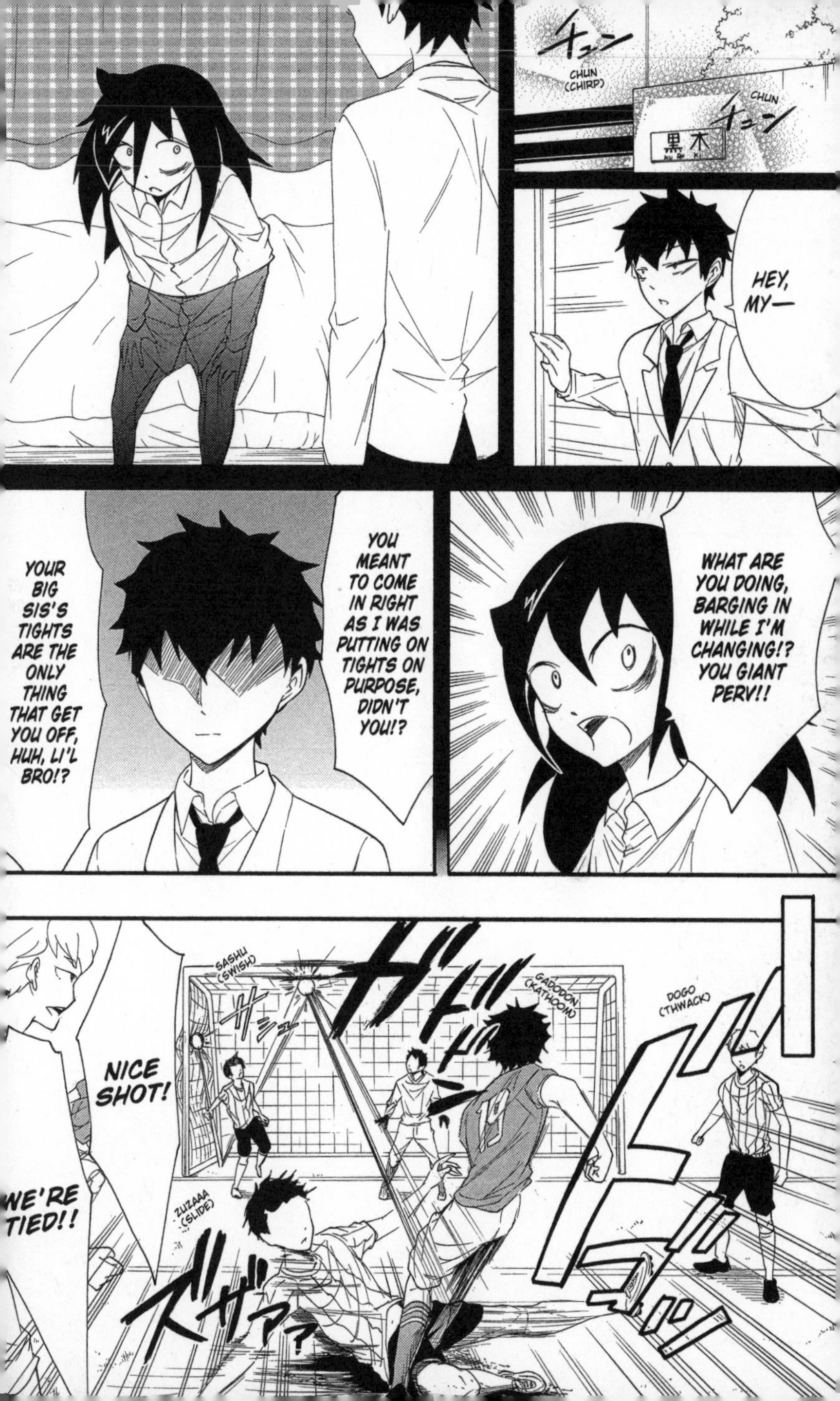

チュン
CHUN (CHIRP)
黒木
KU RO KI
チュン
CHUN
HEY, MY—
WHAT ARE YOU DOING, BARGING IN WHILE I'M CHANGING!? YOU GIANT PERV!!
YOU MEANT TO COME IN RIGHT AS I WAS PUTTING ON TIGHTS ON PURPOSE, DIDN'T YOU!?
YOUR BIG SIS'S TIGHTS ARE THE ONLY THING THAT GET YOU OFF, HUH, LI'L BRO!?
DOGO (THWACK)
GADODON (KATHOOM)
SASHU (SWISH)
NICE SHOT!
ZUZAAA (SLIDE)
WE'RE TIED!!

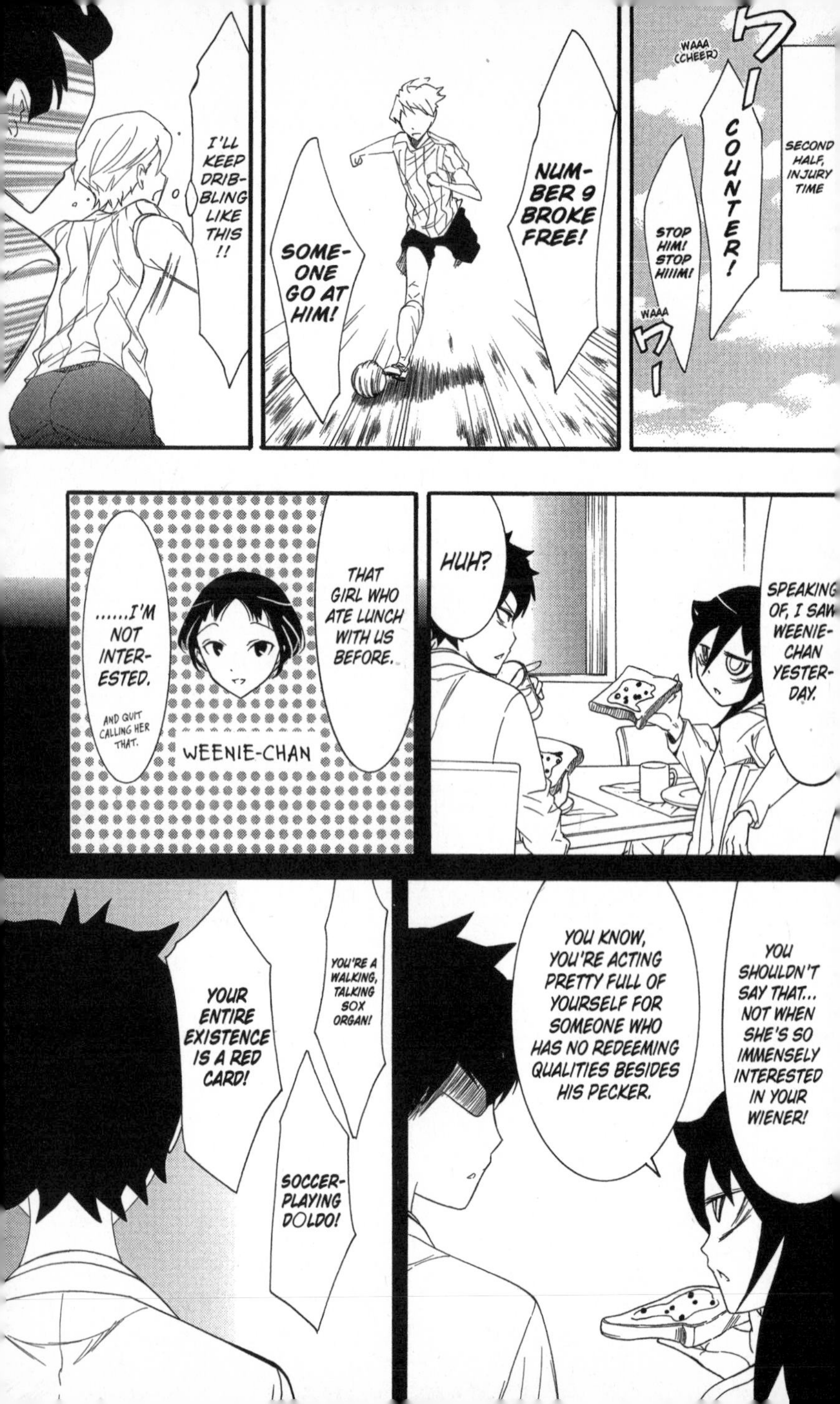
SECOND HALF, INJURY TIME
WAAA (CHEER)
COUNTER!
STOP HIM! STOP HIIIM!
WAAA
NUMBER 9 BROKE FREE!
SOMEONE GO AT HIM!
I'LL KEEP DRIBBLING LIKE THIS!!
SPEAKING OF, I SAW WEENIE-CHAN YESTERDAY.
HUH?
THAT GIRL WHO ATE LUNCH WITH US BEFORE.
WEENIE-CHAN
......I'M NOT INTERESTED.
AND QUIT CALLING HER THAT.
YOU SHOULDN'T SAY THAT... NOT WHEN SHE'S SO IMMENSELY INTERESTED IN YOUR WIENER!
YOU KNOW, YOU'RE ACTING PRETTY FULL OF YOURSELF FOR SOMEONE WHO HAS NO REDEEMING QUALITIES BESIDES HIS PECKER.
YOU'RE A WALKING, TALKING SOX ORGAN!
YOUR ENTIRE EXISTENCE IS A RED CARD!
SOCCER-PLAYING D○LDO!

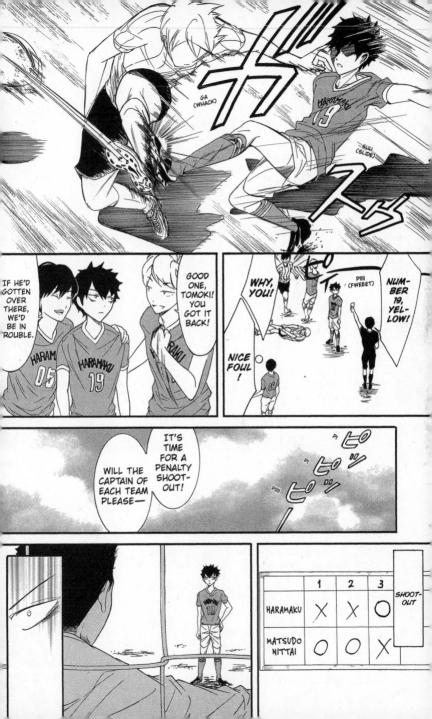

GA
(WHACK)

SUU
(SLIDE)

IF HE'D GOTTEN OVER THERE, WE'D BE IN TROUBLE.

GOOD ONE, TOMOKI! YOU GOT IT BACK!

HARAMAKU
05

HARAMAKU
19

RAKU

WHY, YOU!

NICE FOUL!

PIIII
(FWEET)

NUMBER 19, YELLOW!

WILL THE CAPTAIN OF EACH TEAM PLEASE—

IT'S TIME FOR A PENALTY SHOOT-OUT!

PI
PI
PIIII

PI
PI
PI

	1	2	3	SHOOT-OUT
HARAMAKU	X	X	O	
MATSUDO NITTAI	O	O	X	

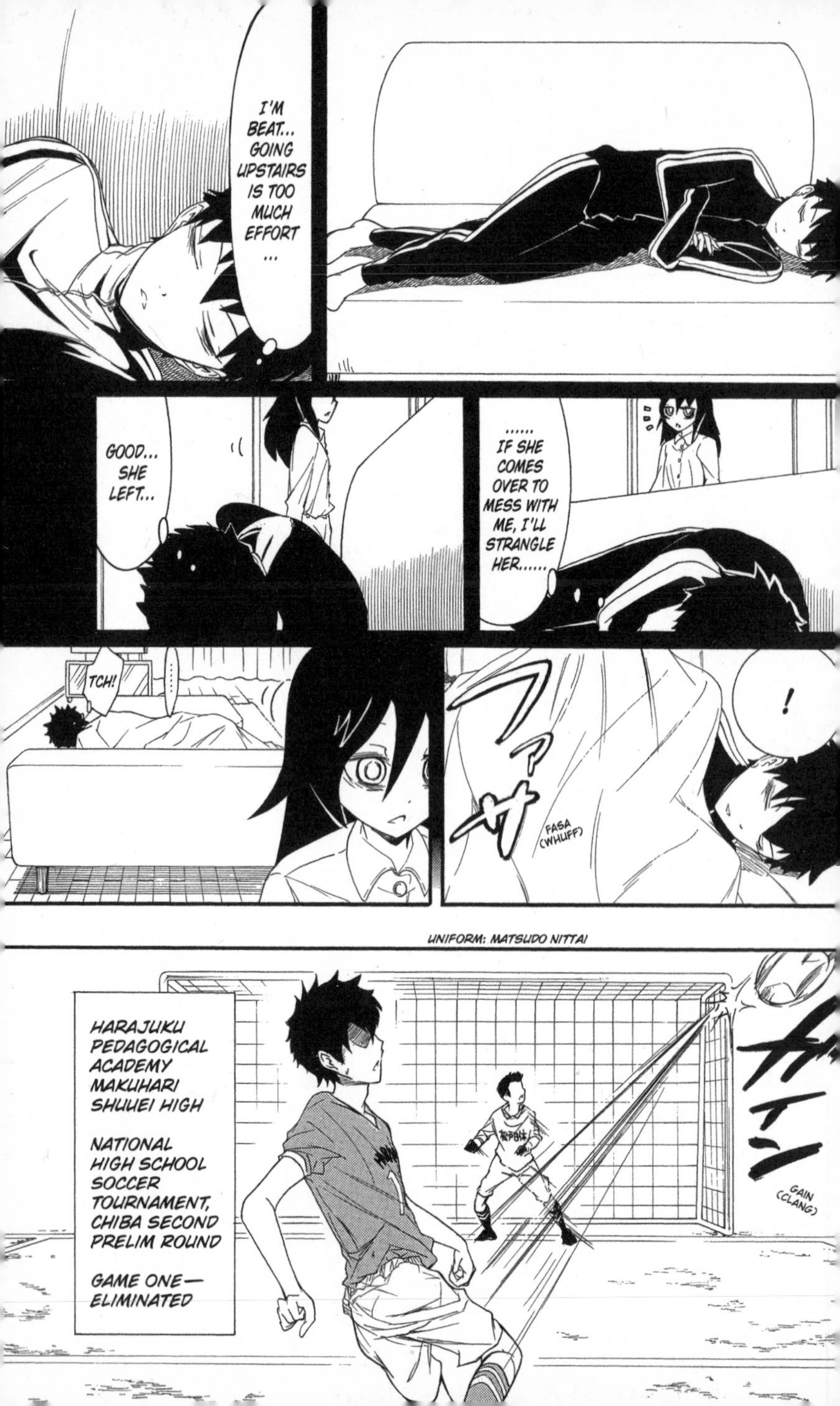
I'M BEAT... GOING UPSTAIRS IS TOO MUCH EFFORT ...
...... IF SHE COMES OVER TO MESS WITH ME, I'LL STRANGLE HER......
GOOD... SHE LEFT...
!
FASA (WHUFF)
TCH!
UNIFORM: MATSUDO NITTAI
GAIN (CLANG)
HARAJUKU PEDAGOGICAL ACADEMY
MAKUHARI SHUUEI HIGH
NATIONAL HIGH SCHOOL SOCCER TOURNAMENT, CHIBA SECOND PRELIM ROUND
GAME ONE—ELIMINATED

No Matter How I Look at It, It's You Guys' Fault I'm Not Popular!

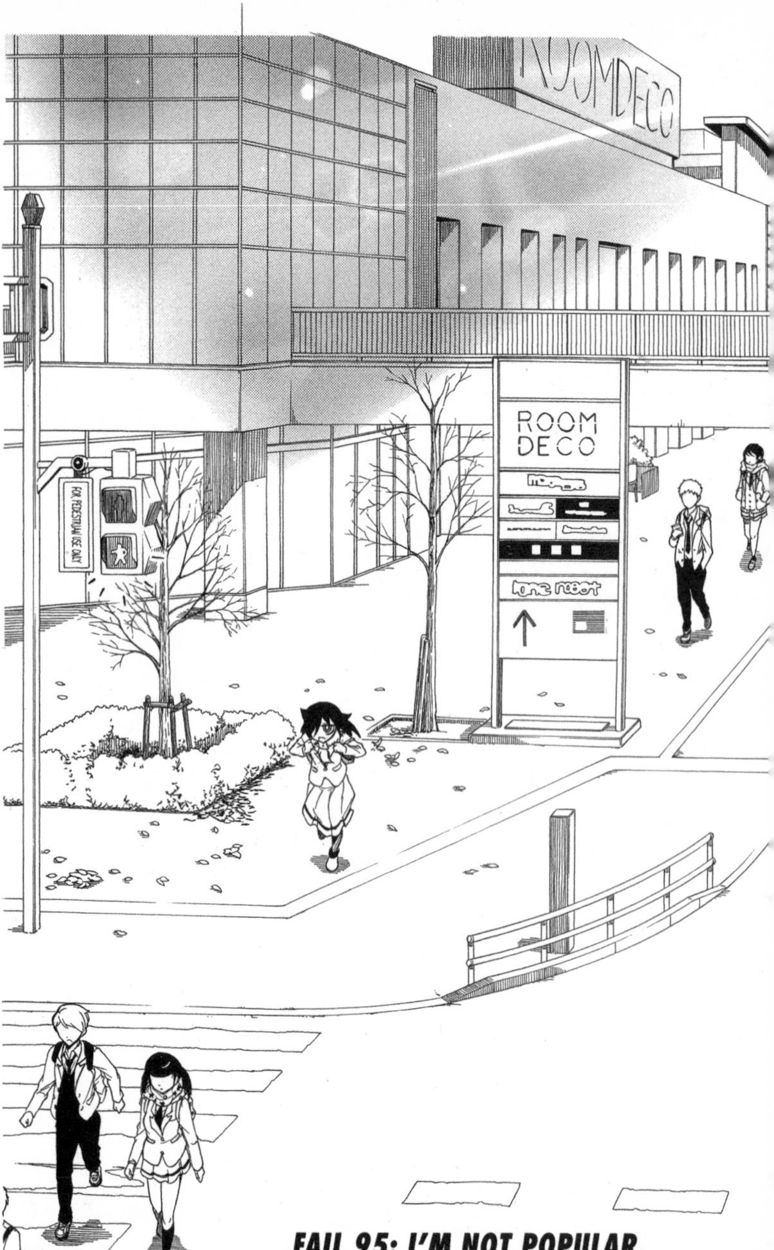
ROOMDECO
FOR PEDESTRIAN USE ONLY
ROOM DECO

FAIL 95: I'M NOT POPULAR, SO IT'S THE END OF AUTUMN.

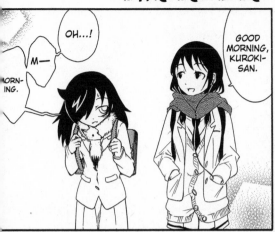

OH...!

M—

MORN-ING.

GOOD MORNING, KUROKI-SAN.

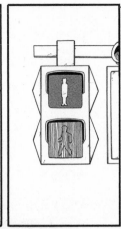

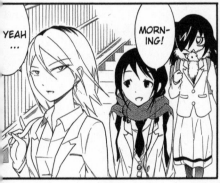

YEAH...

MORN-ING!

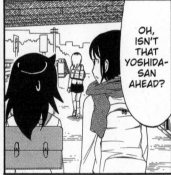

OH, ISN'T THAT YOSHIDA-SAN AHEAD?

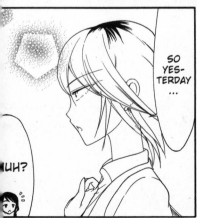

SO YES-TERDAY...

UH?

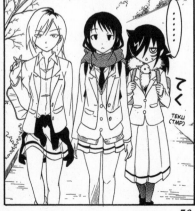

......

TEKU
(TMP)

76

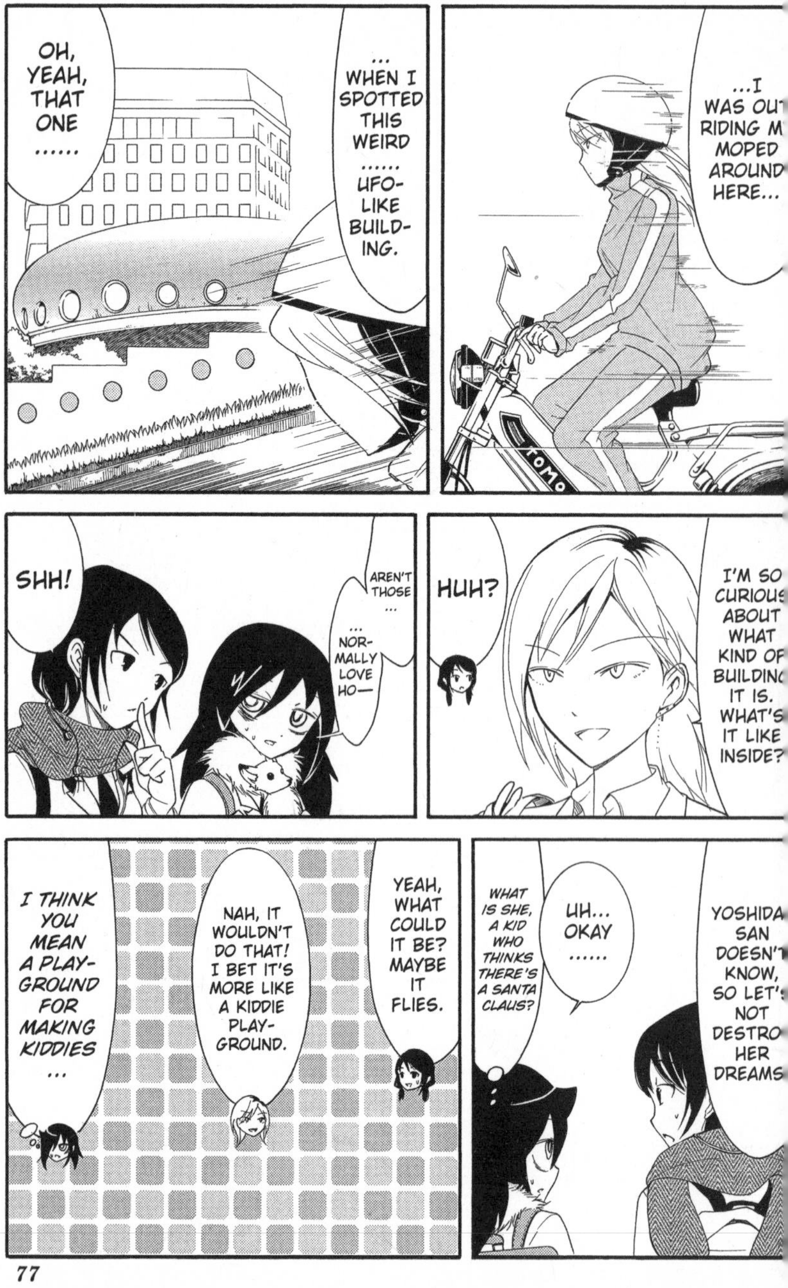

...I WAS OUT RIDING M MOPED AROUND HERE...
... WHEN I SPOTTED THIS WEIRD ...... UFO-LIKE BUILDING.
OH, YEAH, THAT ONE ......
I'M SO CURIOUS ABOUT WHAT KIND OF BUILDING IT IS. WHAT'S IT LIKE INSIDE?
HUH?
AREN'T THOSE ...
... NORMALLY LOVE HO—
SHH!
YOSHIDA SAN DOESN' KNOW, SO LET' NOT DESTRO HER DREAMS
UH... OKAY ......
WHAT IS SHE, A KID WHO THINKS THERE'S A SANTA CLAUS?
YEAH, WHAT COULD IT BE? MAYBE IT FLIES.
NAH, IT WOULDN'T DO THAT! I BET IT'S MORE LIKE A KIDDIE PLAYGROUND.
I THINK YOU MEAN A PLAYGROUND FOR MAKING KIDDIES ...

IMPRESSION

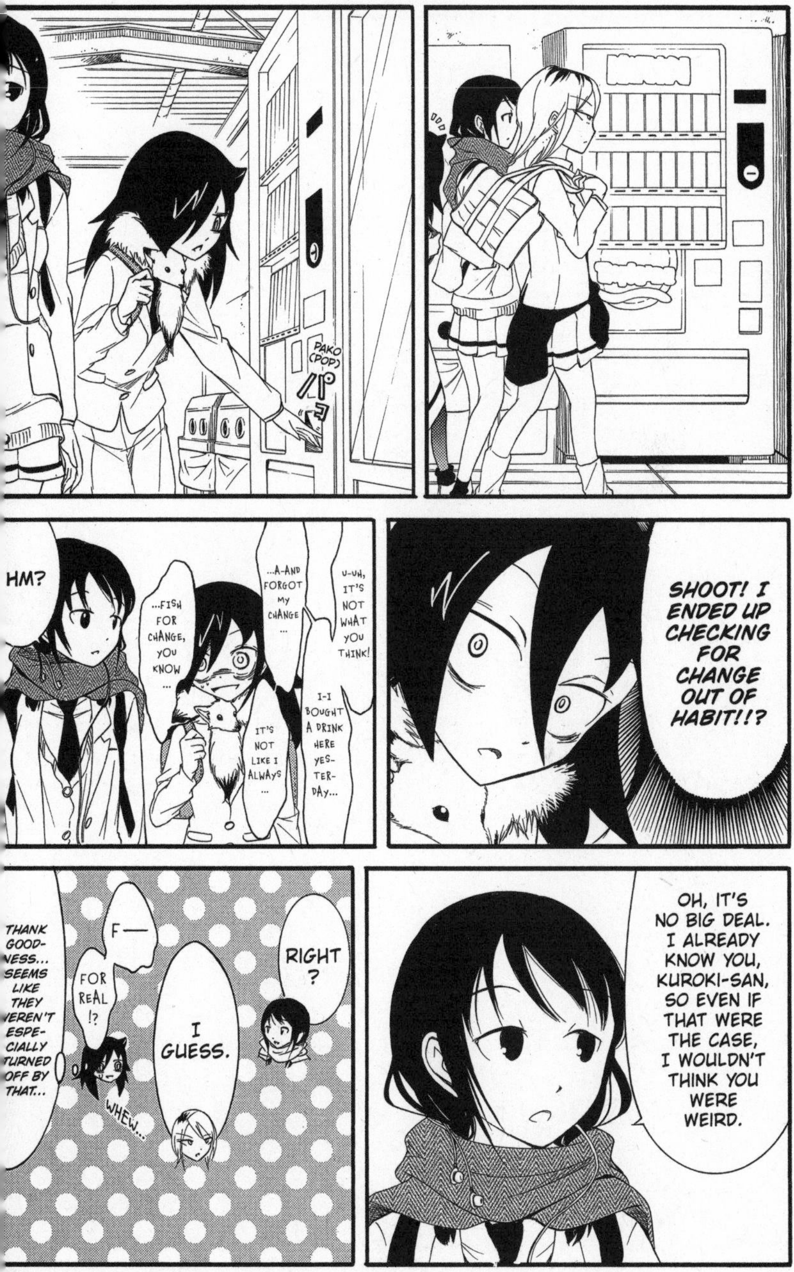
PAKO (POP)
パコ
SHOOT! I ENDED UP CHECKING FOR CHANGE OUT OF HABIT!!?
U-UH, IT'S NOT WHAT YOU THINK!
I-I BOUGHT A DRINK HERE YESTERDAY...
...A-AND FORGOT MY CHANGE...
IT'S NOT LIKE I ALWAYS...
...FISH FOR CHANGE, YOU KNOW...
HM?
OH, IT'S NO BIG DEAL. I ALREADY KNOW YOU, KUROKI-SAN, SO EVEN IF THAT WERE THE CASE, I WOULDN'T THINK YOU WERE WEIRD.
RIGHT?
I GUESS.
F—
FOR REAL!?
WHEW...
THANK GOODNESS... SEEMS LIKE THEY WEREN'T ESPECIALLY TURNED OFF BY THAT...

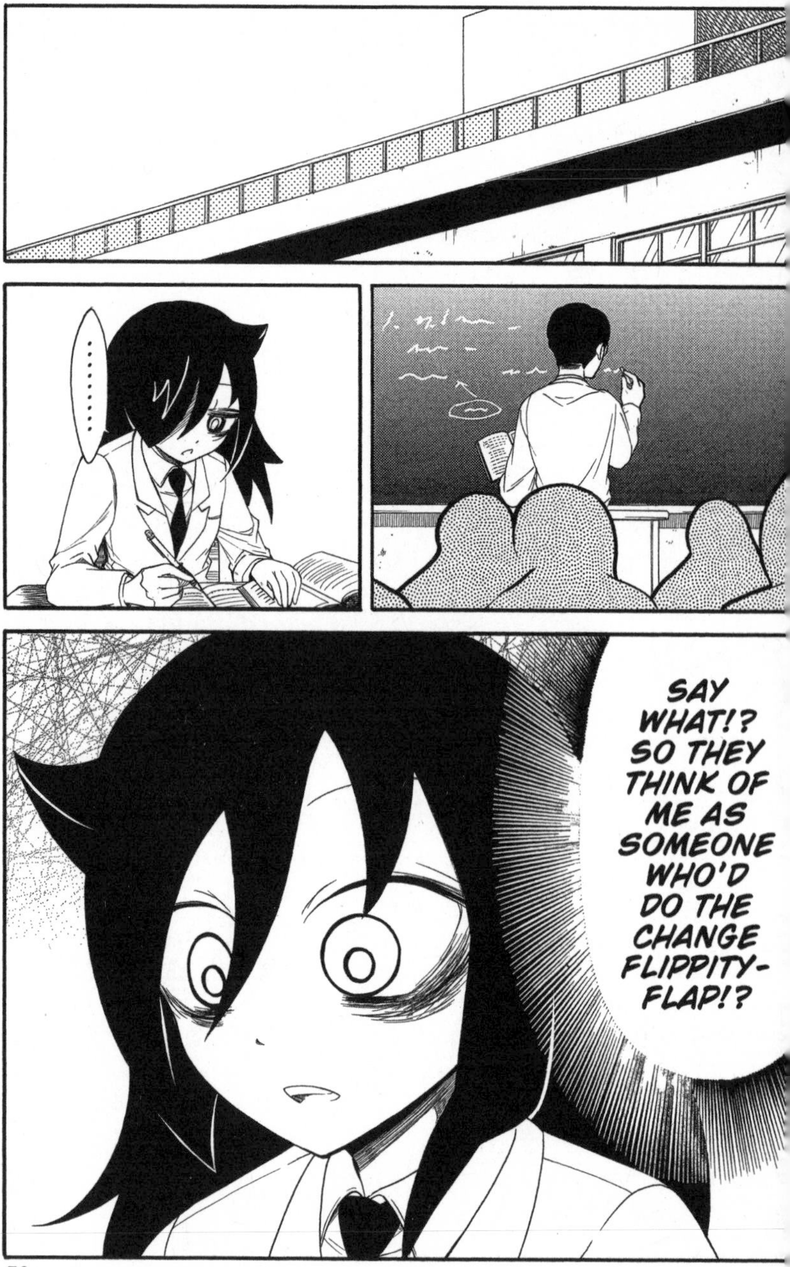
......
SAY WHAT!? SO THEY THINK OF ME AS SOMEONE WHO'D DO THE CHANGE FLIPPITY-FLAP!?

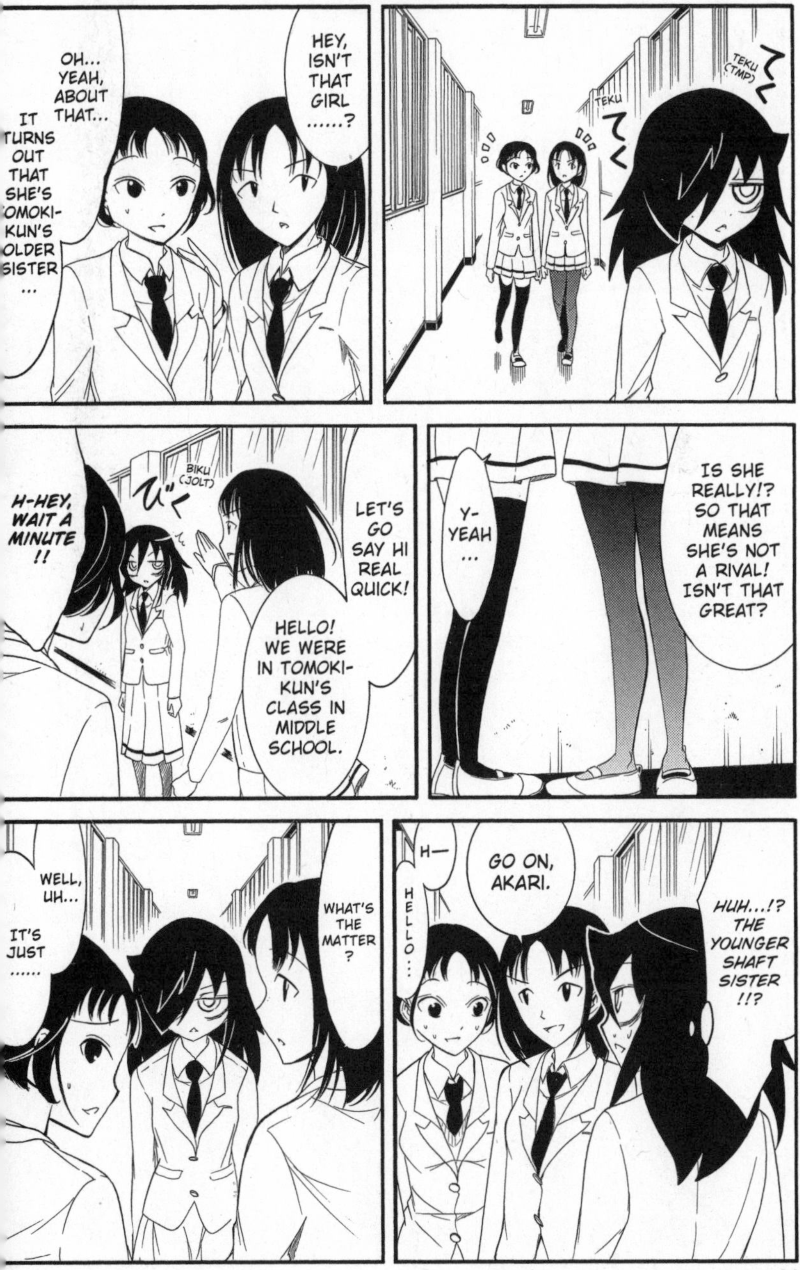
TEKU (TMP)
TEKU
HEY, ISN'T THAT GIRL ......?
OH... YEAH, ABOUT THAT...
IT TURNS OUT THAT SHE'S OMOKI-KUN'S OLDER SISTER ...
IS SHE REALLY!? SO THAT MEANS SHE'S NOT A RIVAL! ISN'T THAT GREAT?
Y-YEAH ...
LET'S GO SAY HI REAL QUICK!
BIKU (JOLT)
H-HEY, WAIT A MINUTE !!
HELLO! WE WERE IN TOMOKI-KUN'S CLASS IN MIDDLE SCHOOL.
HUH...!? THE YOUNGER SHAFT SISTER !!?
GO ON, AKARI.
H—
HELLO...
WHAT'S THE MATTER ?
WELL, UH...
IT'S JUST ......

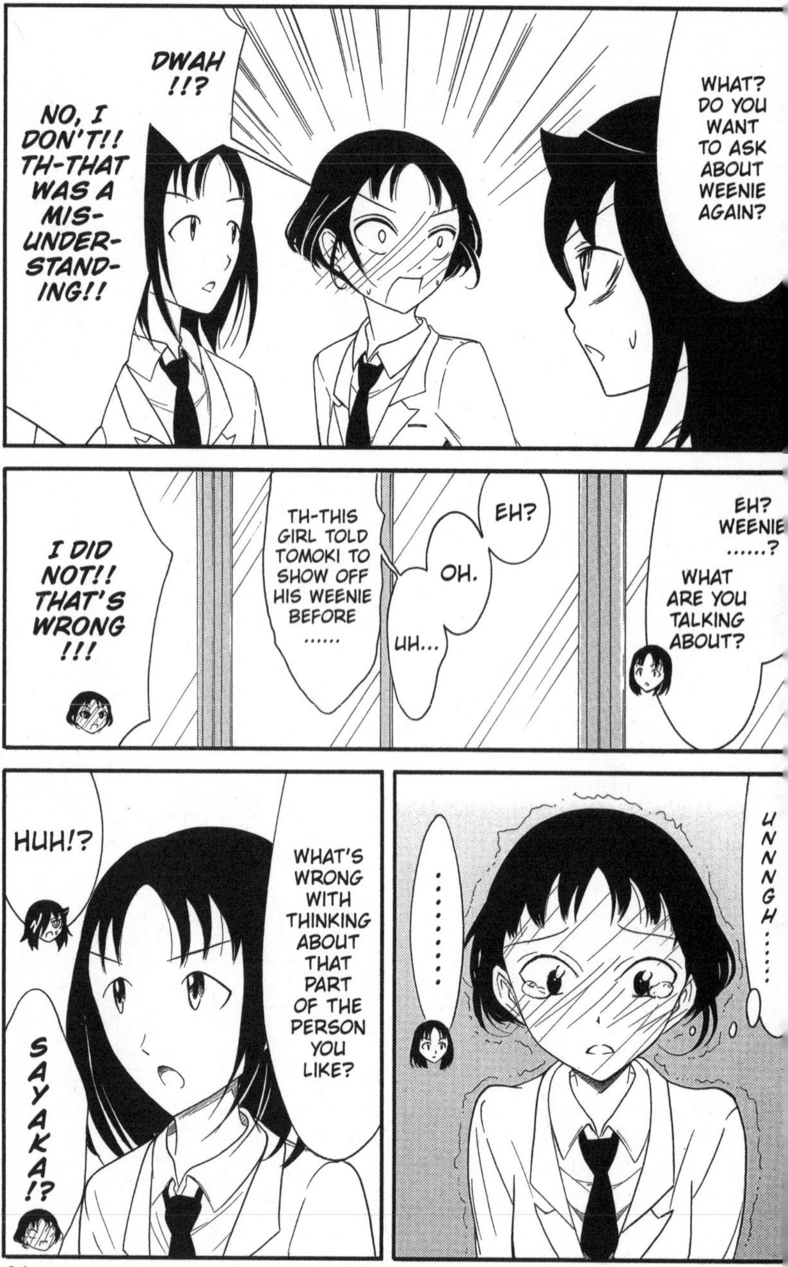

WHAT? DO YOU WANT TO ASK ABOUT WEENIE AGAIN?
DWAH!!?
NO, I DON'T!! TH-THAT WAS A MIS-UNDER-STAND-ING!!
EH? WEENIE ......? WHAT ARE YOU TALKING ABOUT?
EH?
OH.
UH...
TH-THIS GIRL TOLD TOMOKI TO SHOW OFF HIS WEENIE BEFORE ......
I DID NOT!! THAT'S WRONG!!!
UNNNGH......
....
WHAT'S WRONG WITH THINKING ABOUT THAT PART OF THE PERSON YOU LIKE?
HUH!?
SAYAKA!?

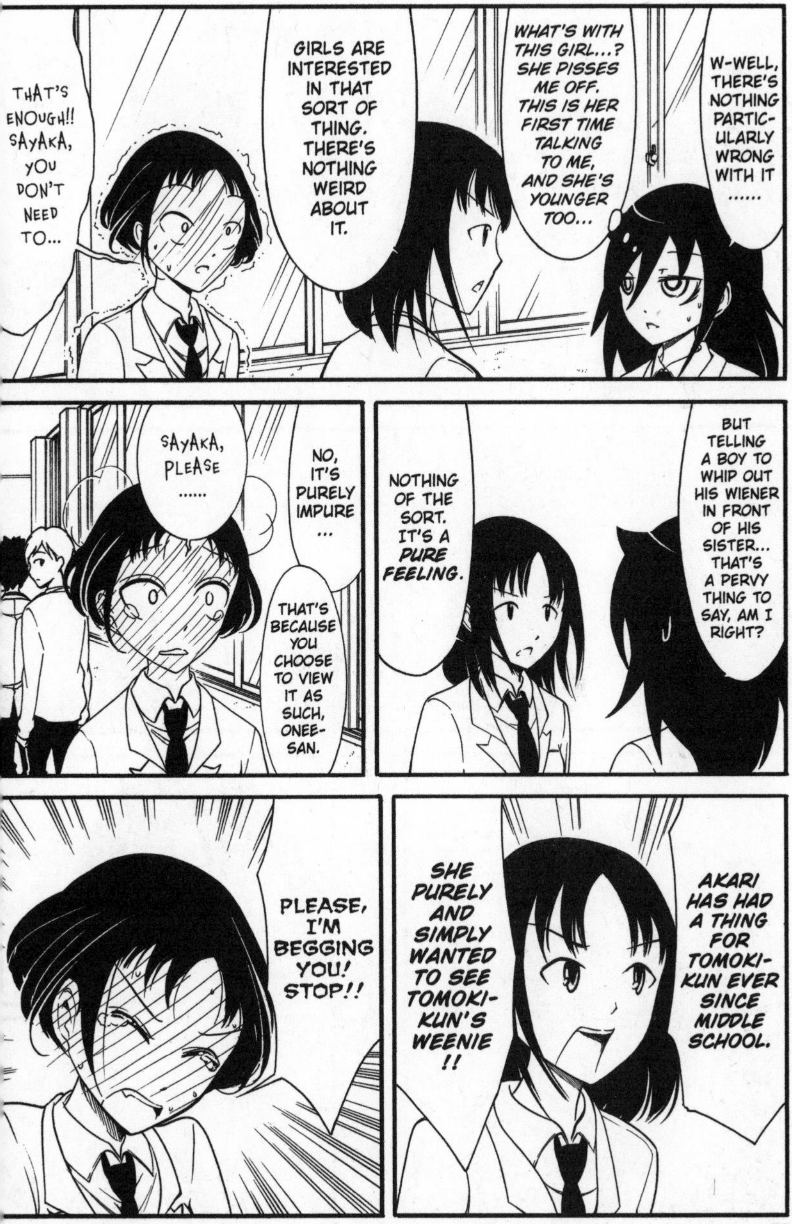
W-WELL, THERE'S NOTHING PARTICULARLY WRONG WITH IT ......
WHAT'S WITH THIS GIRL...? SHE PISSES ME OFF. THIS IS HER FIRST TIME TALKING TO ME, AND SHE'S YOUNGER TOO...
GIRLS ARE INTERESTED IN THAT SORT OF THING. THERE'S NOTHING WEIRD ABOUT IT.
THAT'S ENOUGH!! SAYAKA, YOU DON'T NEED TO...
BUT TELLING A BOY TO WHIP OUT HIS WIENER IN FRONT OF HIS SISTER... THAT'S A PERVY THING TO SAY, AM I RIGHT?
NOTHING OF THE SORT. IT'S A *PURE FEELING*.
NO, IT'S PURELY IMPURE ...
THAT'S BECAUSE YOU CHOOSE TO VIEW IT AS SUCH, ONEE-SAN.
SAYAKA, PLEASE ......
AKARI HAS HAD A THING FOR TOMOKI-KUN EVER SINCE MIDDLE SCHOOL.
SHE PURELY AND SIMPLY WANTED TO SEE TOMOKI-KUN'S WEENIE !!
PLEASE, I'M BEGGING YOU! STOP!!

ANYWHERE BUT THE FACE

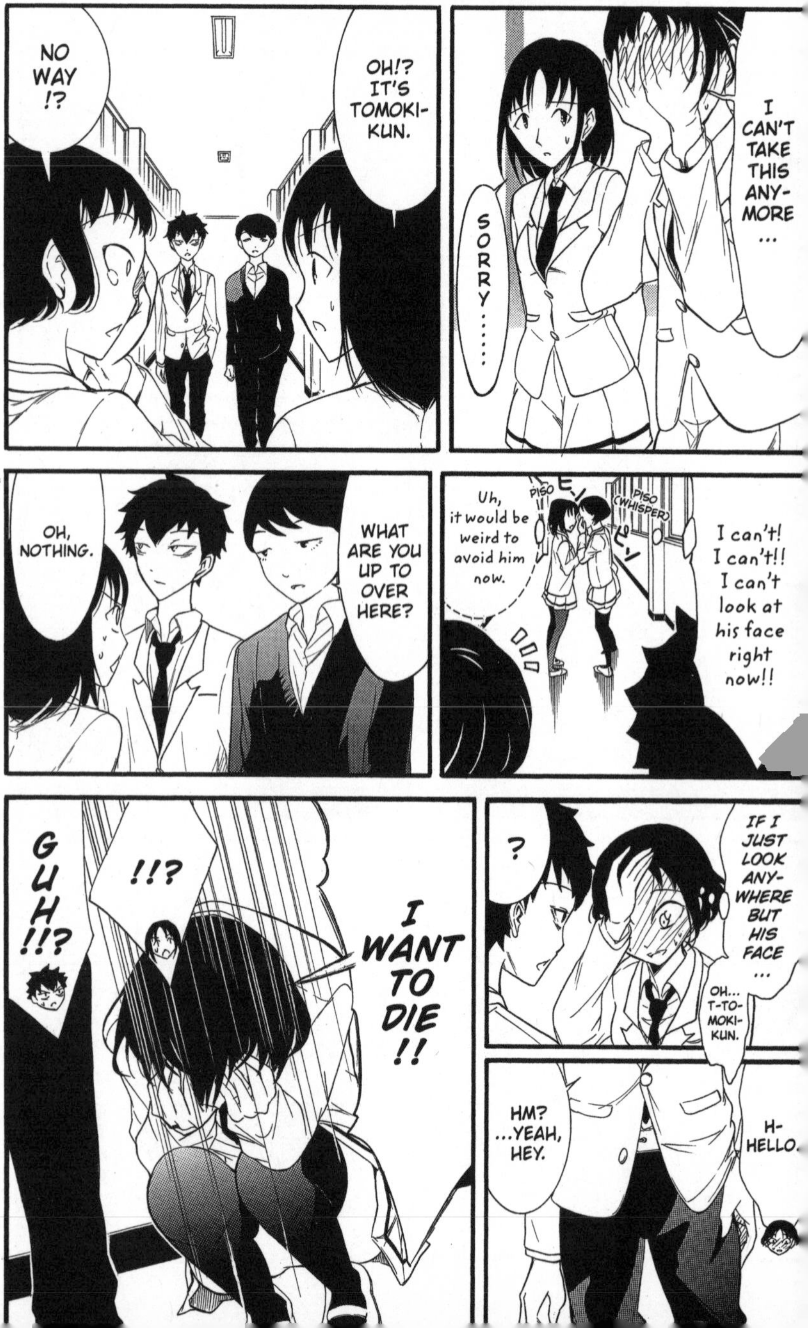

I CAN'T TAKE THIS ANYMORE...
SORRY......
OH!? IT'S TOMOKI-KUN.
NO WAY!?
PISO (WHISPER)
PISO
I can't! I can't!! I can't look at his face right now!!
Uh, it would be weird to avoid him now.
WHAT ARE YOU UP TO OVER HERE?
OH, NOTHING.
IF I JUST LOOK ANYWHERE BUT HIS FACE...
?
OH... T-TOMOKI-KUN.
H-HELLO.
HM? ...YEAH, HEY.
I WANT TO DIE!!
!!?
GUH!!?

FRIGHTENINGLY KNOWLEDGEABLE

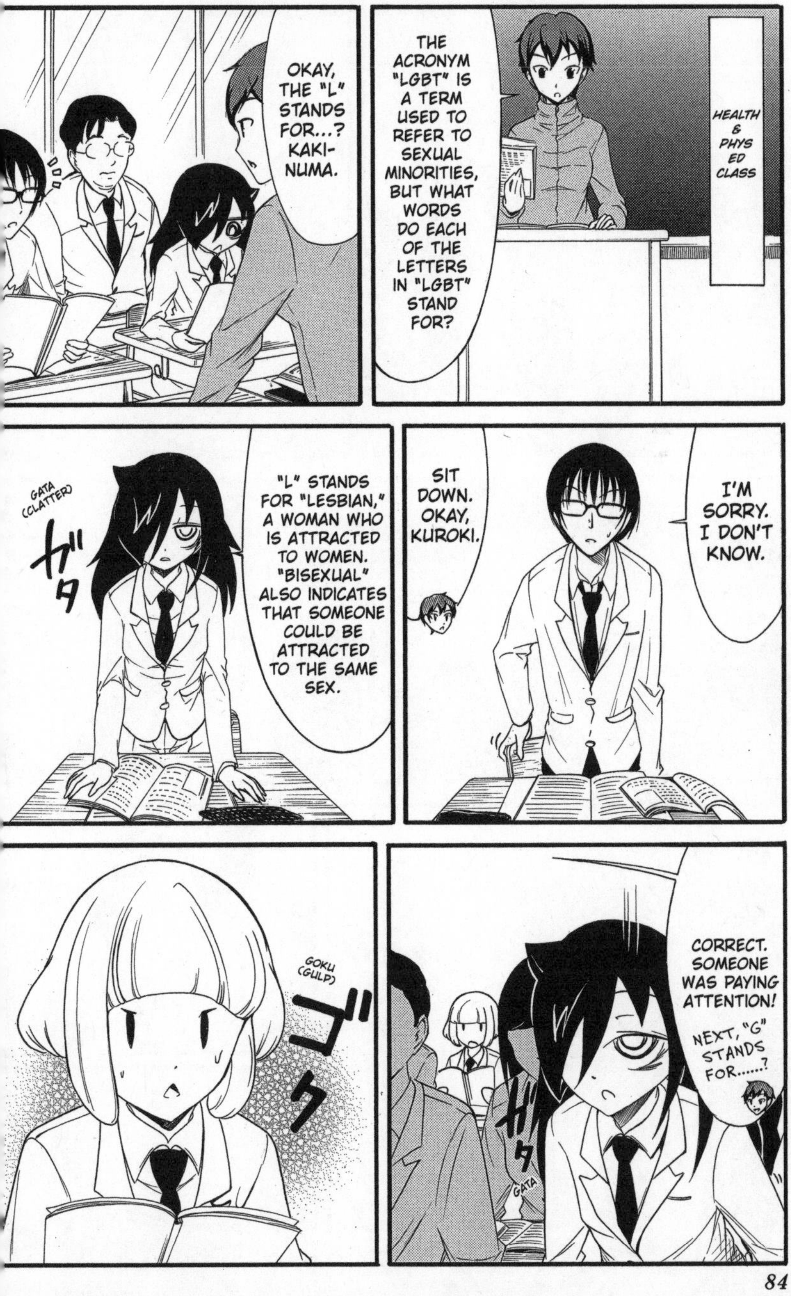
HEALTH & PHYS ED CLASS
THE ACRONYM "LGBT" IS A TERM USED TO REFER TO SEXUAL MINORITIES, BUT WHAT WORDS DO EACH OF THE LETTERS IN "LGBT" STAND FOR?
OKAY, THE "L" STANDS FOR...? KAKI-NUMA.
I'M SORRY. I DON'T KNOW.
SIT DOWN. OKAY, KUROKI.
"L" STANDS FOR "LESBIAN," A WOMAN WHO IS ATTRACTED TO WOMEN. "BISEXUAL" ALSO INDICATES THAT SOMEONE COULD BE ATTRACTED TO THE SAME SEX.
GATA (CLATTER)
CORRECT. SOMEONE WAS PAYING ATTENTION!
NEXT, "G" STANDS FOR......?
GATA
GOKU (GULP)

IDENTIFICATION

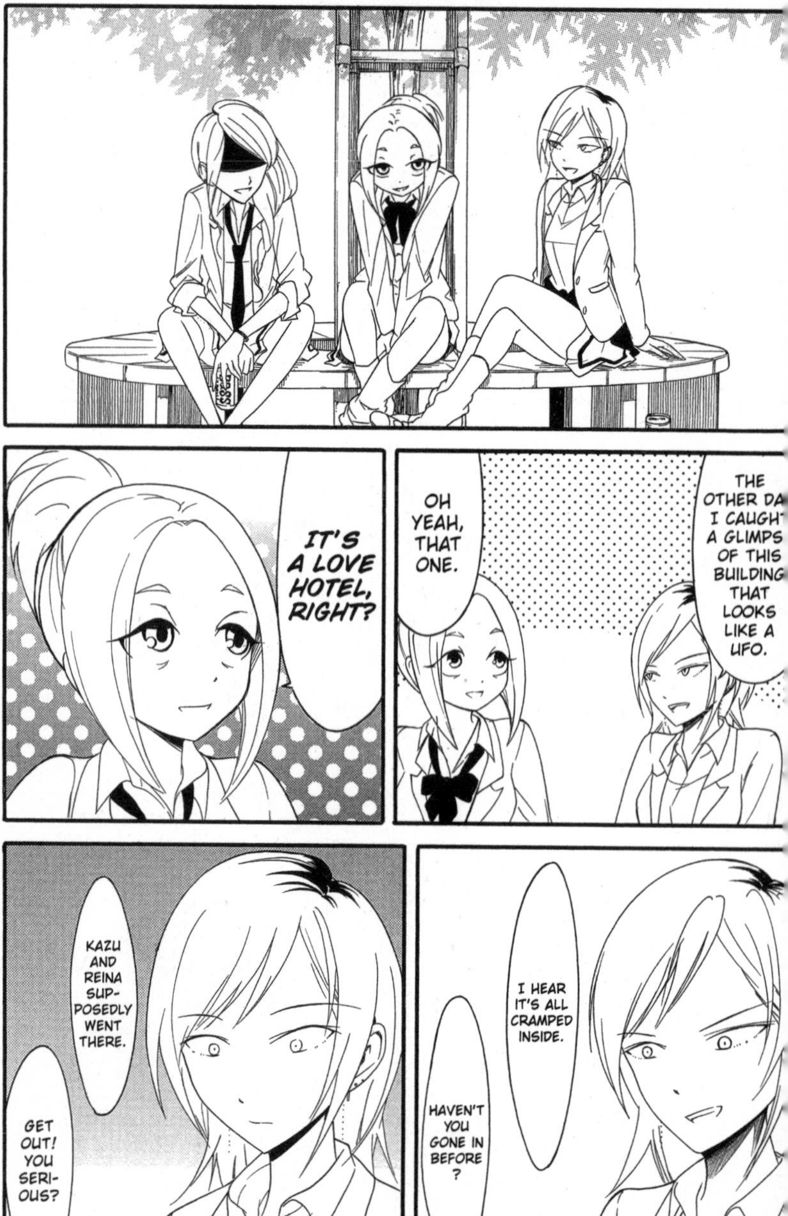
THE OTHER DA I CAUGHT A GLIMPS OF THIS BUILDING THAT LOOKS LIKE A UFO.
OH YEAH, THAT ONE.
IT'S A LOVE HOTEL, RIGHT?
I HEAR IT'S ALL CRAMPED INSIDE.
HAVEN'T YOU GONE IN BEFORE?
KAZU AND REINA SUP-POSEDLY WENT THERE.
GET OUT! YOU SERI-OUS?

MONDAY ROUTINE

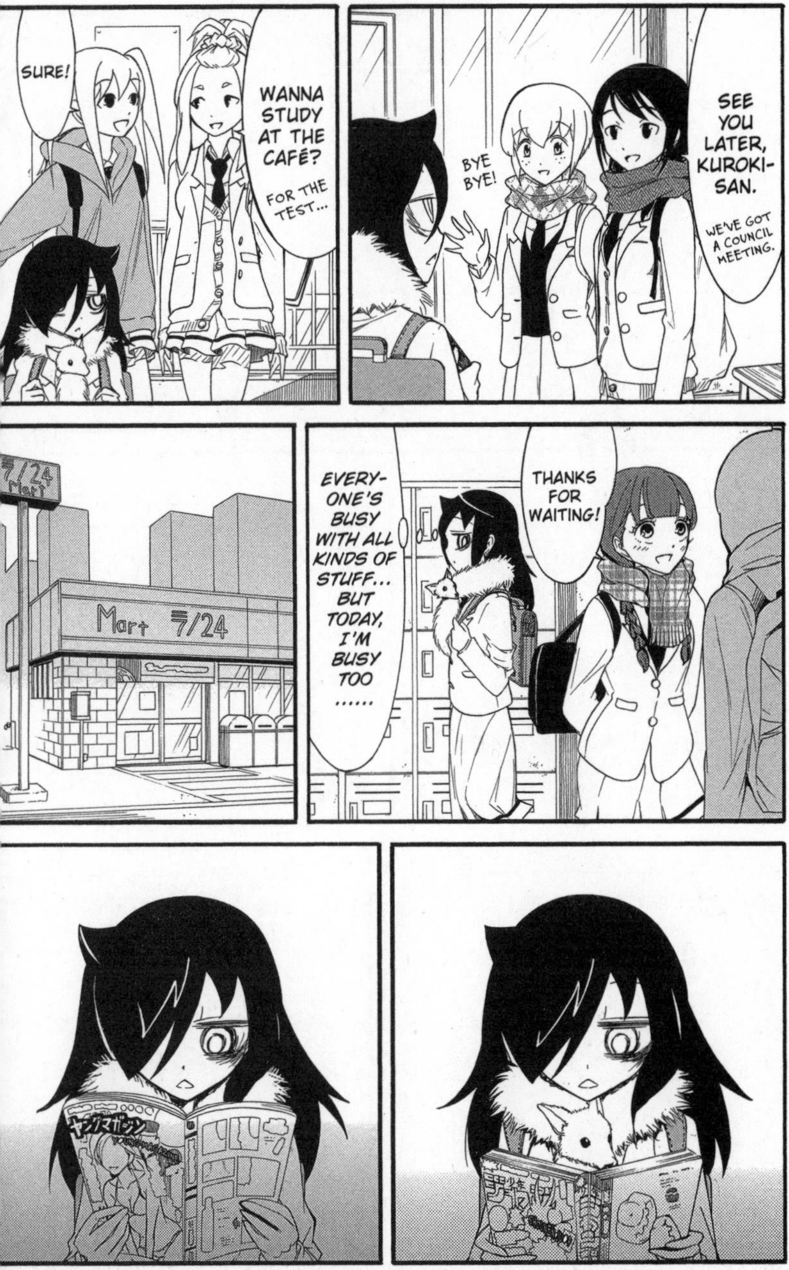
SEE YOU LATER, KUROKI-SAN.
WE'VE GOT A COUNCIL MEETING.
BYE BYE!
WANNA STUDY AT THE CAFÉ?
FOR THE TEST...
SURE!
THANKS FOR WAITING!
EVERY-ONE'S BUSY WITH ALL KINDS OF STUFF... BUT TODAY, I'M BUSY TOO ......
7/24 Mart
Mart 7/24

SIGNS OF WINTER

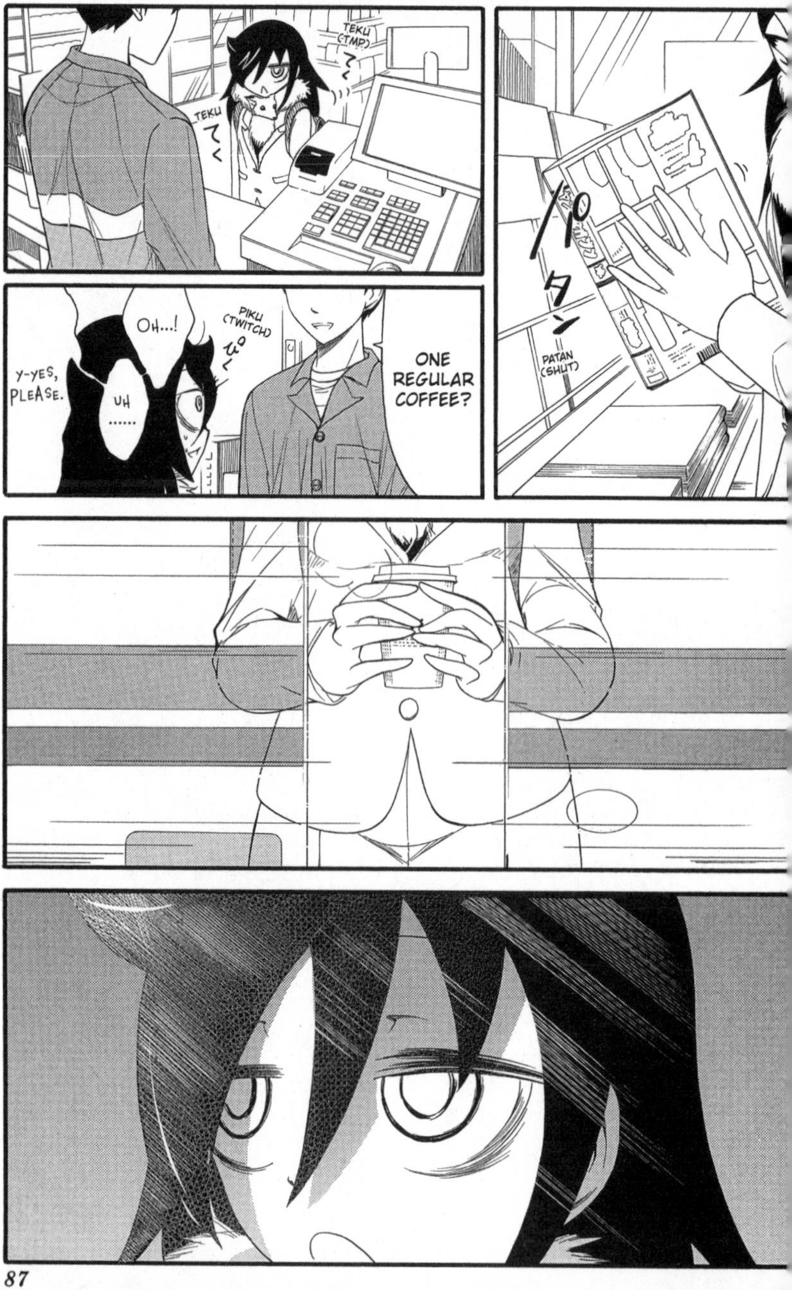

パタン
PATAN (SHUT)
TEKU (TMP)
てく
TEKU
てく
ONE REGULAR COFFEE?
PIKU (TWITCH)
ぴく
OH...!
UH ......
Y-YES, PLEASE.

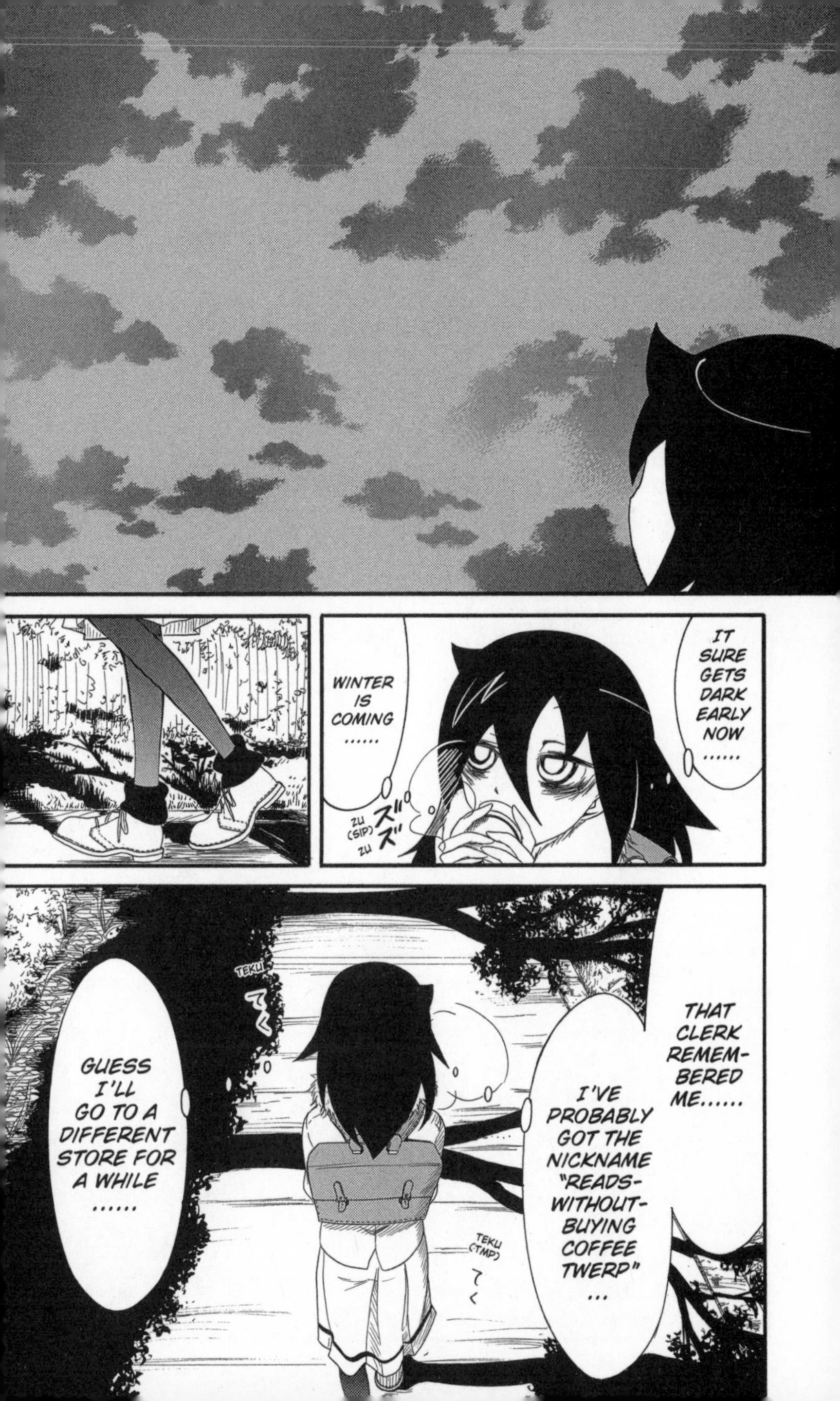
IT SURE GETS DARK EARLY NOW......
WINTER IS COMING......
ZU (SIP) ZU
THAT CLERK REMEMBERED ME......
I'VE PROBABLY GOT THE NICKNAME "READS-WITHOUT-BUYING COFFEE TWERP"...
TEKU (TMP)
GUESS I'LL GO TO A DIFFERENT STORE FOR A WHILE......
TEKU

No Matter How I Look at It, It's You Guys' Fault I'm Not Popular!

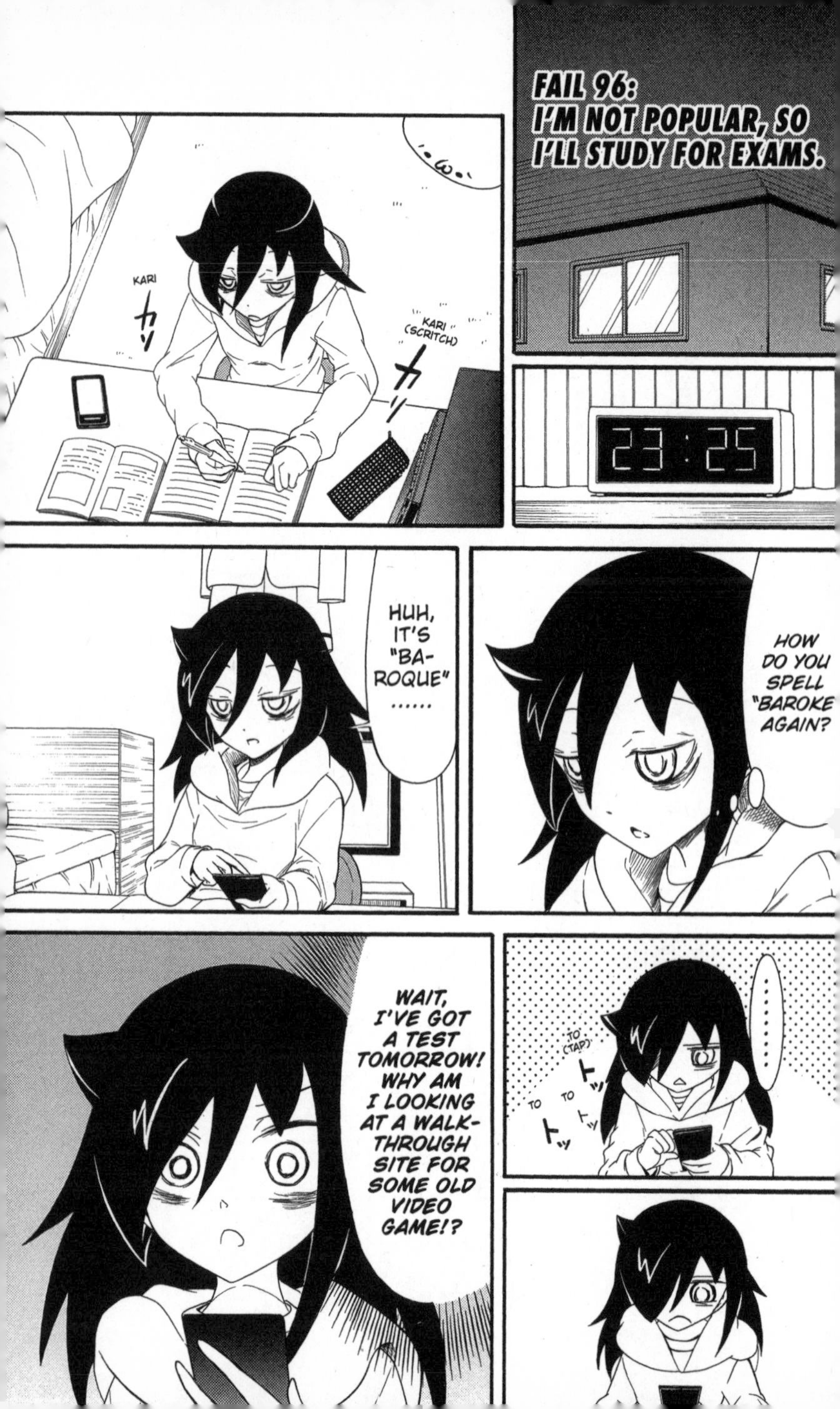

FAIL 96:
I'M NOT POPULAR, SO I'LL STUDY FOR EXAMS.
23:25
KARI (SCRITCH)
カリ
KARI
カリ
HOW DO YOU SPELL "BAROKE AGAIN?
HUH, IT'S "BA-ROQUE" ......
......
TO (TAP)
トッ
TO
トッ
TO
トッ
WAIT, I'VE GOT A TEST TOMORROW! WHY AM I LOOKING AT A WALK-THROUGH SITE FOR SOME OLD VIDEO GAME!?

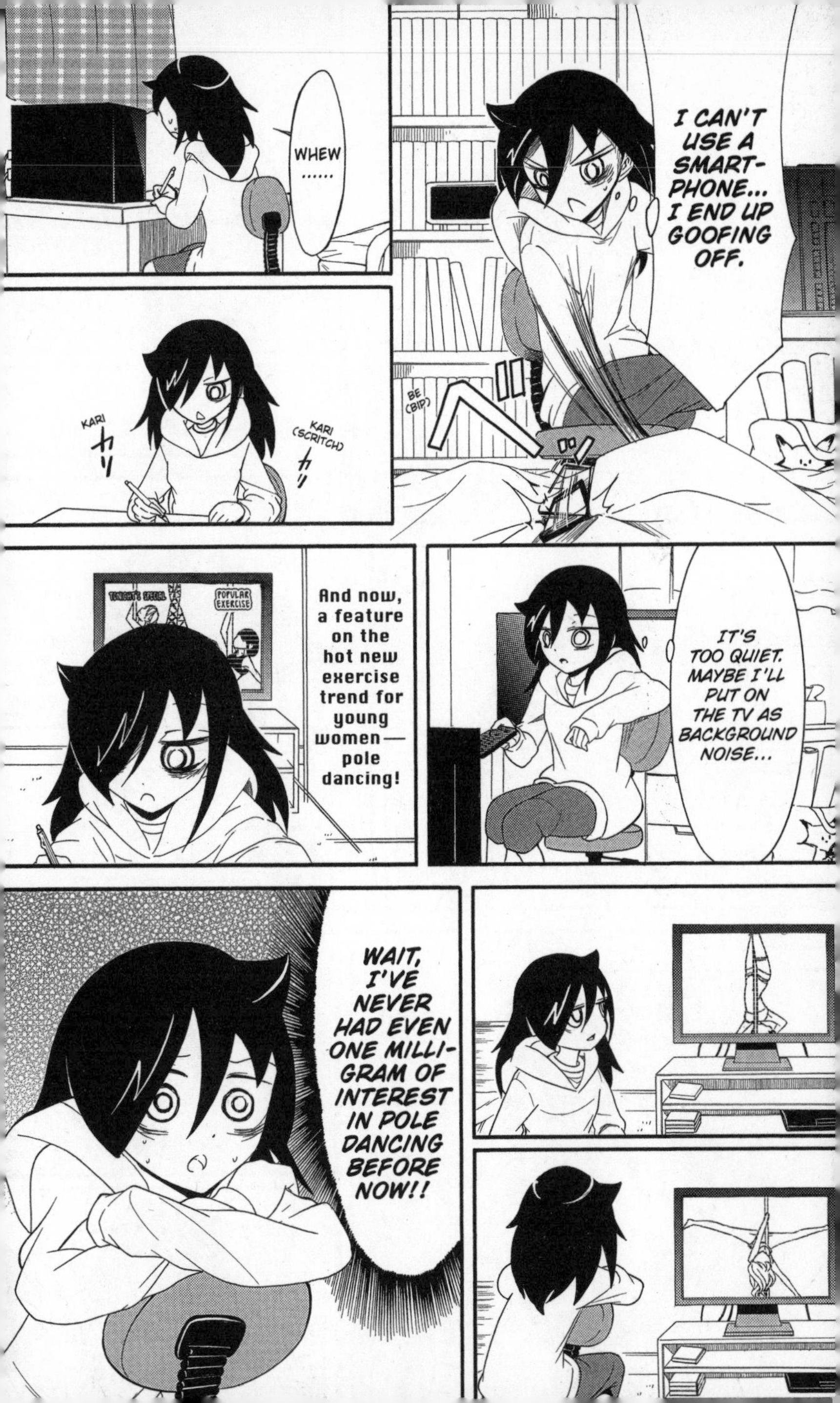

I CAN'T USE A SMART-PHONE... I END UP GOOFING OFF.
BE (BIP)
WHEW ......
KARI (SCRITCH)
カリ
KARI
カリ
IT'S TOO QUIET. MAYBE I'LL PUT ON THE TV AS BACKGROUND NOISE...
TONIGHT'S SPECIAL
POPULAR EXERCISE
And now, a feature on the hot new exercise trend for young women—pole dancing!
WAIT, I'VE NEVER HAD EVEN ONE MILLI-GRAM OF INTEREST IN POLE DANCING BEFORE NOW!!

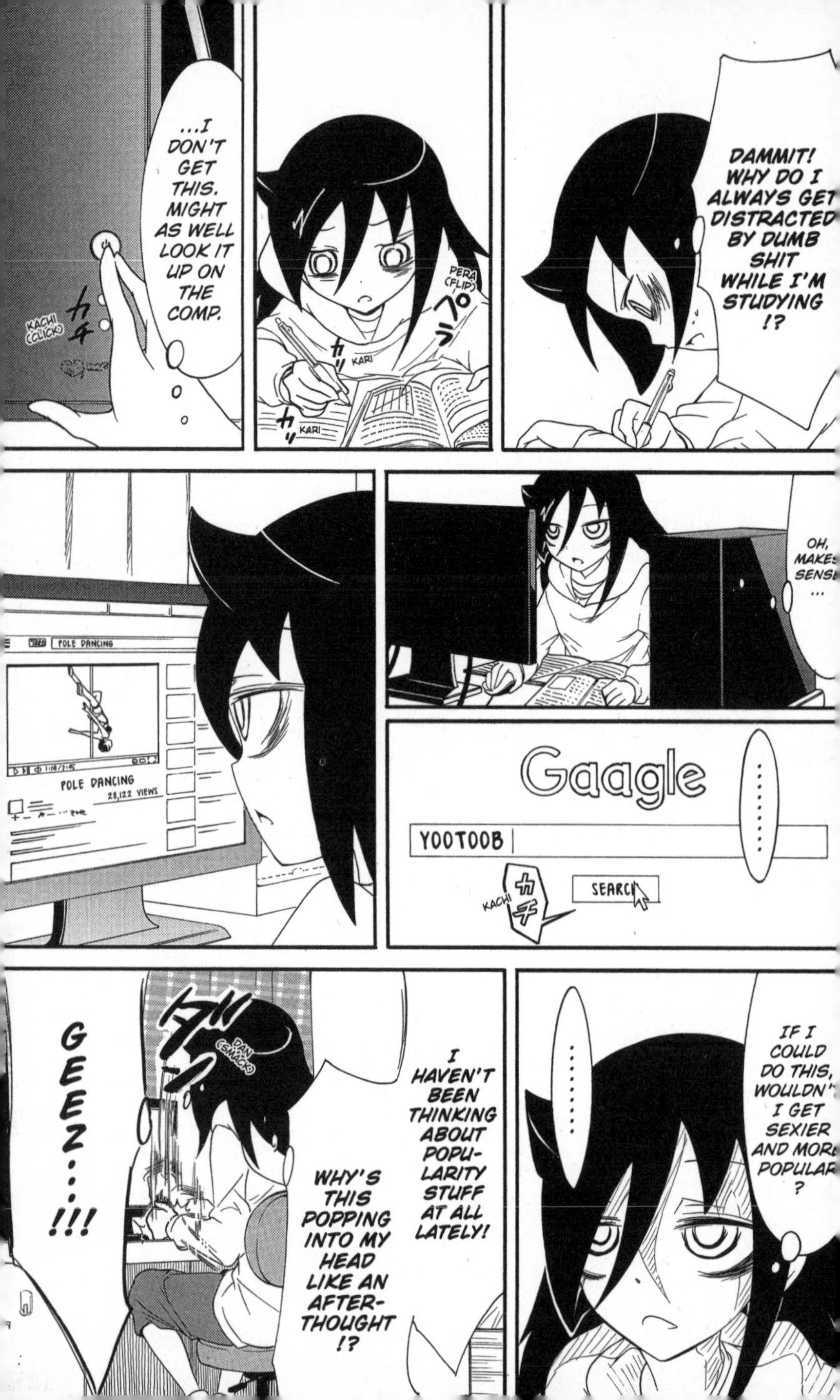
DAMMIT! WHY DO I ALWAYS GET DISTRACTED BY DUMB SHIT WHILE I'M STUDYING !?
PERA (FLIP)
KARI
KARI
...I DON'T GET THIS. MIGHT AS WELL LOOK IT UP ON THE COMP.
KACHI (CLICK)
OH, MAKES SENS ...
......
Gaagle
YOOTOOB
SEARC
KACHI
POLE DANCING
POLE DANCING
28,122 VIEWS
......
IF I COULD DO THIS, WOULDN'T I GET SEXIER AND MORE POPULAR ?
I HAVEN'T BEEN THINKING ABOUT POPULARITY STUFF AT ALL LATELY!
WHY'S THIS POPPING INTO MY HEAD LIKE AN AFTERTHOUGHT !?
DAN (SMACK)
GEEZ...!!!

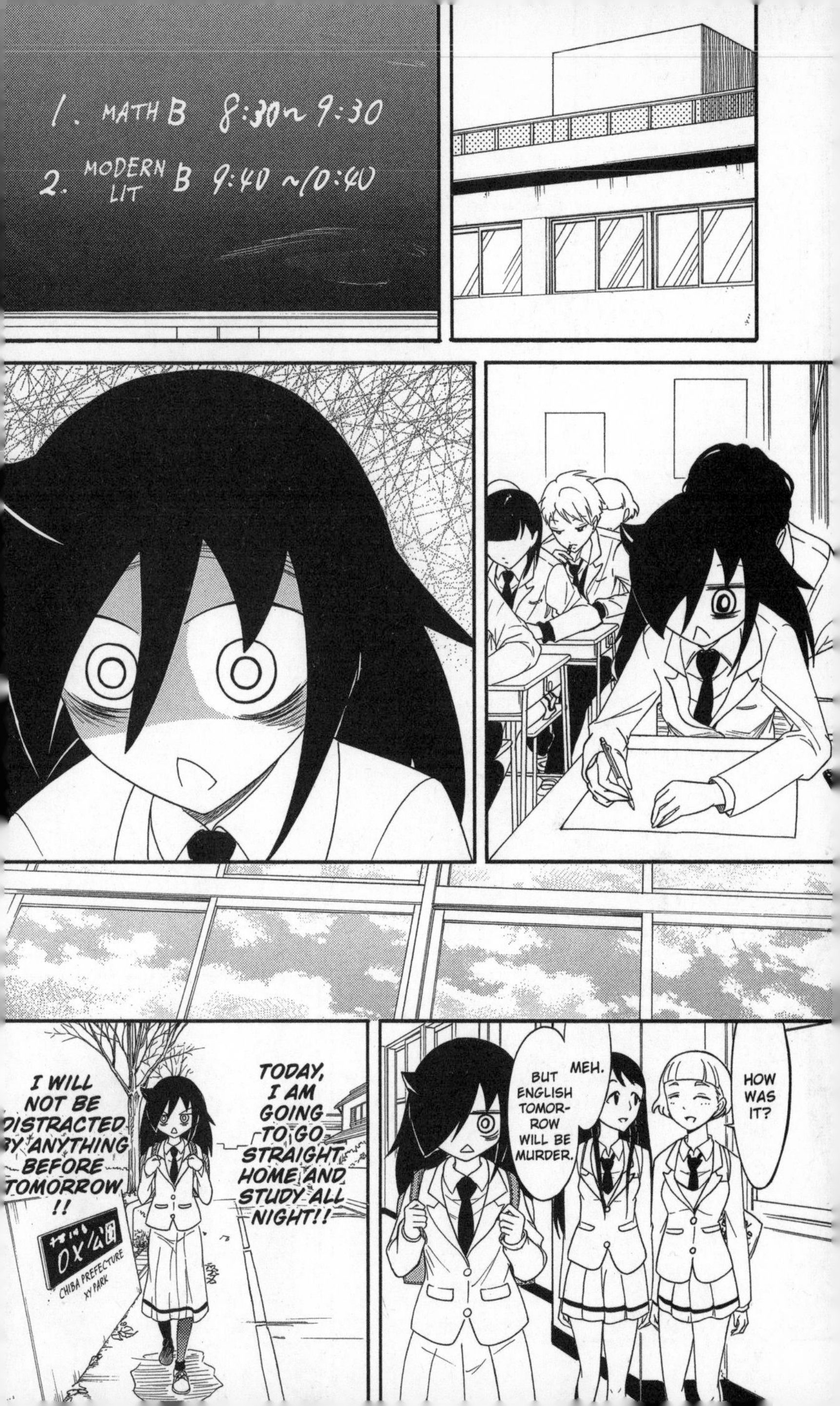

1. MATH B 8:30~9:30
2. MODERN LIT B 9:40~10:40
HOW WAS IT?
MEH.
BUT ENGLISH TOMORROW WILL BE MURDER.
TODAY, I AM GOING TO GO STRAIGHT HOME AND STUDY ALL NIGHT!!
I WILL NOT BE DISTRACTED BY ANYTHING BEFORE TOMORROW!!
○×公園
CHIBA PREFECTURE XY PARK

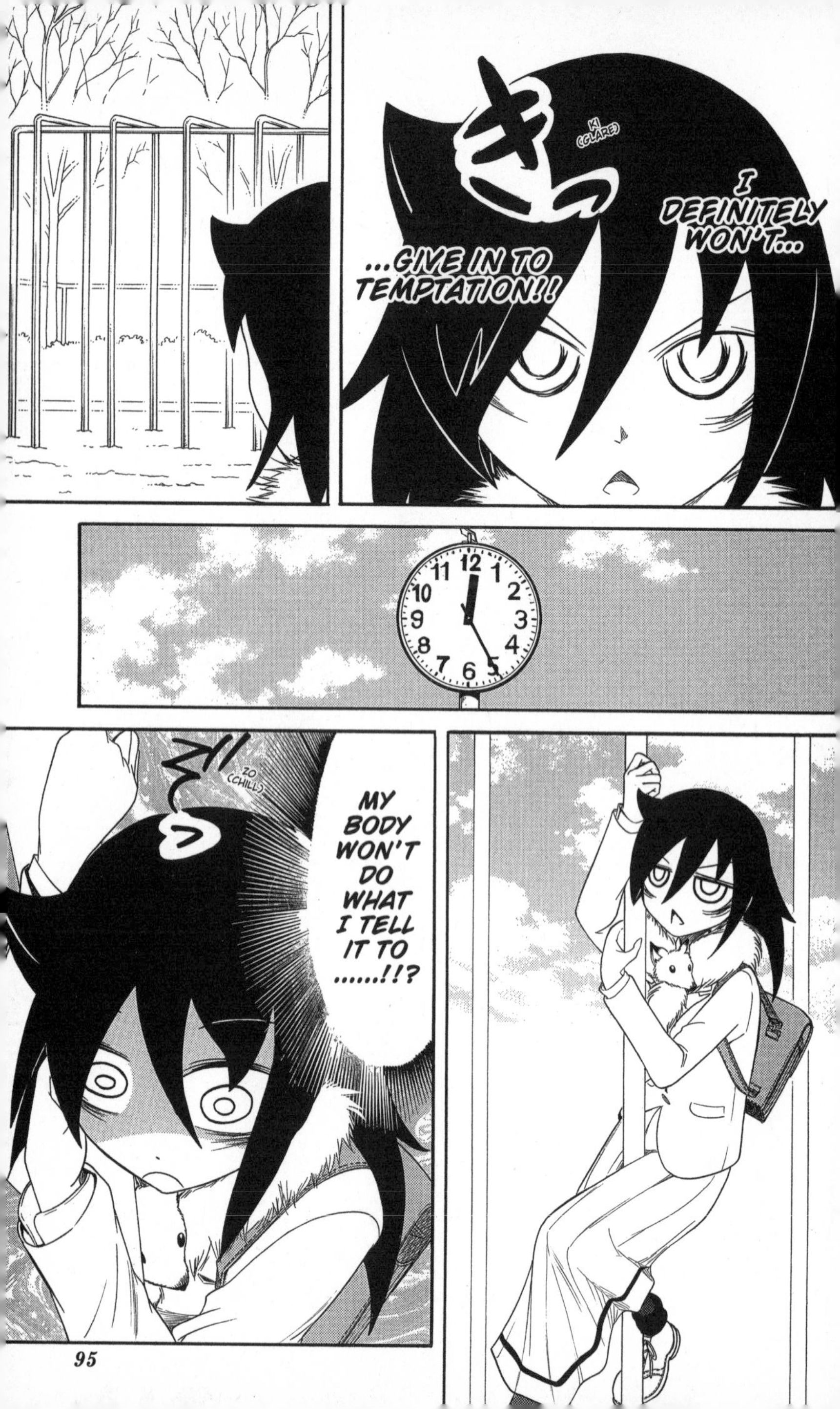
KI (GLARE)
I DEFINITELY WON'T...
...GIVE IN TO TEMPTATION!!
ZO (CHILL)
MY BODY WON'T DO WHAT I TELL IT TO ......!!?

No Matter How I Look at It, It's You Guys' Fault I'm Not Popular!

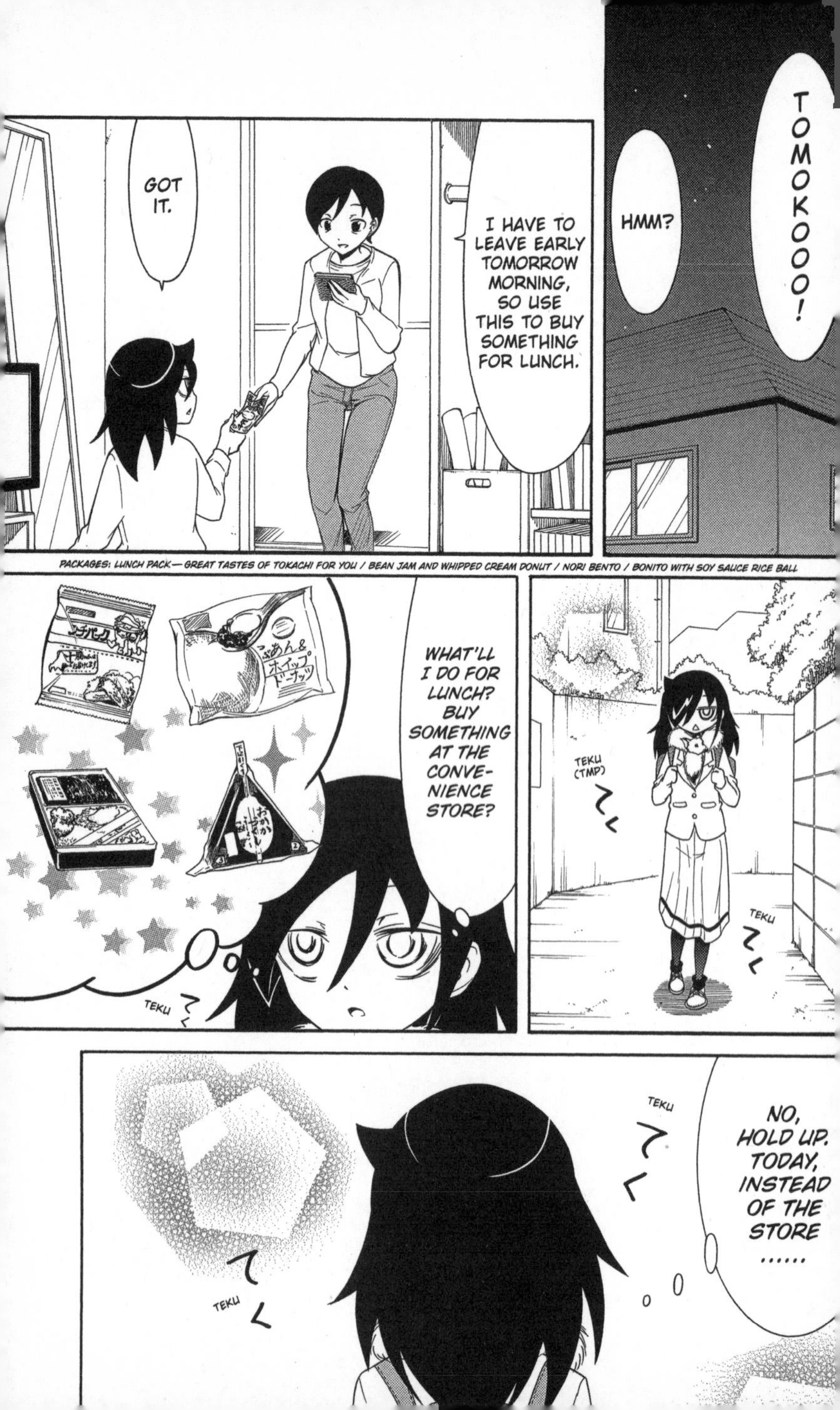
TOMOKOOO!
HMM?
I HAVE TO LEAVE EARLY TOMORROW MORNING, SO USE THIS TO BUY SOMETHING FOR LUNCH.
GOT IT.
PACKAGES: LUNCH PACK— GREAT TASTES OF TOKACHI FOR YOU / BEAN JAM AND WHIPPED CREAM DONUT / NORI BENTO / BONITO WITH SOY SAUCE RICE BALL
TEKU (TMP)
TEKU
WHAT'LL I DO FOR LUNCH? BUY SOMETHING AT THE CONVE-NIENCE STORE?
TEKU
NO, HOLD UP. TODAY, INSTEAD OF THE STORE ......
TEKU
TEKU

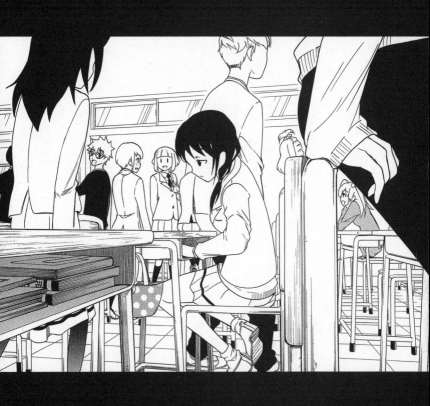

FAIL 97: I'M NOT POPULAR, SO I'LL EAT IN THE CAFETERIA.

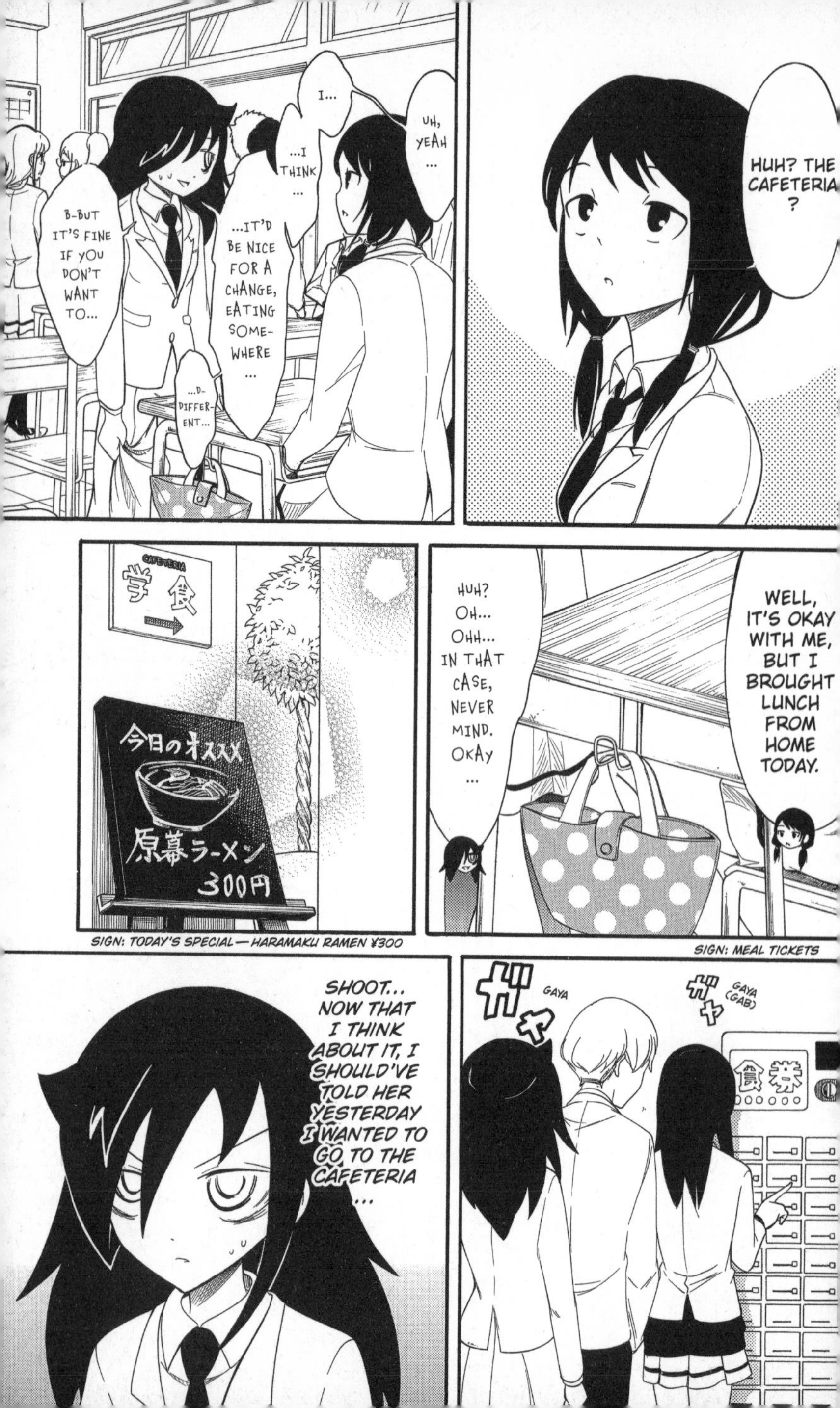
HUH? THE CAFETERIA ?
UH, YEAH ...
I...
...I THINK ...
...IT'D BE NICE FOR A CHANGE, EATING SOME-WHERE ...
...D-DIFFER-ENT...
B-BUT IT'S FINE IF YOU DON'T WANT TO...
WELL, IT'S OKAY WITH ME, BUT I BROUGHT LUNCH FROM HOME TODAY.
HUH? OH... OHH... IN THAT CASE, NEVER MIND. OKAY ...
CAFETERIA
学食
今日のオススメ
原幕ラーメン
300円
SIGN: TODAY'S SPECIAL—HARAMAKU RAMEN ¥300
SIGN: MEAL TICKETS
ガヤ
GAYA
ガヤ
GAYA (GAB)
食券
SHOOT... NOW THAT I THINK ABOUT IT, I SHOULD'VE TOLD HER YESTERDAY I WANTED TO GO TO THE CAFETERIA ...

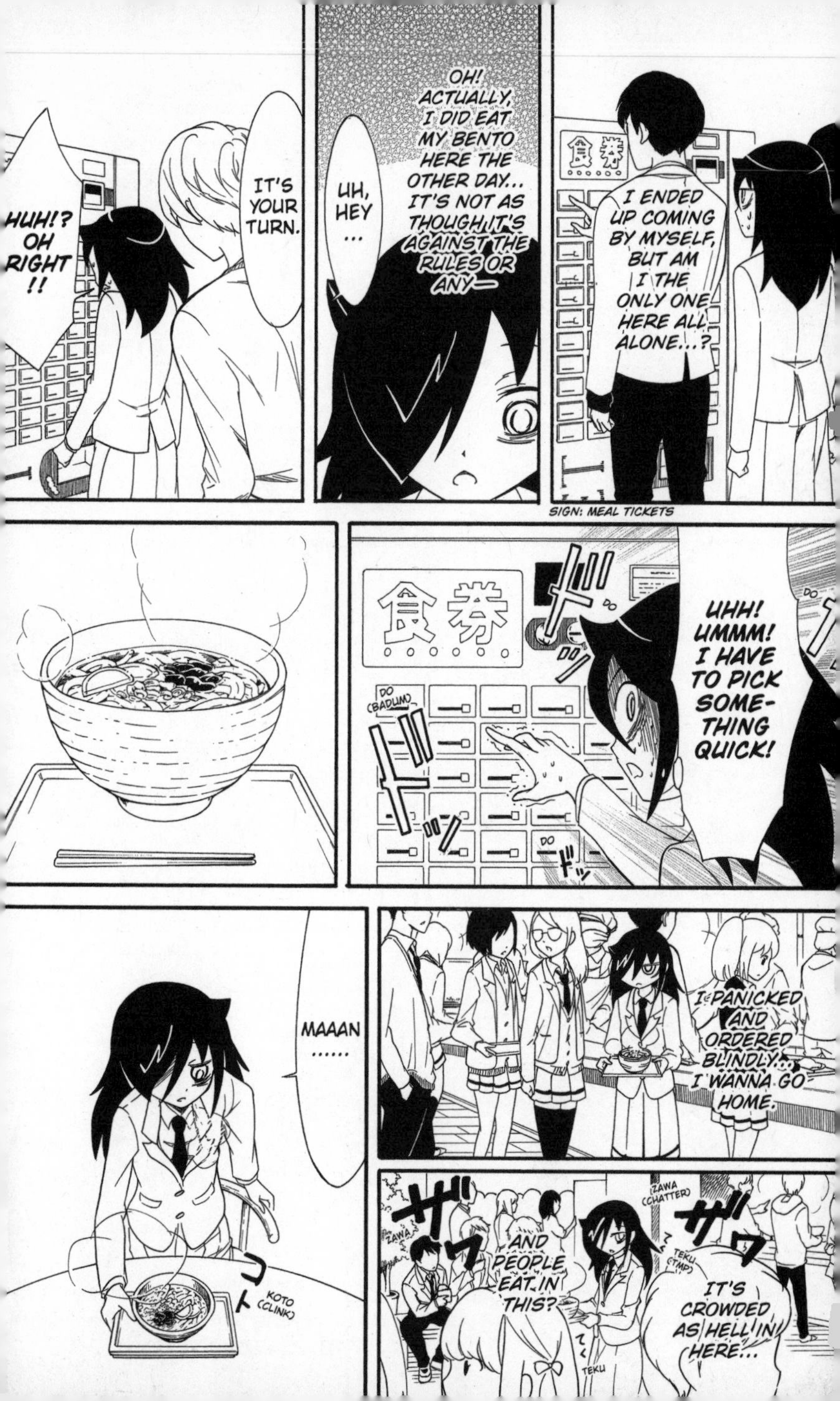

I ENDED UP COMING BY MYSELF, BUT AM I THE ONLY ONE HERE ALL ALONE...?
食券
SIGN: MEAL TICKETS
OH! ACTUALLY, I DID EAT MY BENTO HERE THE OTHER DAY... IT'S NOT AS THOUGH IT'S AGAINST THE RULES OR ANY—
UH, HEY ...
IT'S YOUR TURN.
HUH!? OH RIGHT !!
DO
UHH! UMMM! I HAVE TO PICK SOMETHING QUICK!
食券
DO (BADUM)
DO
I PANICKED AND ORDERED BLINDLY... I WANNA GO HOME.
ZAWA (CHATTER)
ZAWA
TEKU (TMP)
IT'S CROWDED AS HELL IN HERE...
AND PEOPLE EAT IN THIS?
TEKU
MAAAN ......
KOTO (CLINK)

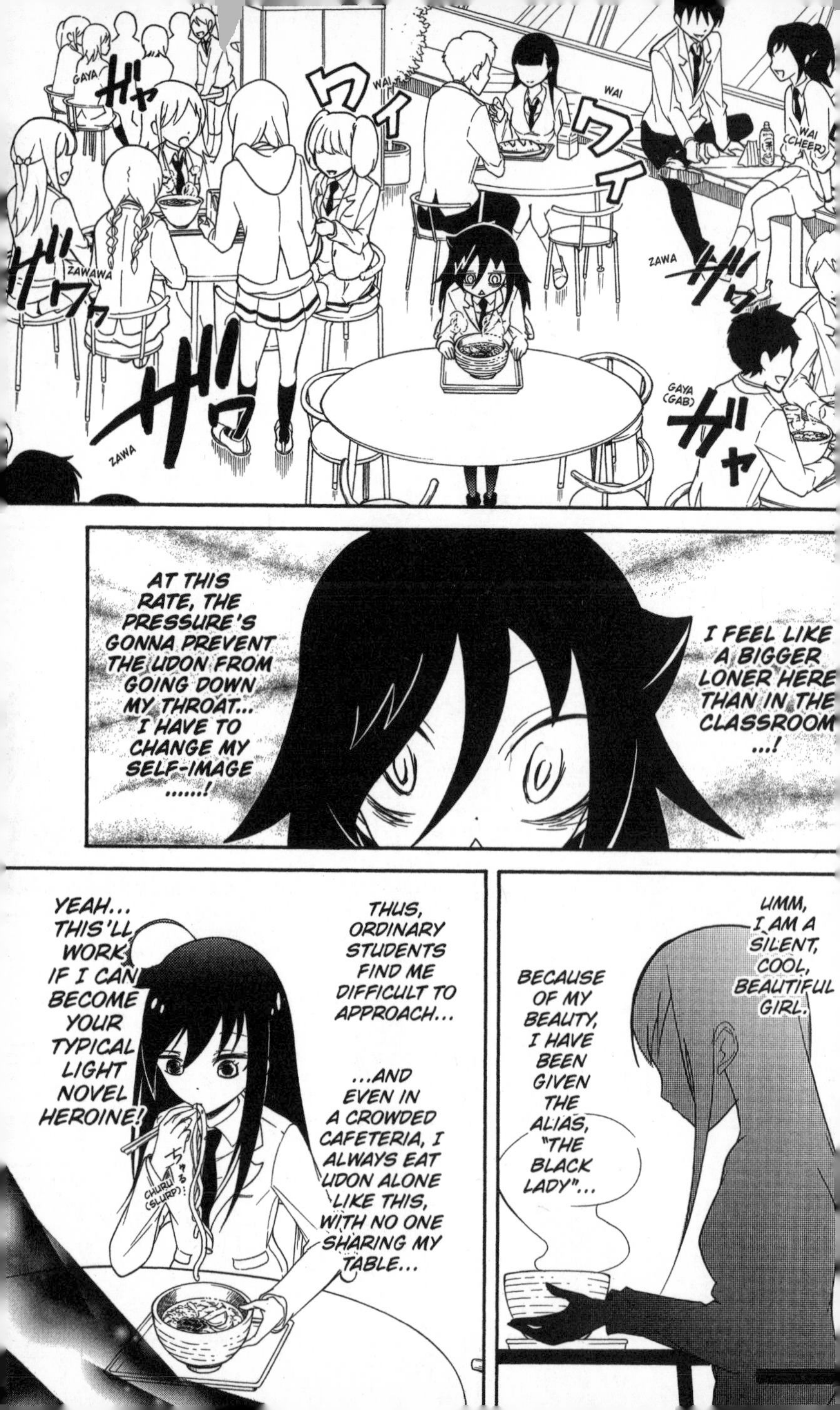

WAI (CHEER)
WAI
WAI
GAYA
ZAWA
GAYA (GAB)
ZAWAWA
ZAWA
I FEEL LIKE A BIGGER LONER HERE THAN IN THE CLASSROOM...!
AT THIS RATE, THE PRESSURE'S GONNA PREVENT THE UDON FROM GOING DOWN MY THROAT... I HAVE TO CHANGE MY SELF-IMAGE......!
UMM, I AM A SILENT, COOL, BEAUTIFUL GIRL.
BECAUSE OF MY BEAUTY, I HAVE BEEN GIVEN THE ALIAS, "THE BLACK LADY"...
THUS, ORDINARY STUDENTS FIND ME DIFFICULT TO APPROACH...
...AND EVEN IN A CROWDED CAFETERIA, I ALWAYS EAT UDON ALONE LIKE THIS, WITH NO ONE SHARING MY TABLE...
CHURU (SLURP)
YEAH... THIS'LL WORK IF I CAN BECOME YOUR TYPICAL LIGHT NOVEL HEROINE!

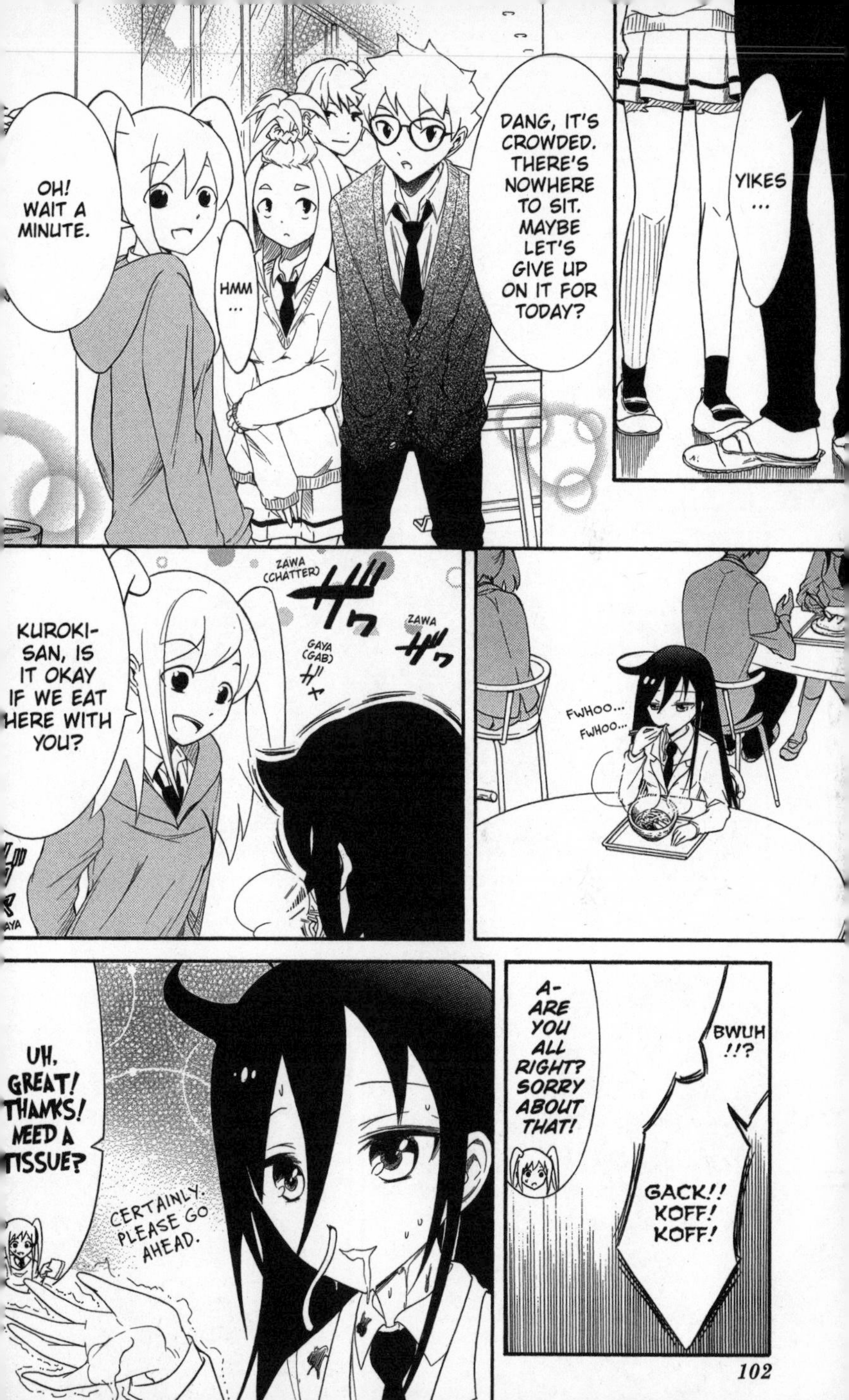
YIKES ...
DANG, IT'S CROWDED. THERE'S NOWHERE TO SIT. MAYBE LET'S GIVE UP ON IT FOR TODAY?
HMM ...
OH! WAIT A MINUTE.
FWHOO... FWHOO...
ZAWA (CHATTER)
ZAWA
GAYA (GAB)
KUROKI-SAN, IS IT OKAY IF WE EAT HERE WITH YOU?
BWUH !!?
A-ARE YOU ALL RIGHT? SORRY ABOUT THAT!
GACK!! KOFF! KOFF!
CERTAINLY. PLEASE GO AHEAD.
UH, GREAT! THANKS! NEED A TISSUE?

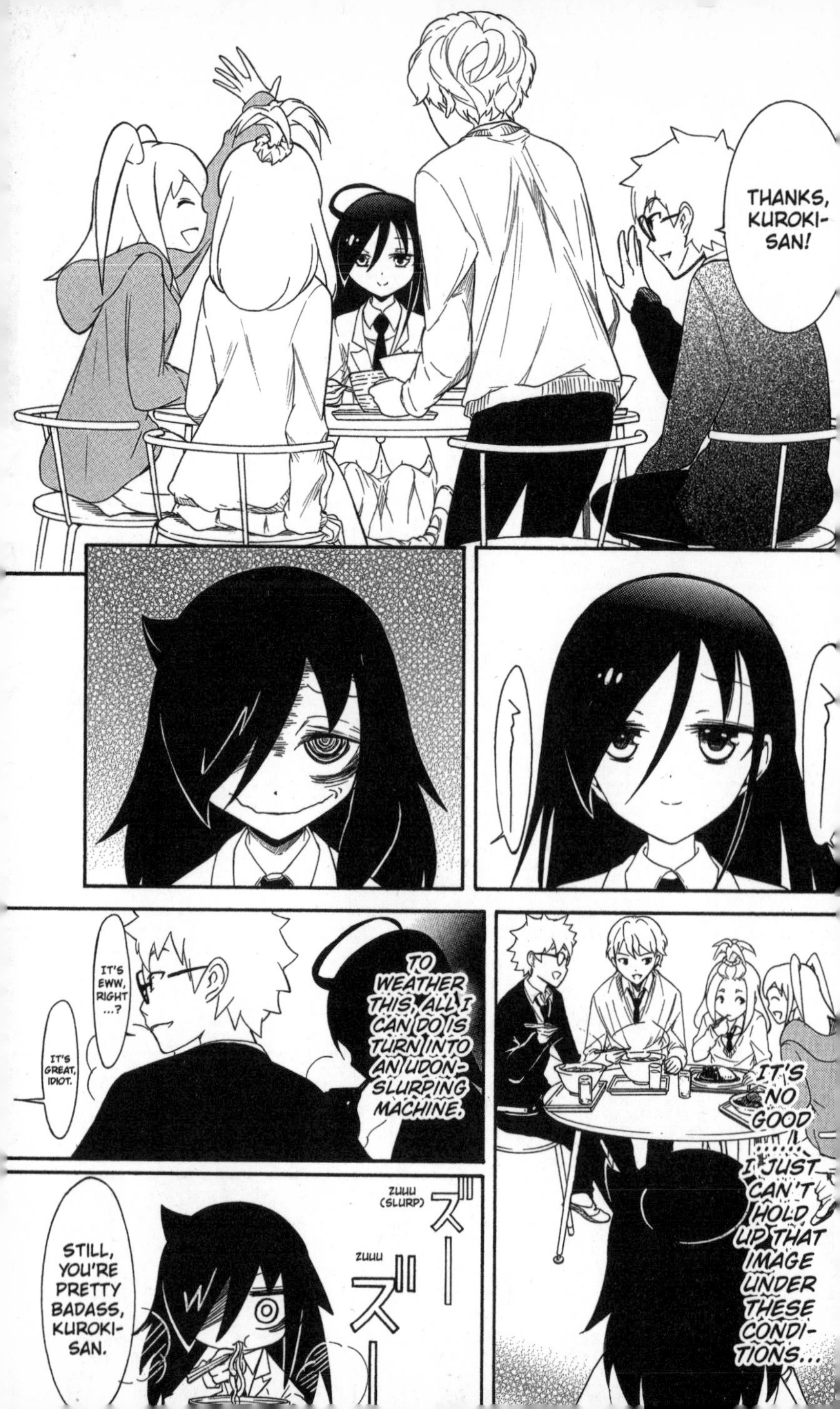
THANKS, KUROKI-SAN!
IT'S NO GOOD..... I JUST CAN'T HOLD UP THAT IMAGE UNDER THESE CONDITIONS...
IT'S EWW, RIGHT...?
IT'S GREAT, IDIOT.
TO WEATHER THIS, ALL I CAN DO IS TURN INTO AN UDON-SLURPING MACHINE.
ZUUU (SLURP)
ズー
ZUUU
ズー
STILL, YOU'RE PRETTY BADASS, KUROKI-SAN.

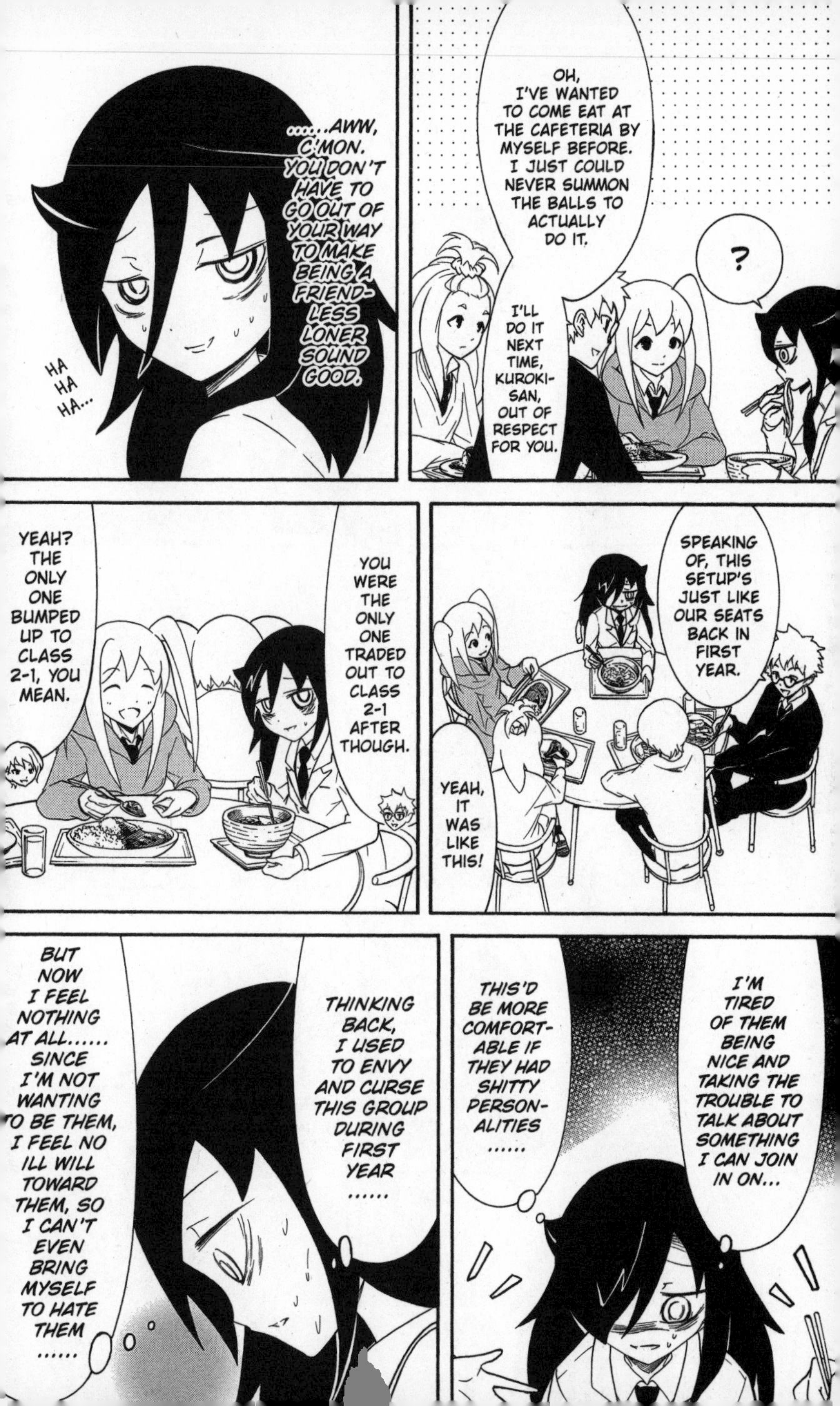
OH, I'VE WANTED TO COME EAT AT THE CAFETERIA BY MYSELF BEFORE. I JUST COULD NEVER SUMMON THE BALLS TO ACTUALLY DO IT.
?
I'LL DO IT NEXT TIME, KUROKI-SAN, OUT OF RESPECT FOR YOU.
......AWW, C'MON. YOU DON'T HAVE TO GO OUT OF YOUR WAY TO MAKE BEING A FRIEND-LESS LONER SOUND GOOD.
HA HA HA...
SPEAKING OF, THIS SETUP'S JUST LIKE OUR SEATS BACK IN FIRST YEAR.
YEAH, IT WAS LIKE THIS!
YOU WERE THE ONLY ONE TRADED OUT TO CLASS 2-1 AFTER THOUGH.
YEAH? THE ONLY ONE BUMPED UP TO CLASS 2-1, YOU MEAN.
I'M TIRED OF THEM BEING NICE AND TAKING THE TROUBLE TO TALK ABOUT SOMETHING I CAN JOIN IN ON...
THIS'D BE MORE COMFORT-ABLE IF THEY HAD SHITTY PERSON-ALITIES ......
THINKING BACK, I USED TO ENVY AND CURSE THIS GROUP DURING FIRST YEAR ......
BUT NOW I FEEL NOTHING AT ALL...... SINCE I'M NOT WANTING TO BE THEM, I FEEL NO ILL WILL TOWARD THEM, SO I CAN'T EVEN BRING MYSELF TO HATE THEM ......

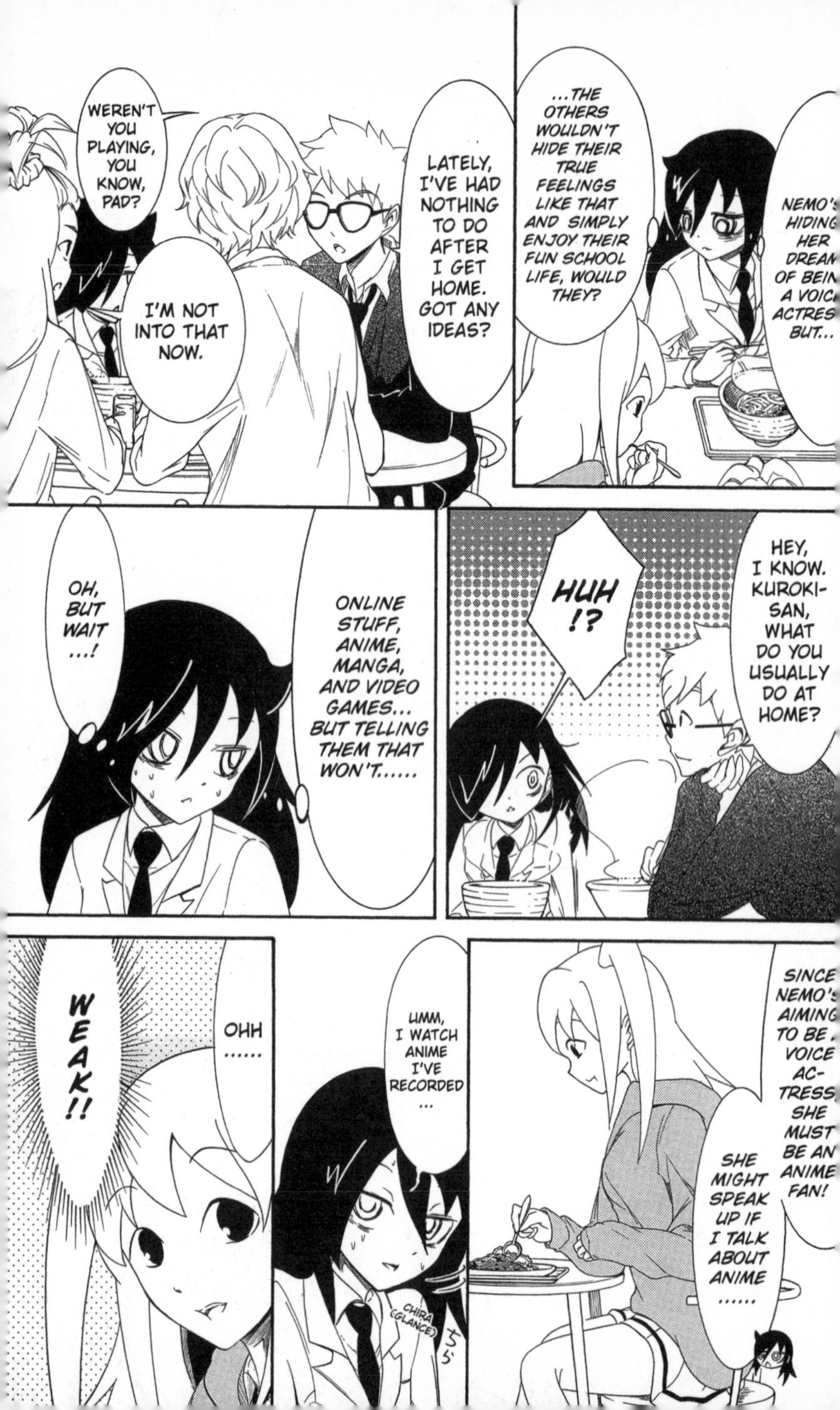
NEMO's HIDING HER DREAM OF BEIN A VOIC ACTRES BUT...
...THE OTHERS WOULDN'T HIDE THEIR TRUE FEELINGS LIKE THAT AND SIMPLY ENJOY THEIR FUN SCHOOL LIFE, WOULD THEY?
LATELY, I'VE HAD NOTHING TO DO AFTER I GET HOME. GOT ANY IDEAS?
WEREN'T YOU PLAYING, YOU KNOW, PAD?
I'M NOT INTO THAT NOW.
HEY, I KNOW. KUROKI-SAN, WHAT DO YOU USUALLY DO AT HOME?
HUH !?
ONLINE STUFF, ANIME, MANGA, AND VIDEO GAMES... BUT TELLING THEM THAT WON'T......
OH, BUT WAIT ...!
SINCE NEMO's AIMING TO BE VOICE AC-TRESS SHE MUST BE AN ANIME FAN!
SHE MIGHT SPEAK UP IF I TALK ABOUT ANIME ......
UMM, I WATCH ANIME I'VE RECORDED ...
CHIRA (GLANCE)
OHH ......
WEAK!!

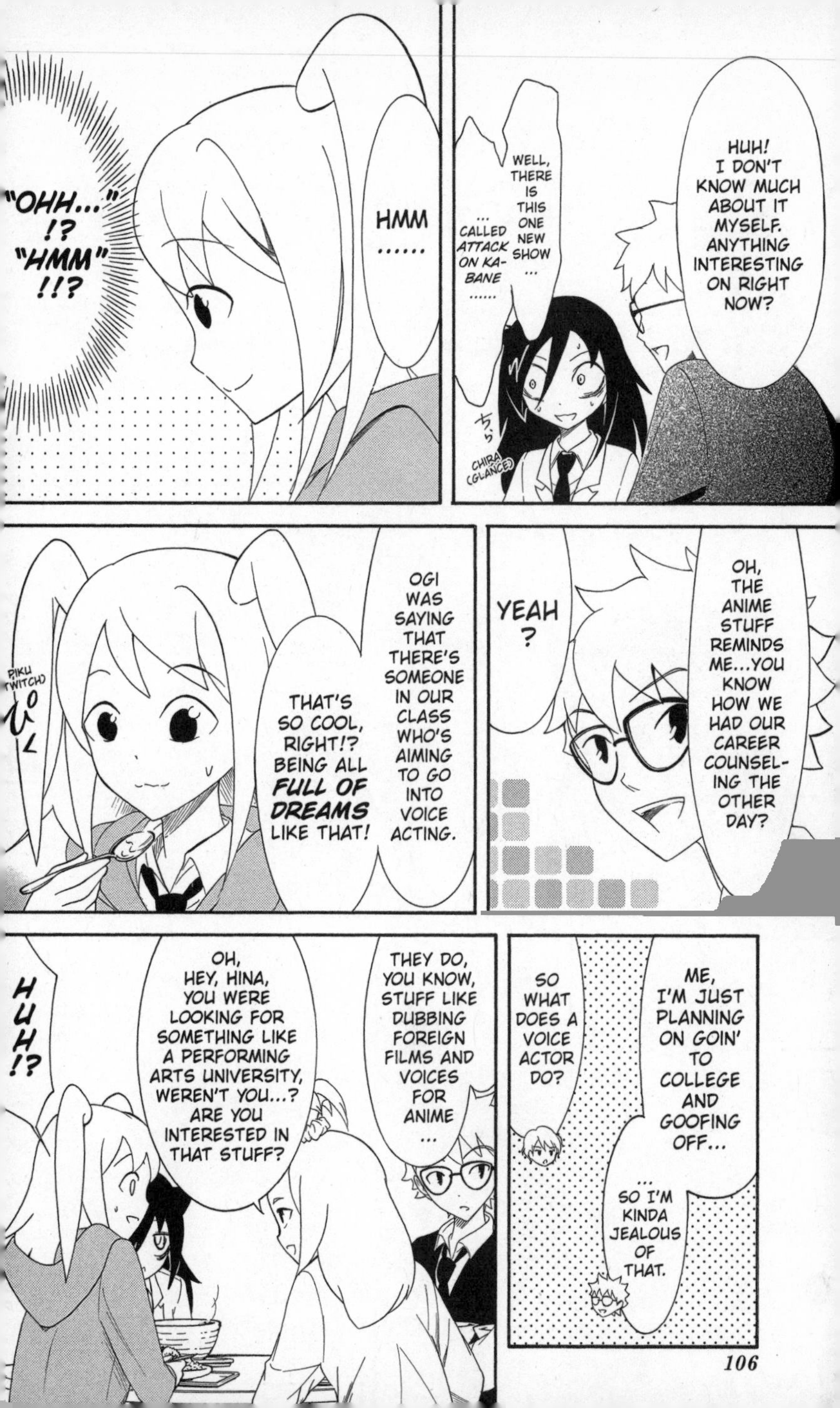
HUH! I DON'T KNOW MUCH ABOUT IT MYSELF. ANYTHING INTERESTING ON RIGHT NOW?
WELL, THERE IS THIS ONE NEW SHOW ...
... CALLED ATTACK ON KA-BANE ......
ちら
CHIRA (GLANCE)
HMM ......
"OHH..." !? "HMM" !!?
OH, THE ANIME STUFF REMINDS ME...YOU KNOW HOW WE HAD OUR CAREER COUNSEL-ING THE OTHER DAY?
YEAH ?
OGI WAS SAYING THAT THERE'S SOMEONE IN OUR CLASS WHO'S AIMING TO GO INTO VOICE ACTING.
THAT'S SO COOL, RIGHT!? BEING ALL FULL OF DREAMS LIKE THAT!
PIKU (TWITCH)
ME, I'M JUST PLANNING ON GOIN' TO COLLEGE AND GOOFING OFF...
... SO I'M KINDA JEALOUS OF THAT.
SO WHAT DOES A VOICE ACTOR DO?
THEY DO, YOU KNOW, STUFF LIKE DUBBING FOREIGN FILMS AND VOICES FOR ANIME ...
OH, HEY, HINA, YOU WERE LOOKING FOR SOMETHING LIKE A PERFORMING ARTS UNIVERSITY, WEREN'T YOU...? ARE YOU INTERESTED IN THAT STUFF?
HUH!?

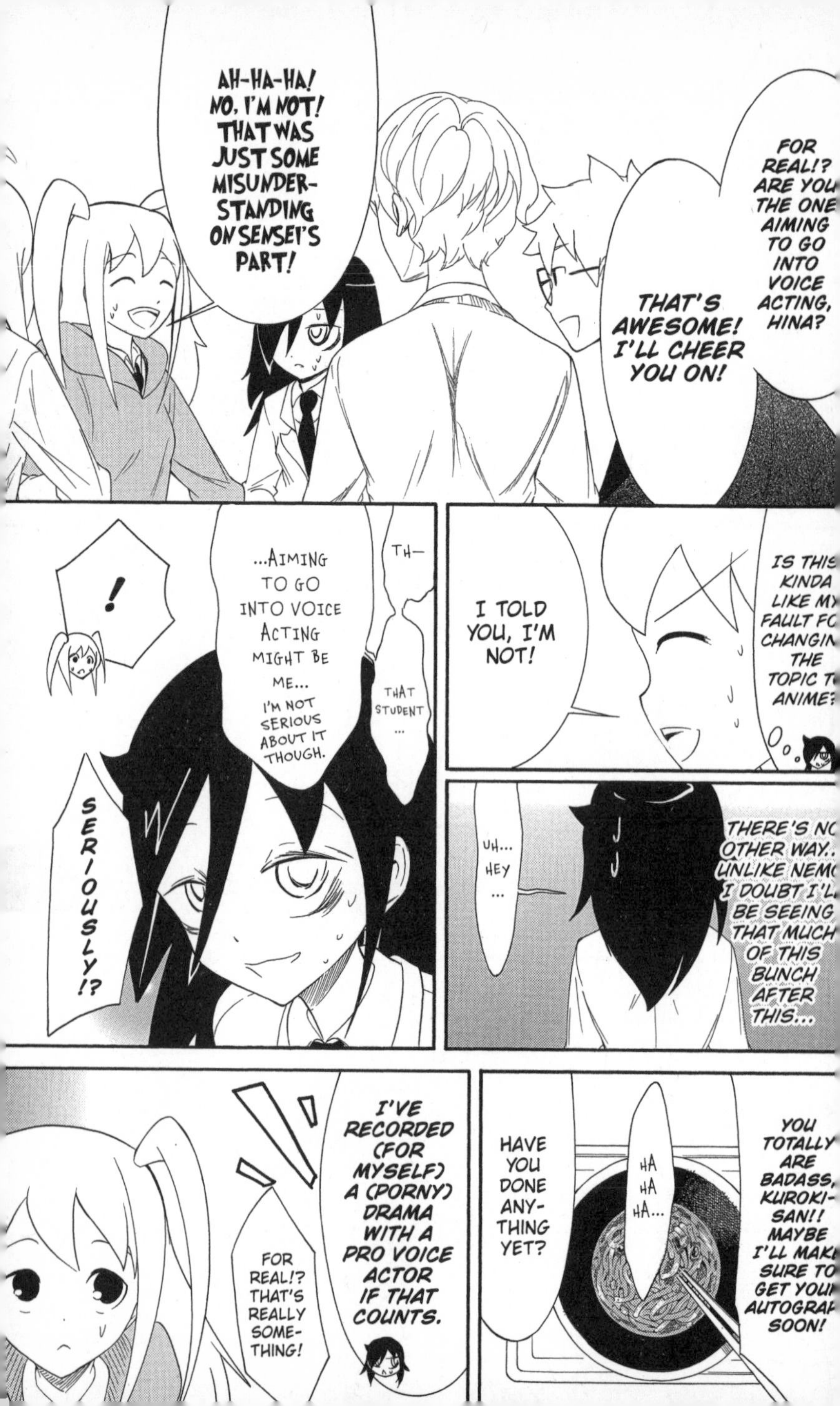
FOR REAL!? ARE YOU THE ONE AIMING TO GO INTO VOICE ACTING, HINA?
THAT'S AWESOME! I'LL CHEER YOU ON!
AH-HA-HA! NO, I'M NOT! THAT WAS JUST SOME MISUNDER-STANDING ON SENSEI'S PART!
IS THIS KINDA LIKE MY FAULT FO CHANGIN THE TOPIC T ANIME?
I TOLD YOU, I'M NOT!
THERE'S NO OTHER WAY.. UNLIKE NEMO I DOUBT I'L BE SEEING THAT MUCH OF THIS BUNCH AFTER THIS...
UH... HEY ...
TH—
THAT STUDENT ...
...AIMING TO GO INTO VOICE ACTING MIGHT BE ME... I'M NOT SERIOUS ABOUT IT THOUGH.
!
SERIOUSLY!?
YOU TOTALLY ARE BADASS, KUROKI-SAN!! MAYBE I'LL MAK SURE TO GET YOU AUTOGRAP SOON!
HA HA HA...
HAVE YOU DONE ANY-THING YET?
I'VE RECORDED (FOR MYSELF) A (PORNY) DRAMA WITH A PRO VOICE ACTOR IF THAT COUNTS.
FOR REAL!? THAT'S REALLY SOME-THING!

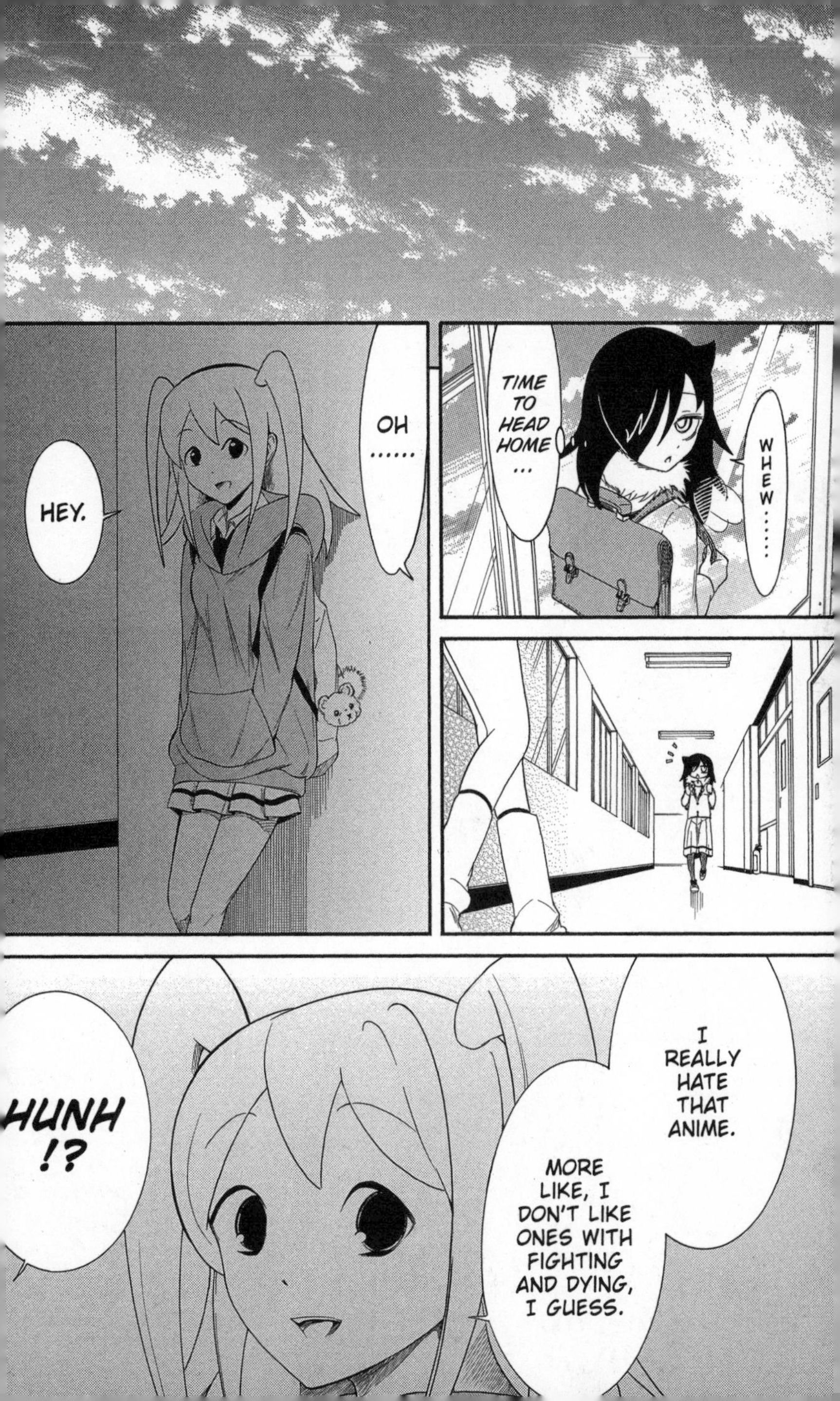
WHEW......
TIME TO HEAD HOME...
OH......
HEY.
I REALLY HATE THAT ANIME.
MORE LIKE, I DON'T LIKE ONES WITH FIGHTING AND DYING, I GUESS.
HUNH!?

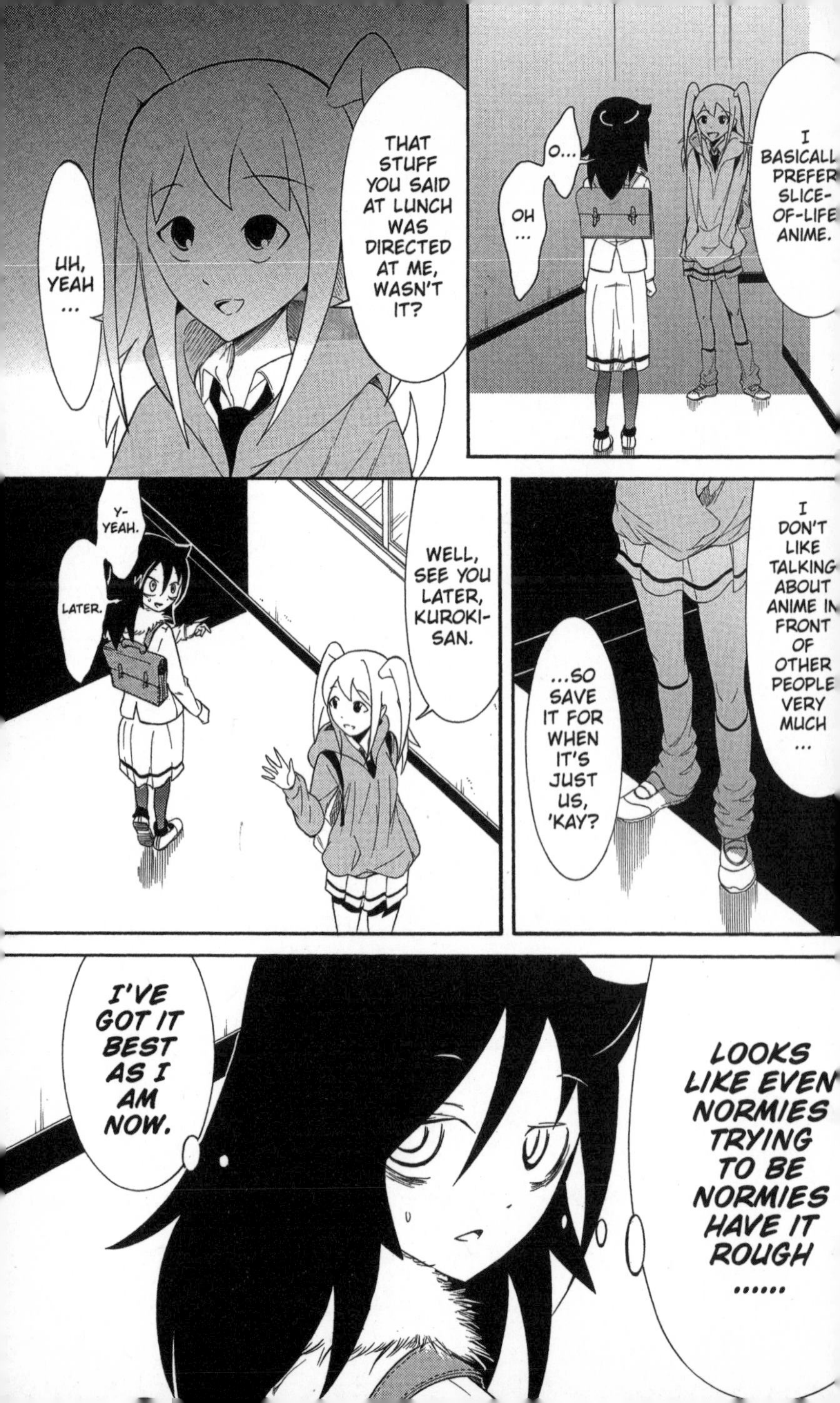
I BASICALL PREFER SLICE-OF-LIFE ANIME.
O...
OH ...
THAT STUFF YOU SAID AT LUNCH WAS DIRECTED AT ME, WASN'T IT?
UH, YEAH ...
I DON'T LIKE TALKING ABOUT ANIME IN FRONT OF OTHER PEOPLE VERY MUCH ...
...SO SAVE IT FOR WHEN IT'S JUST US, 'KAY?
WELL, SEE YOU LATER, KUROKI-SAN.
Y-YEAH.
LATER.
LOOKS LIKE EVEN NORMIES TRYING TO BE NORMIES HAVE IT ROUGH ......
I'VE GOT IT BEST AS I AM NOW.

No Matter How I Look at It, It's You Guys' Fault I'm Not Popular!

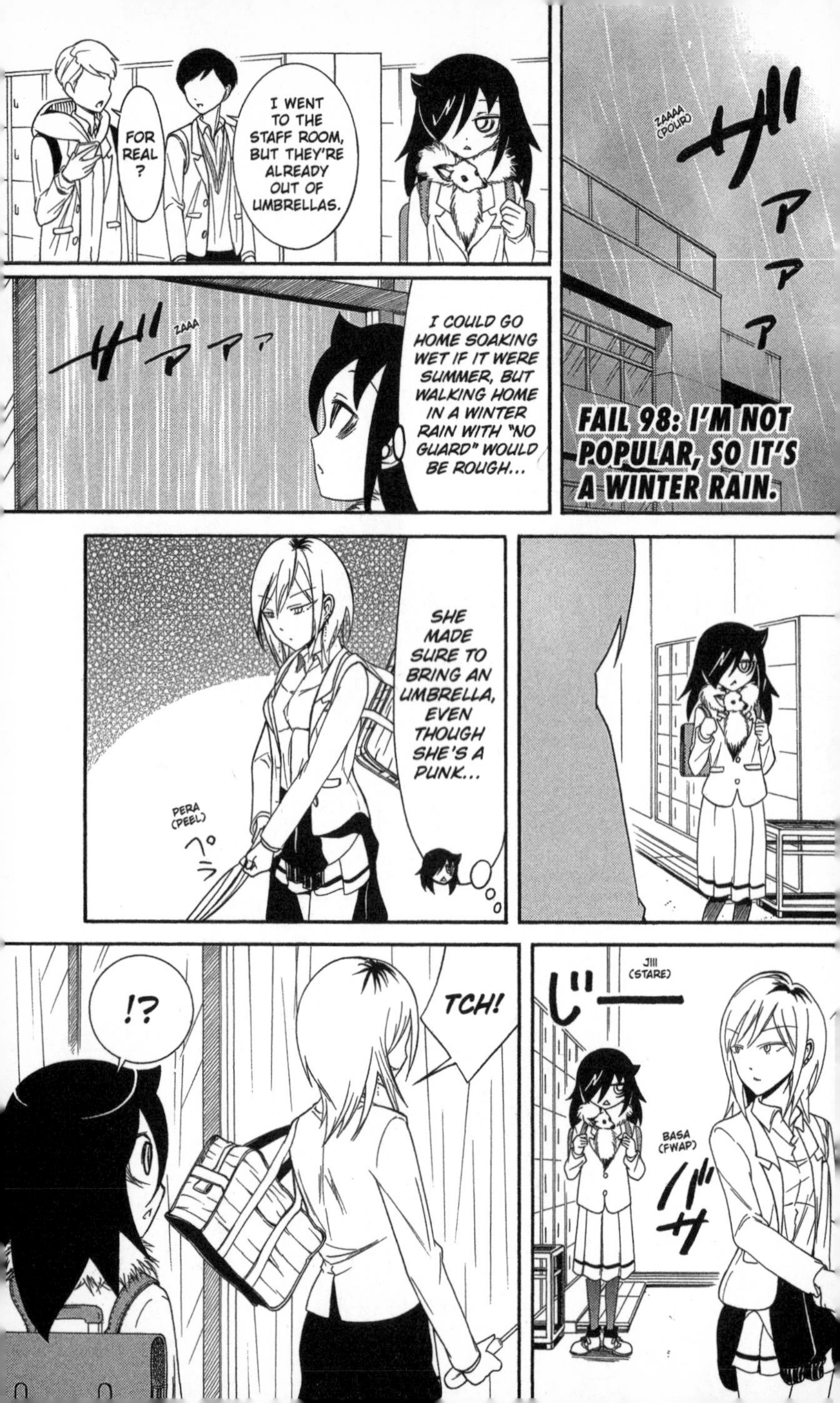

ZAAAA (POUR)
ザァァァ
FAIL 98: I'M NOT POPULAR, SO IT'S A WINTER RAIN.
I WENT TO THE STAFF ROOM, BUT THEY'RE ALREADY OUT OF UMBRELLAS.
FOR REAL ?
ZAAA
ザァァァ
I COULD GO HOME SOAKING WET IF IT WERE SUMMER, BUT WALKING HOME IN A WINTER RAIN WITH "NO GUARD" WOULD BE ROUGH...
SHE MADE SURE TO BRING AN UMBRELLA, EVEN THOUGH SHE'S A PUNK...
PERA (PEEL)
ペラ
JIII (STARE)
じー
BASA (FWAP)
バサ
TCH!
!?

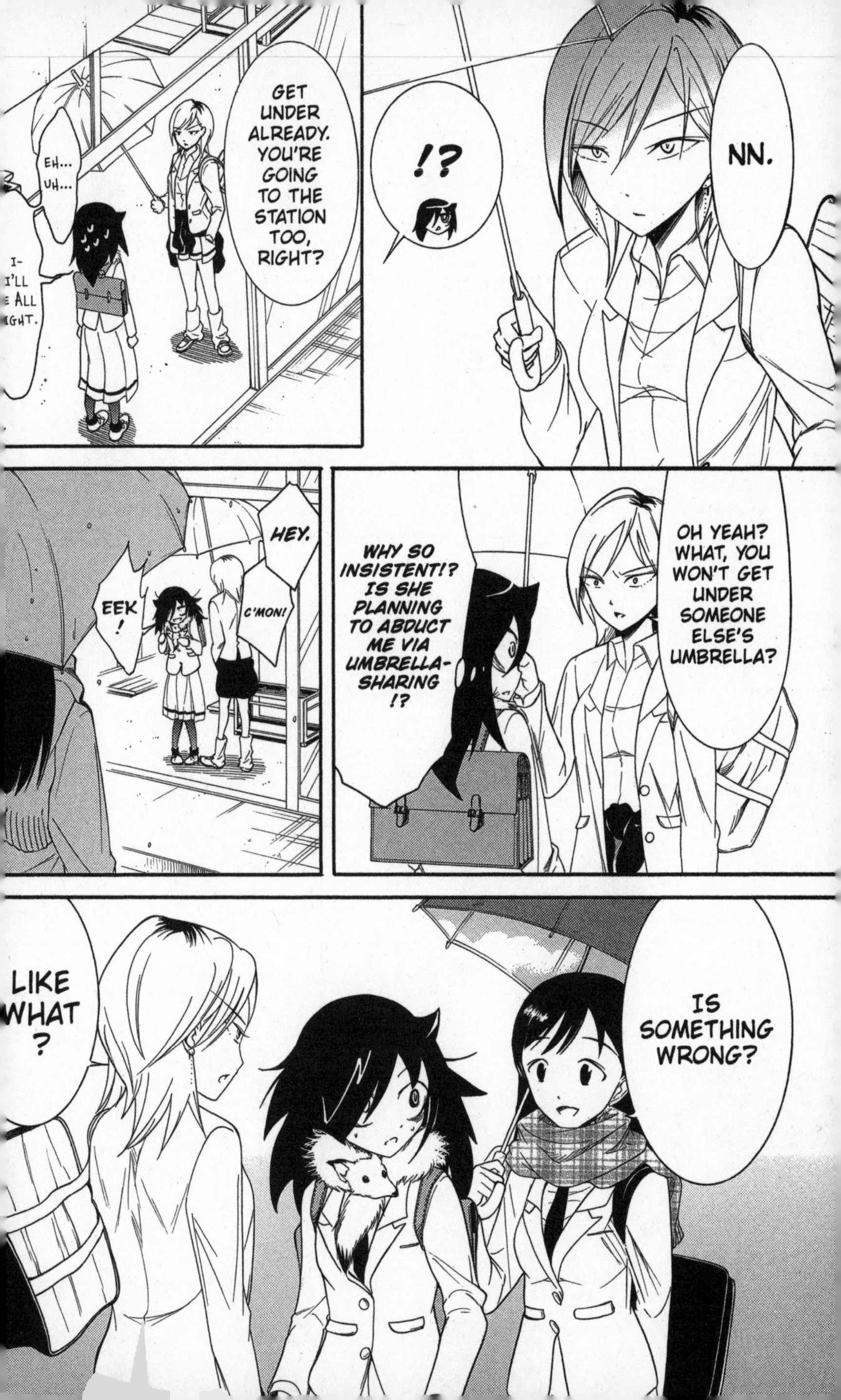
NN.
!?
GET UNDER ALREADY. YOU'RE GOING TO THE STATION TOO, RIGHT?
EH... UH...
I- I'LL E ALL IGHT.
OH YEAH? WHAT, YOU WON'T GET UNDER SOMEONE ELSE'S UMBRELLA?
WHY SO INSISTENT!? IS SHE PLANNING TO ABDUCT ME VIA UMBRELLA-SHARING!?
HEY.
C'MON!
EEK!
IS SOMETHING WRONG?
LIKE WHAT?

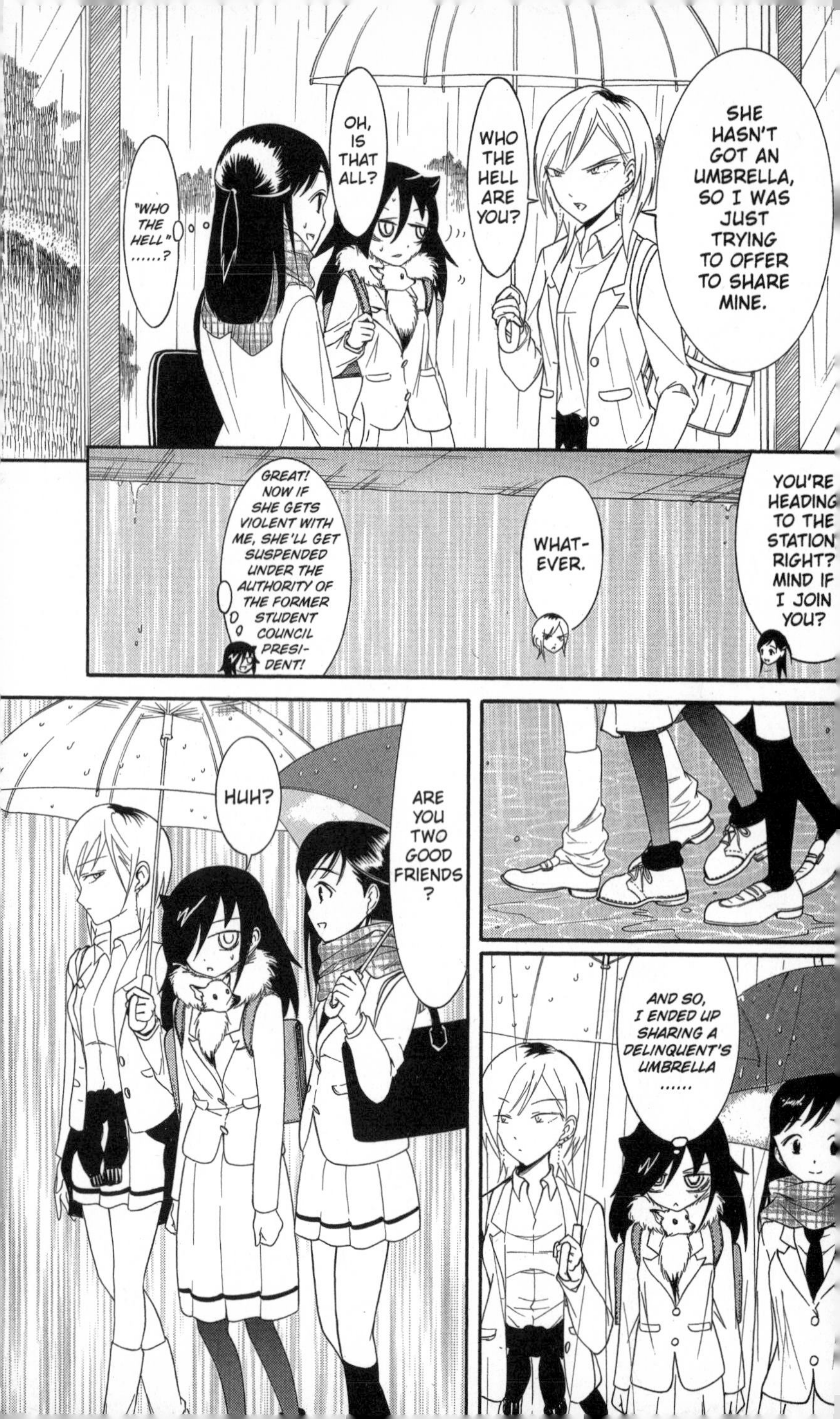
SHE HASN'T GOT AN UMBRELLA, SO I WAS JUST TRYING TO OFFER TO SHARE MINE.
WHO THE HELL ARE YOU?
OH, IS THAT ALL?
"WHO THE HELL"......?
YOU'RE HEADING TO THE STATION RIGHT? MIND IF I JOIN YOU?
WHAT-EVER.
GREAT! NOW IF SHE GETS VIOLENT WITH ME, SHE'LL GET SUSPENDED UNDER THE AUTHORITY OF THE FORMER STUDENT COUNCIL PRESI-DENT!
AND SO, I ENDED UP SHARING A DELINQUENT'S UMBRELLA ......
ARE YOU TWO GOOD FRIENDS?
HUH?

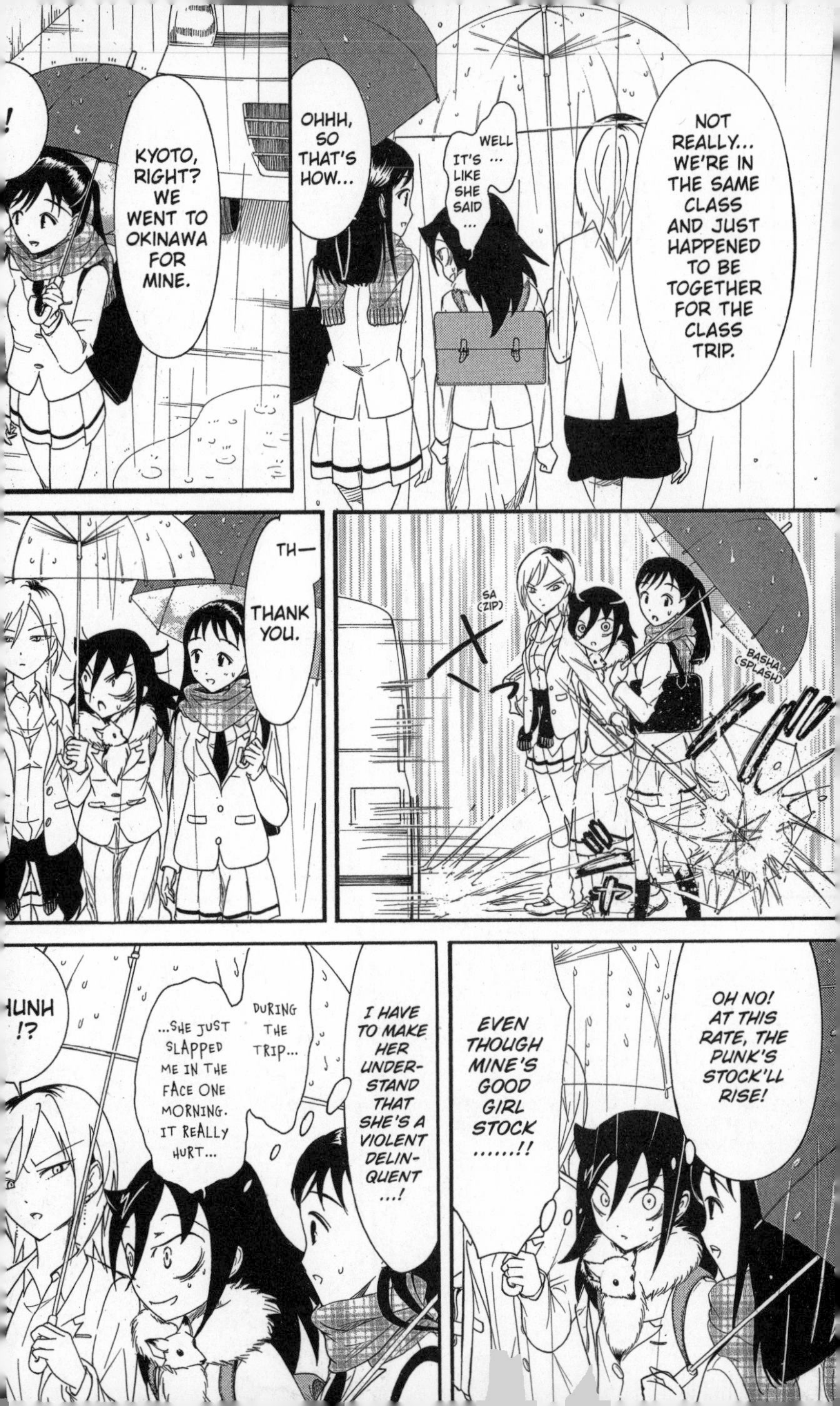
NOT REALLY... WE'RE IN THE SAME CLASS AND JUST HAPPENED TO BE TOGETHER FOR THE CLASS TRIP.
WELL ... IT'S LIKE SHE SAID ...
OHHH, SO THAT'S HOW...
!
KYOTO, RIGHT? WE WENT TO OKINAWA FOR MINE.
SA (ZIP)
BASHA (SPLASH)
TH—
THANK YOU.
OH NO! AT THIS RATE, THE PUNK'S STOCK'LL RISE!
EVEN THOUGH MINE'S GOOD GIRL STOCK ......!!
I HAVE TO MAKE HER UNDERSTAND THAT SHE'S A VIOLENT DELINQUENT ...!
DURING THE TRIP...
...SHE JUST SLAPPED ME IN THE FACE ONE MORNING. IT REALLY HURT...
HUNH !?

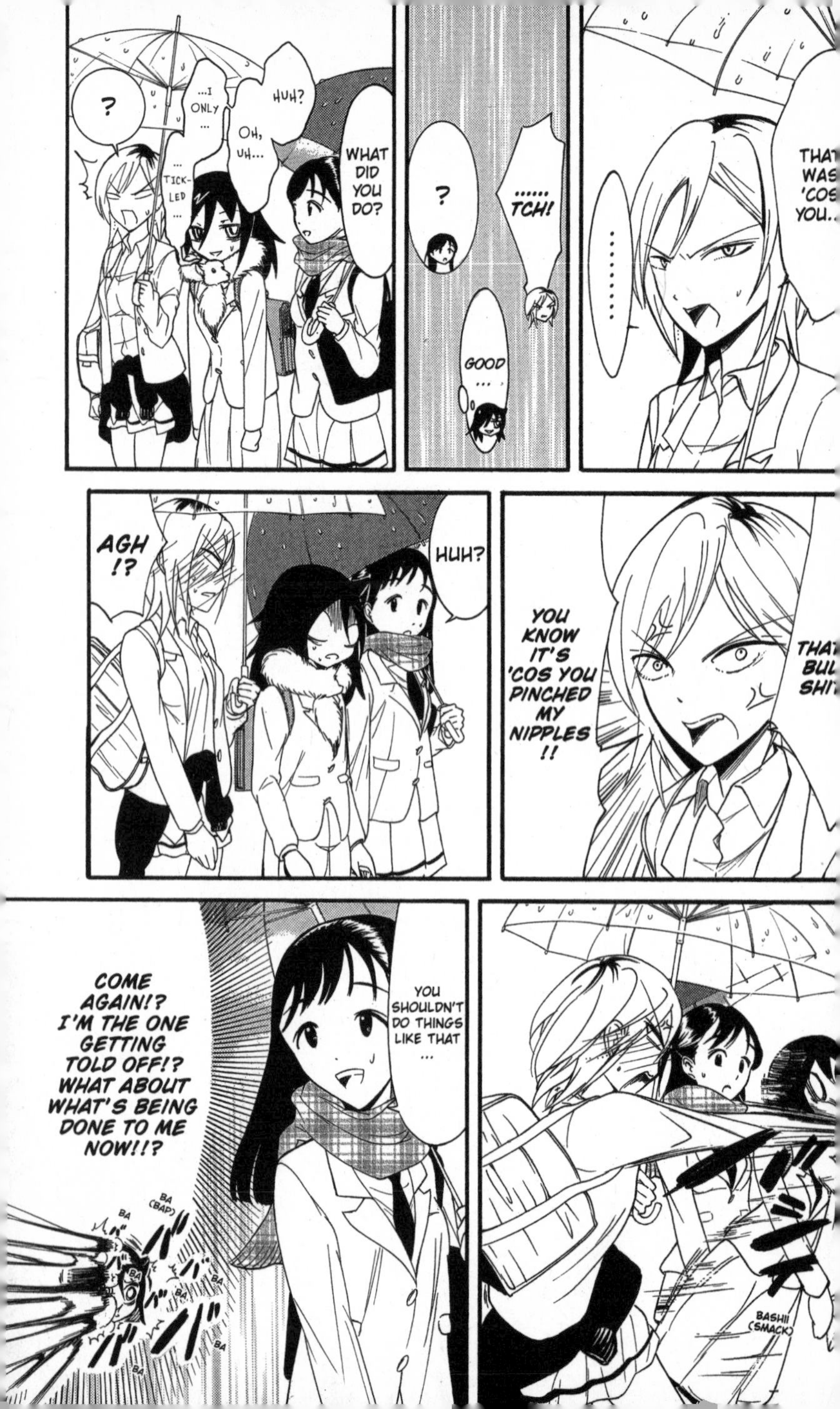
THAT WAS 'COS YOU...
....
......TCH!
?
GOOD...
WHAT DID YOU DO?
HUH?
OH, UH...
...I ONLY ...
...TICK-LED ...
?
THA BUL SHI
YOU KNOW IT'S 'COS YOU PINCHED MY NIPPLES !!
HUH?
AGH !?
BASHII (SMACK)
YOU SHOULDN'T DO THINGS LIKE THAT ...
COME AGAIN!? I'M THE ONE GETTING TOLD OFF!? WHAT ABOUT WHAT'S BEING DONE TO ME NOW!!?
BA (BAP)
BA
BA
BA
BA
BA
BA

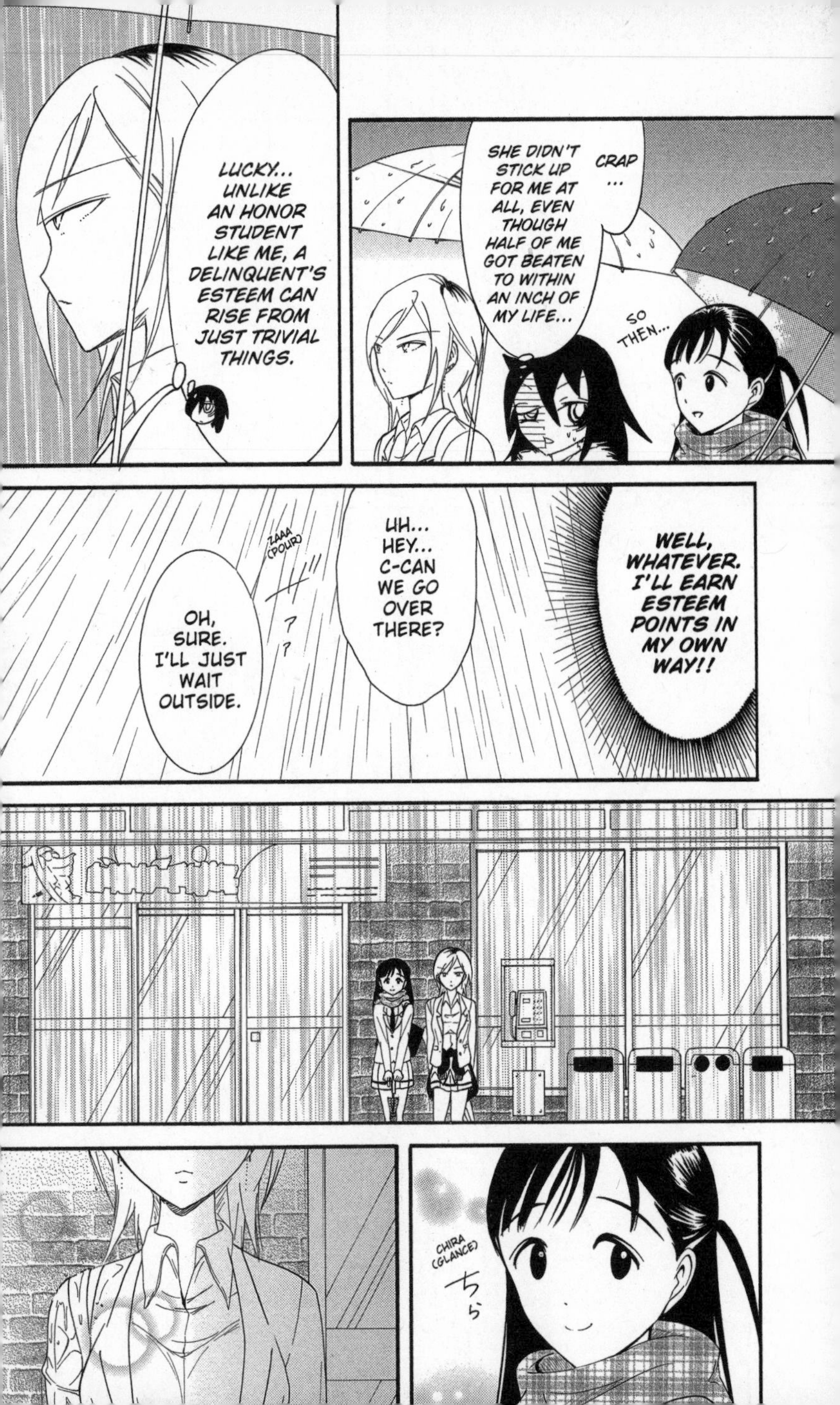
CRAP...
SHE DIDN'T STICK UP FOR ME AT ALL, EVEN THOUGH HALF OF ME GOT BEATEN TO WITHIN AN INCH OF MY LIFE...
SO THEN...
LUCKY... UNLIKE AN HONOR STUDENT LIKE ME, A DELINQUENT'S ESTEEM CAN RISE FROM JUST TRIVIAL THINGS.
WELL, WHATEVER. I'LL EARN ESTEEM POINTS IN MY OWN WAY!!
UH... HEY... C-CAN WE GO OVER THERE?
ZAAA (POUR)
OH, SURE. I'LL JUST WAIT OUTSIDE.
CHIRA (GLANCE)

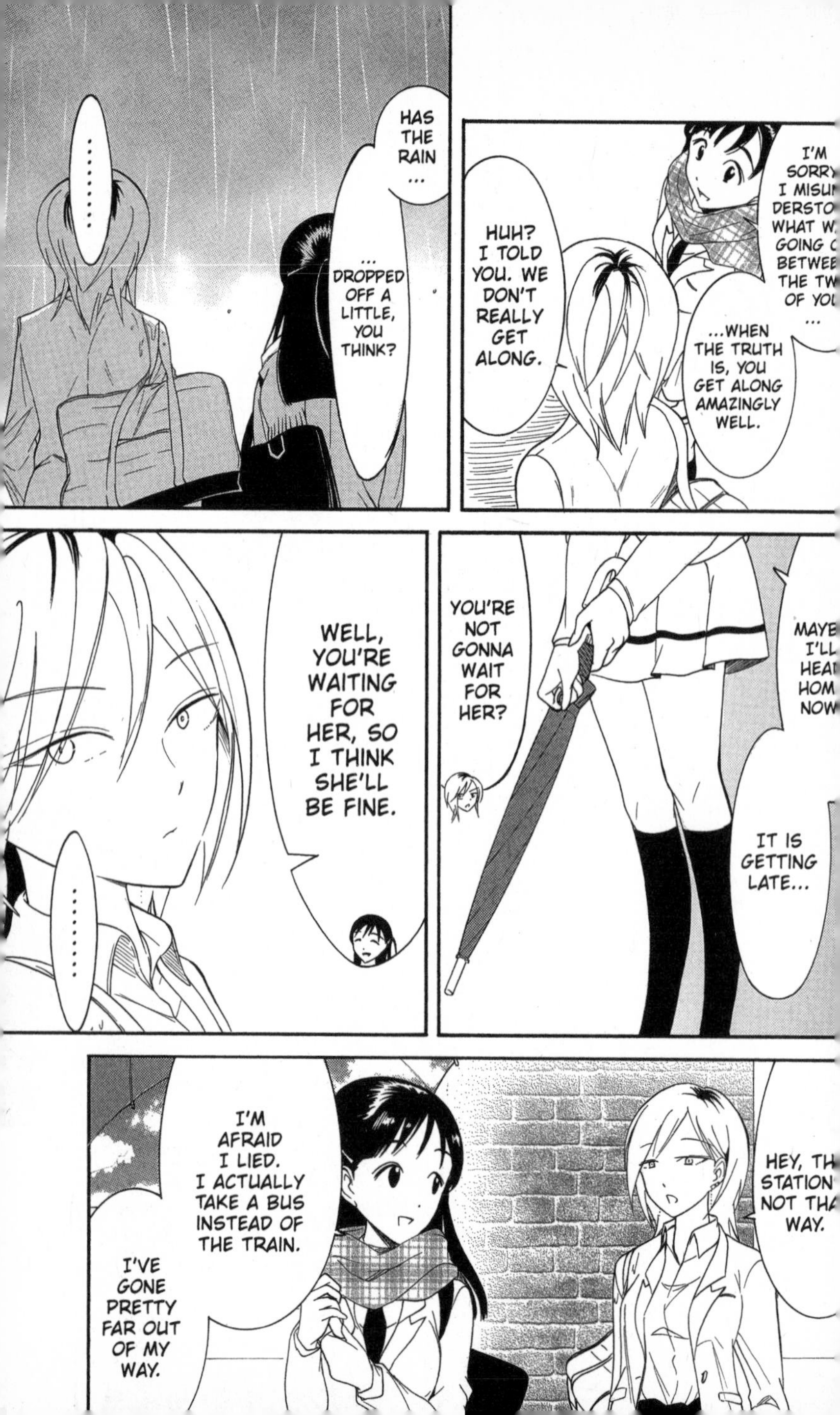
I'M SORRY I MISUN DERSTO WHAT W GOING C BETWEE THE TW OF YOU ...
...WHEN THE TRUTH IS, YOU GET ALONG AMAZINGLY WELL.
HUH? I TOLD YOU. WE DON'T REALLY GET ALONG.
HAS THE RAIN ...
... DROPPED OFF A LITTLE, YOU THINK?
......
MAYE I'LL HEA HOM NOW
IT IS GETTING LATE...
YOU'RE NOT GONNA WAIT FOR HER?
WELL, YOU'RE WAITING FOR HER, SO I THINK SHE'LL BE FINE.
......
HEY, TH STATION NOT THA WAY.
I'M AFRAID I LIED. I ACTUALLY TAKE A BUS INSTEAD OF THE TRAIN.
I'VE GONE PRETTY FAR OUT OF MY WAY.

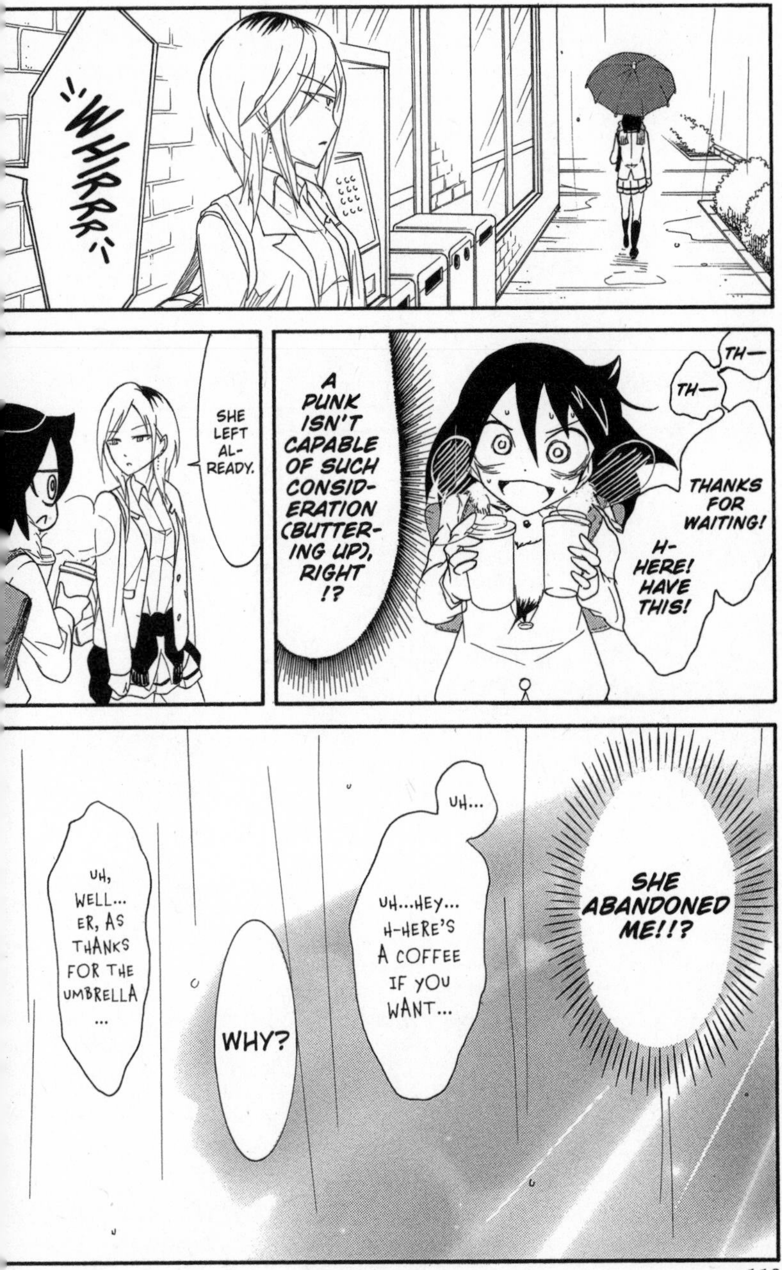
WHIRRR
TH— TH—
THANKS FOR WAITING!
H-HERE! HAVE THIS!
A PUNK ISN'T CAPABLE OF SUCH CONSID-ERATION (BUTTER-ING UP), RIGHT!?
SHE LEFT AL-READY.
SHE ABANDONED ME!!?
UH...
UH...HEY... H-HERE'S A COFFEE IF YOU WANT...
WHY?
UH, WELL... ER, AS THANKS FOR THE UMBRELLA...

No Matter How I Look at It, It's You Guys' Fault I'm Not Popular!

SPECIAL CHAPTER 6

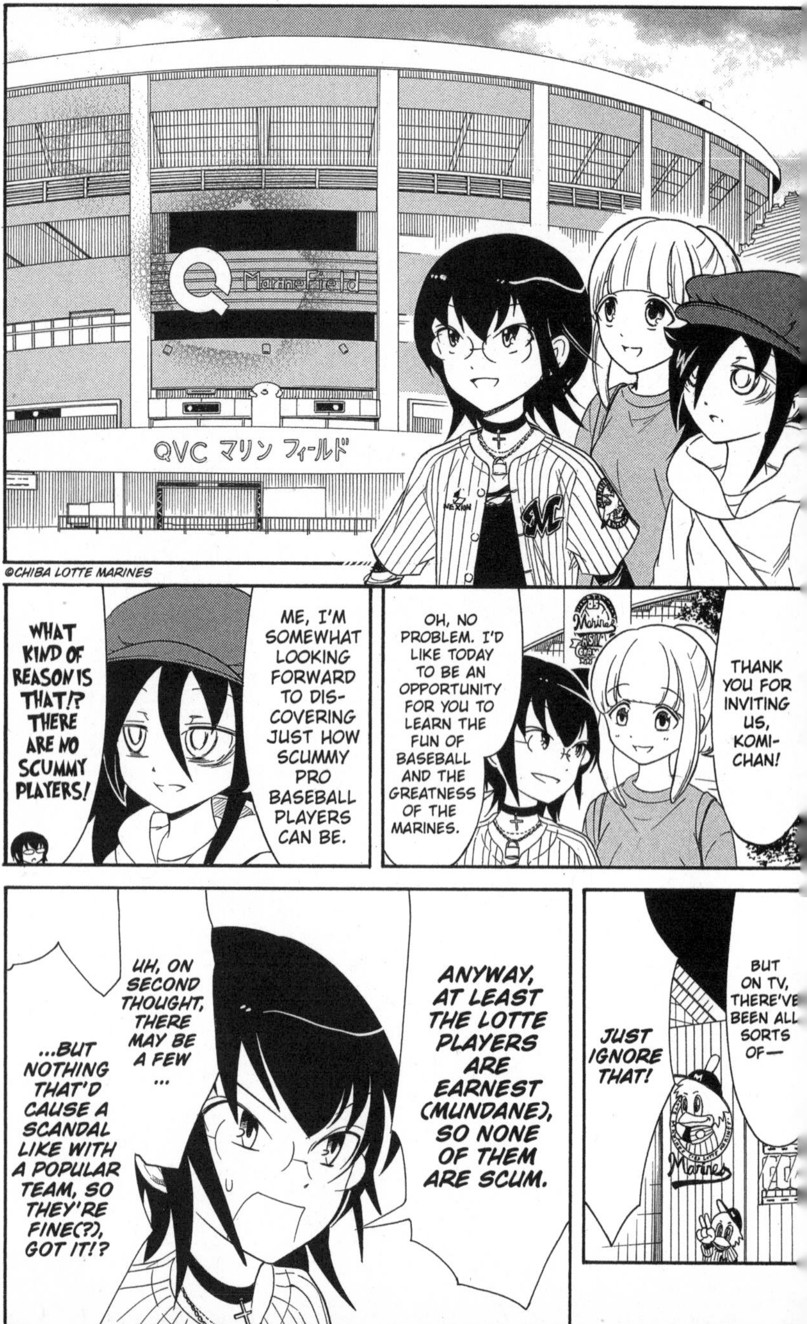
MarineField
QVC マリン フィールド
©CHIBA LOTTE MARINES
THANK YOU FOR INVITING US, KOMI-CHAN!
OH, NO PROBLEM. I'D LIKE TODAY TO BE AN OPPORTUNITY FOR YOU TO LEARN THE FUN OF BASEBALL AND THE GREATNESS OF THE MARINES.
ME, I'M SOMEWHAT LOOKING FORWARD TO DIS-COVERING JUST HOW SCUMMY PRO BASEBALL PLAYERS CAN BE.
WHAT KIND OF REASON IS THAT!? THERE ARE NO SCUMMY PLAYERS!
BUT ON TV, THERE'VE BEEN ALL SORTS OF—
JUST IGNORE THAT!
ANYWAY, AT LEAST THE LOTTE PLAYERS ARE EARNEST (MUNDANE), SO NONE OF THEM ARE SCUM.
UH, ON SECOND THOUGHT, THERE MAY BE A FEW ...
...BUT NOTHING THAT'D CAUSE A SCANDAL LIKE WITH A POPULAR TEAM, SO THEY'RE FINE(?), GOT IT!?

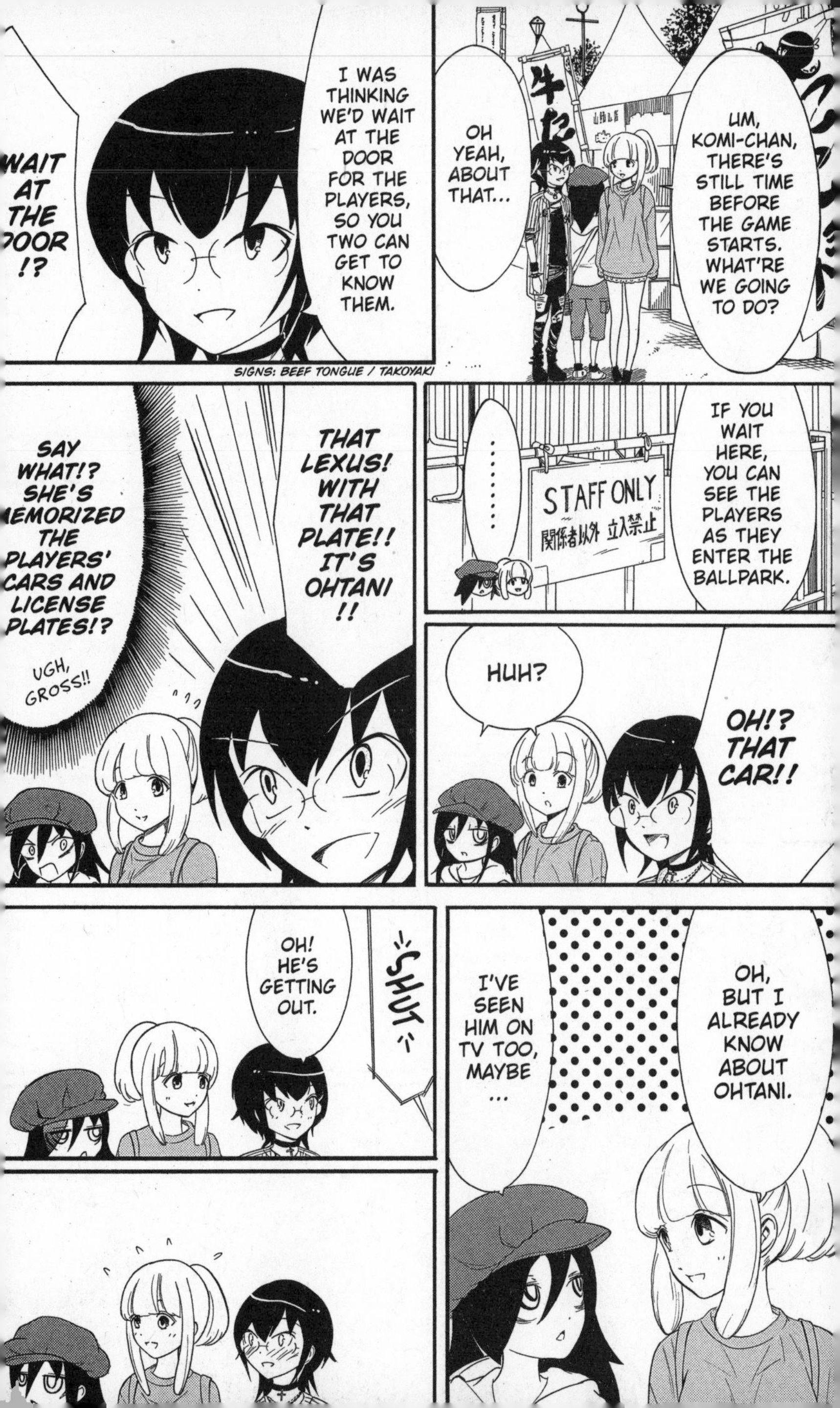
UM, KOMI-CHAN, THERE'S STILL TIME BEFORE THE GAME STARTS. WHAT'RE WE GOING TO DO?
OH YEAH, ABOUT THAT...
I WAS THINKING WE'D WAIT AT THE DOOR FOR THE PLAYERS, SO YOU TWO CAN GET TO KNOW THEM.
WAIT AT THE DOOR !?
SIGNS: BEEF TONGUE / TAKOYAKI
IF YOU WAIT HERE, YOU CAN SEE THE PLAYERS AS THEY ENTER THE BALLPARK.
STAFF ONLY
関係者以外 立入禁止
......
OH!? THAT CAR!!
HUH?
THAT LEXUS! WITH THAT PLATE!! IT'S OHTANI!!
SAY WHAT!? SHE'S MEMORIZED THE PLAYERS' CARS AND LICENSE PLATES!?
UGH, GROSS!!
OH, BUT I ALREADY KNOW ABOUT OHTANI.
I'VE SEEN HIM ON TV TOO, MAYBE...
SHUT
OH! HE'S GETTING OUT.

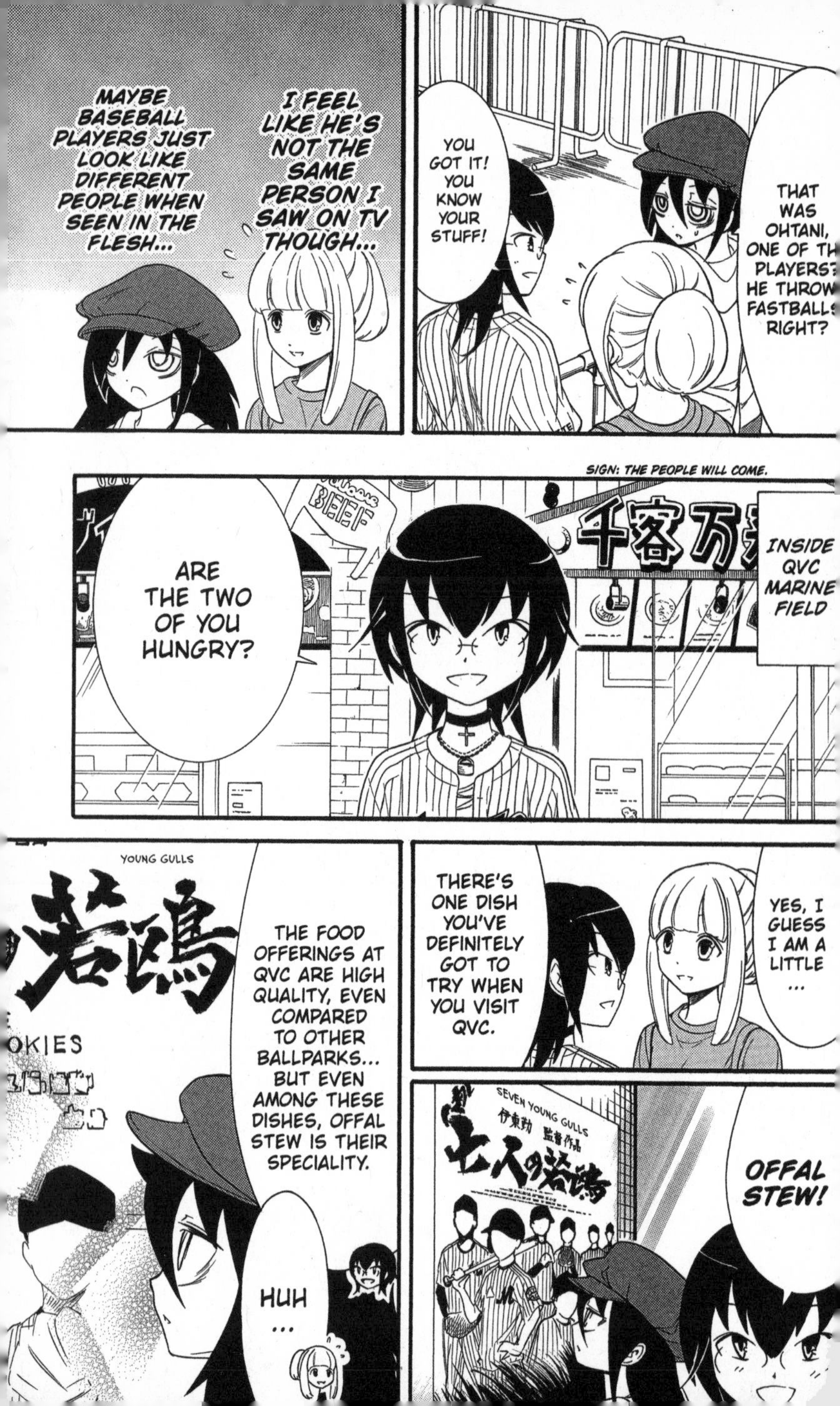

THAT WAS OHTANI, ONE OF TH PLAYERS? HE THROW FASTBALLS RIGHT?
YOU GOT IT! YOU KNOW YOUR STUFF!
I FEEL LIKE HE'S NOT THE SAME PERSON I SAW ON TV THOUGH...
MAYBE BASEBALL PLAYERS JUST LOOK LIKE DIFFERENT PEOPLE WHEN SEEN IN THE FLESH...
SIGN: THE PEOPLE WILL COME.
千客万
INSIDE QVC MARINE FIELD
BEEF
ARE THE TWO OF YOU HUNGRY?
YES, I GUESS I AM A LITTLE ...
THERE'S ONE DISH YOU'VE DEFINITELY GOT TO TRY WHEN YOU VISIT QVC.
SEVEN YOUNG GULLS
伊東勤 監督作品
七人の若鴎
OFFAL STEW!
YOUNG GULLS
若鴎
OKIES
THE FOOD OFFERINGS AT QVC ARE HIGH QUALITY, EVEN COMPARED TO OTHER BALLPARKS... BUT EVEN AMONG THESE DISHES, OFFAL STEW IS THEIR SPECIALITY.
HUH ...

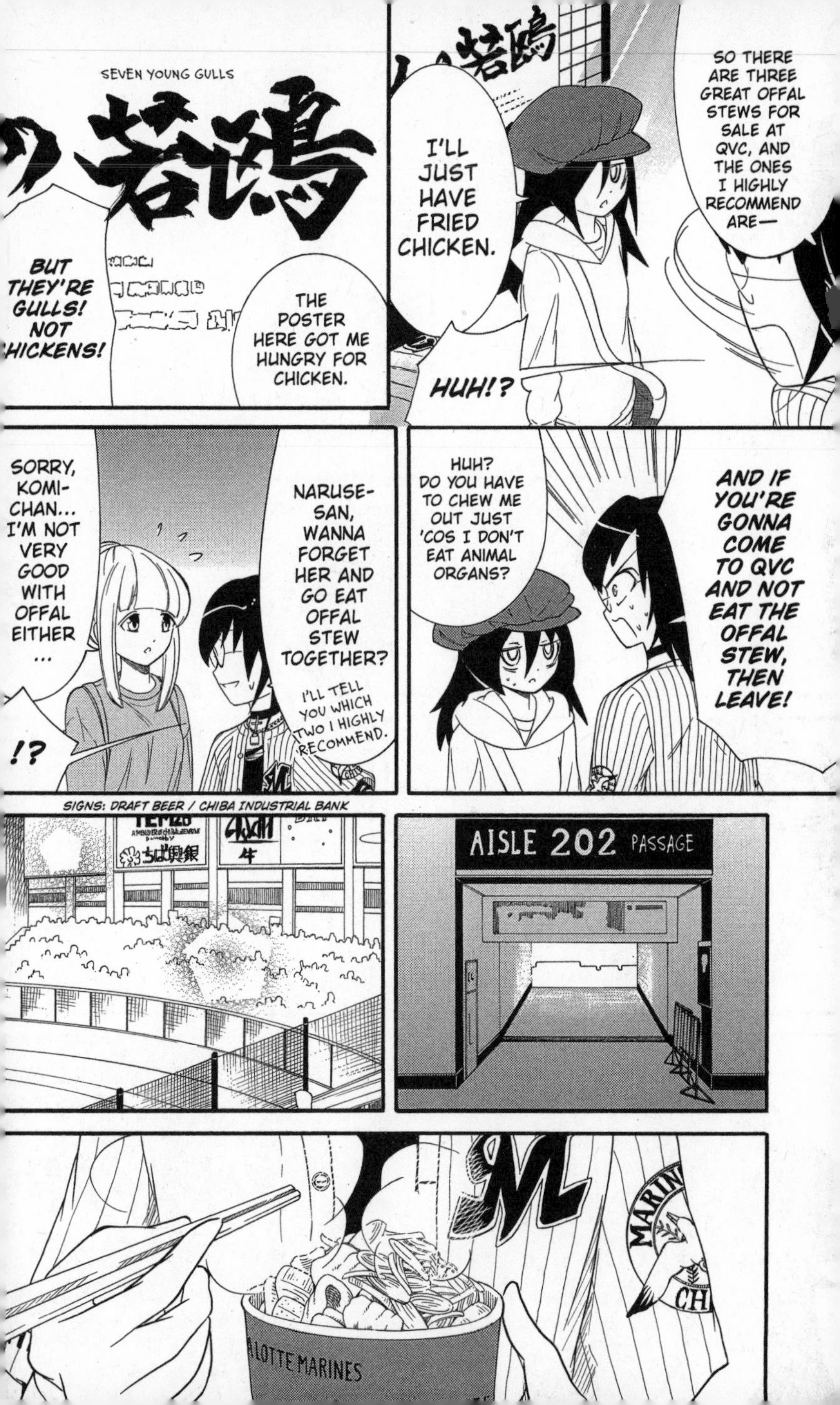
SO THERE ARE THREE GREAT OFFAL STEWS FOR SALE AT QVC, AND THE ONES I HIGHLY RECOMMEND ARE—
I'LL JUST HAVE FRIED CHICKEN.
HUH!?
SEVEN YOUNG GULLS
THE POSTER HERE GOT ME HUNGRY FOR CHICKEN.
BUT THEY'RE GULLS! NOT HICKENS!
AND IF YOU'RE GONNA COME TO QVC AND NOT EAT THE OFFAL STEW, THEN LEAVE!
HUH? DO YOU HAVE TO CHEW ME OUT JUST 'COS I DON'T EAT ANIMAL ORGANS?
NARUSE-SAN, WANNA FORGET HER AND GO EAT OFFAL STEW TOGETHER?
I'LL TELL YOU WHICH TWO I HIGHLY RECOMMEND.
SORRY, KOMI-CHAN... I'M NOT VERY GOOD WITH OFFAL EITHER...
!?
AISLE 202 PASSAGE
SIGNS: DRAFT BEER / CHIBA INDUSTRIAL BANK
LOTTE MARINES

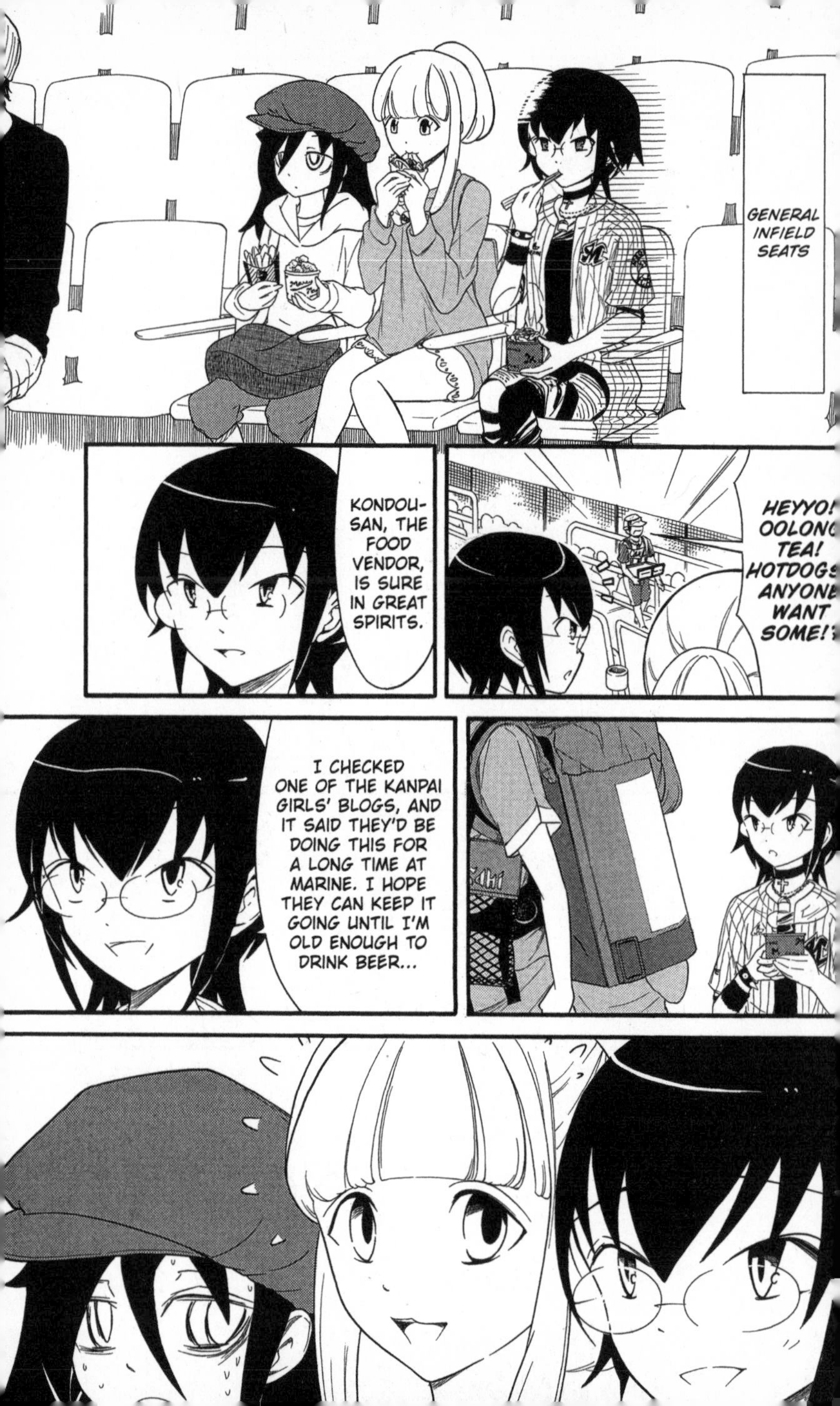

GENERAL INFIELD SEATS
HEYYO! OOLONG TEA! HOTDOGS ANYONE WANT SOME!?
KONDOU-SAN, THE FOOD VENDOR, IS SURE IN GREAT SPIRITS.
I CHECKED ONE OF THE KANPAI GIRLS' BLOGS, AND IT SAID THEY'D BE DOING THIS FOR A LONG TIME AT MARINE. I HOPE THEY CAN KEEP IT GOING UNTIL I'M OLD ENOUGH TO DRINK BEER...

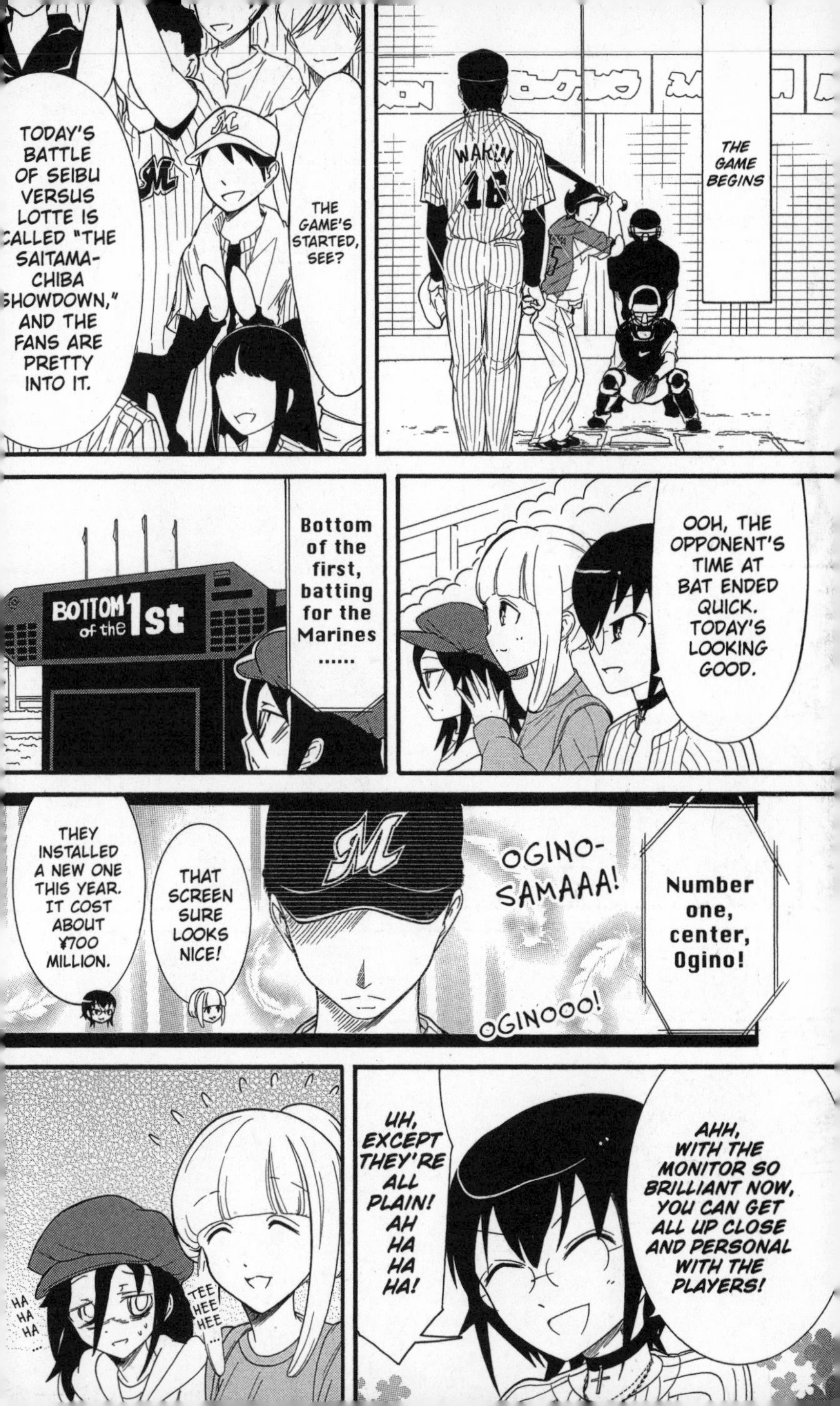
THE GAME BEGINS
THE GAME'S STARTED, SEE?
TODAY'S BATTLE OF SEIBU VERSUS LOTTE IS CALLED "THE SAITAMA-CHIBA SHOWDOWN," AND THE FANS ARE PRETTY INTO IT.
OOH, THE OPPONENT'S TIME AT BAT ENDED QUICK. TODAY'S LOOKING GOOD.
Bottom of the first, batting for the Marines ......
BOTTOM of the 1st
Number one, center, Ogino!
OGINO-SAMAAA!
OGINOOO!
THAT SCREEN SURE LOOKS NICE!
THEY INSTALLED A NEW ONE THIS YEAR. IT COST ABOUT ¥700 MILLION.
AHH, WITH THE MONITOR SO BRILLIANT NOW, YOU CAN GET ALL UP CLOSE AND PERSONAL WITH THE PLAYERS!
UH, EXCEPT THEY'RE ALL PLAIN! AH HA HA HA!
TEE HEE HEE ...
HA HA HA ...

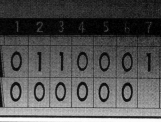

1	2	3	4	5	6	7
0	1	1	0	0	0	1
0	0	0	0	0	0	

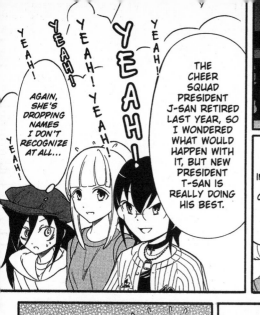

YEAH! YEAH! YEAH! YEAH! YEAH! YEAH!

Again, she's dropping names I don't recognize at all...

THE CHEER SQUAD PRESIDENT J-SAN RETIRED LAST YEAR, SO I WONDERED WHAT WOULD HAPPEN WITH IT, BUT NEW PRESIDENT T-SAN IS REALLY DOING HIS BEST.

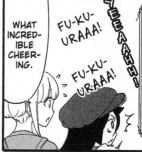

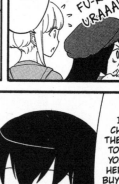

WHAT INCREDIBLE CHEERING.

FU-KU-URAAA!

FU-KU-UR-AAA!

YEEAAHH!

Now pinch-hitting for Hosoya Fukuur

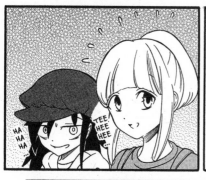

HA HA HA

TEE HEE HEE...

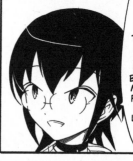

I WENT WITH CHEERING FROM THE INFIELD SEATS TODAY SINCE IT'S YOUR FIRST TIME HERE, BUT YOU'LL BUY UNIFORMS AND MEMORIZE ALL THE FIGHT SONGS, AND WE'LL SIT BY THE LIGHT STAND NEXT TIME, OKAY?

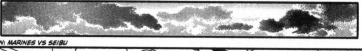

SIGN: MARINES VS SEIBU

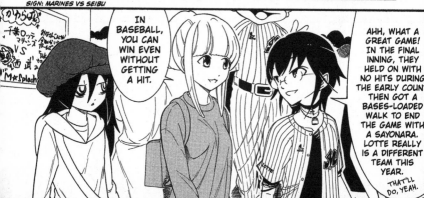

IN BASEBALL, YOU CAN WIN EVEN WITHOUT GETTING A HIT.

AHH, WHAT A GREAT GAME! IN THE FINAL INNING, THEY HELD ON WITH NO HITS DURING THE EARLY COUNT THEN GOT A BASES-LOADED WALK TO END THE GAME WITH A SAYONARA. LOTTE REALLY IS A DIFFERENT TEAM THIS YEAR.

THAT'LL DO, YEAH.

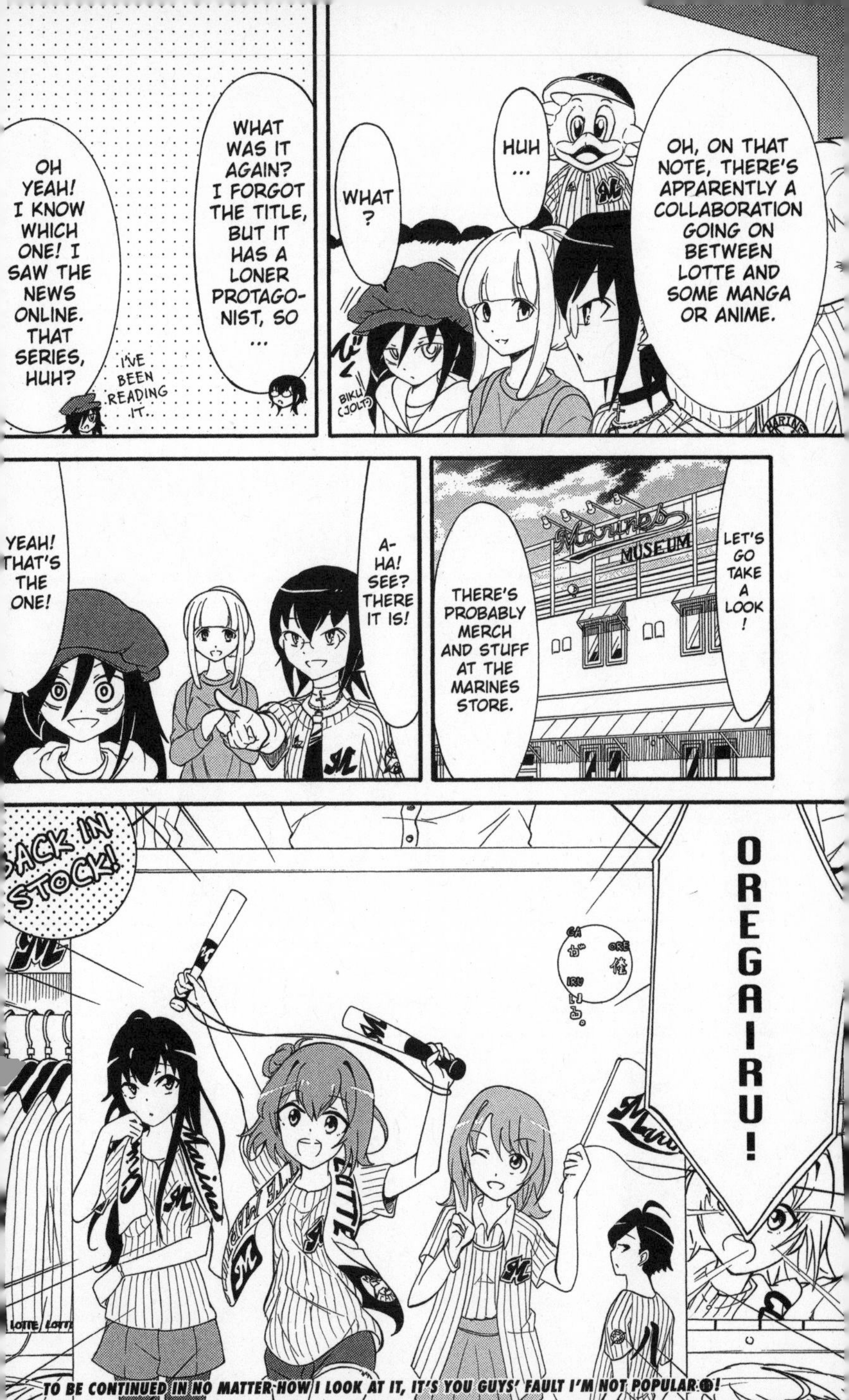

OH, ON THAT NOTE, THERE'S APPARENTLY A COLLABORATION GOING ON BETWEEN LOTTE AND SOME MANGA OR ANIME.
HUH ...
WHAT ?
BIKU (JOLT)
WHAT WAS IT AGAIN? I FORGOT THE TITLE, BUT IT HAS A LONER PROTAGO-NIST, SO ...
OH YEAH! I KNOW WHICH ONE! I SAW THE NEWS ONLINE. THAT SERIES, HUH?
I'VE BEEN READING IT.
LET'S GO TAKE A LOOK!
Marines MUSEUM
THERE'S PROBABLY MERCH AND STUFF AT THE MARINES STORE.
A-HA! SEE? THERE IT IS!
YEAH! THAT'S THE ONE!
OREGAIRU!
ORE 俺 GA が IRU いる。
BACK IN STOCK!

TO BE CONTINUED IN NO MATTER HOW I LOOK AT IT, IT'S YOU GUYS' FAULT I'M NOT POPULAR ⑪!

No Matter How I Look at It, It's You Guys' Fault I'm Not Popular!

AFTER FAIL 89...

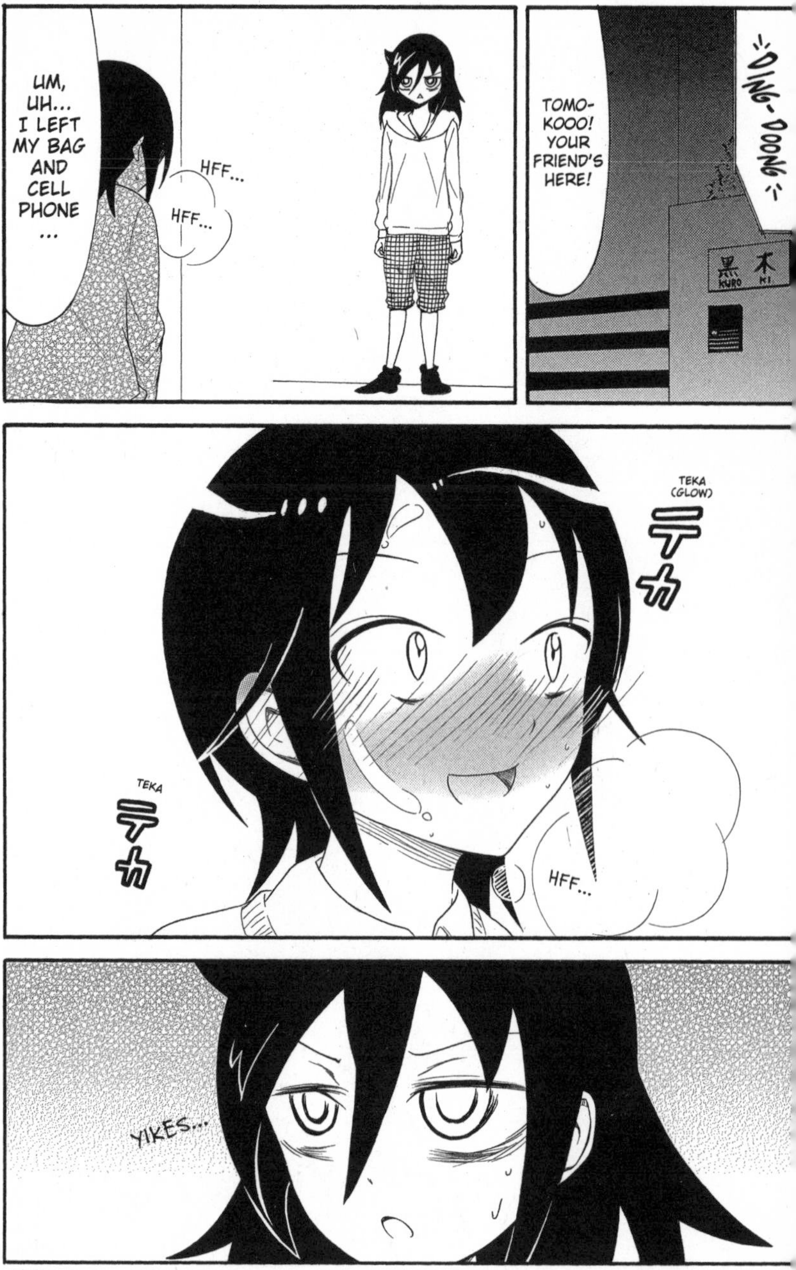
DING-DOONG
黒 木
KURO KI
TOMO-KOOO! YOUR FRIEND'S HERE!
HFF...
HFF...
UM, UH... I LEFT MY BAG AND CELL PHONE ...
テカ
TEKA (GLOW)
テカ
TEKA
HFF...
YIKES...

AFTER FAIL 91...

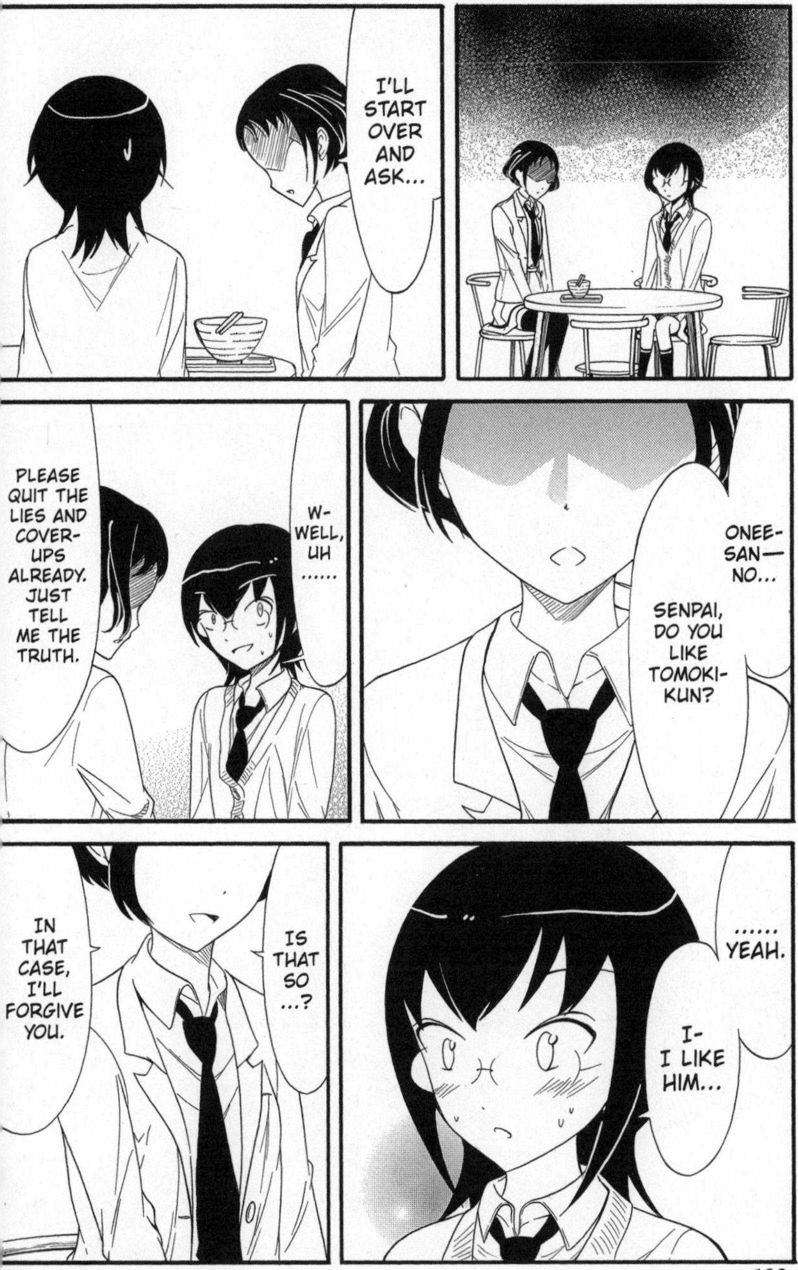
I'LL START OVER AND ASK...
ONEE-SAN— NO...
SENPAI, DO YOU LIKE TOMOKI-KUN?
W-WELL, UH ......
PLEASE QUIT THE LIES AND COVER-UPS ALREADY. JUST TELL ME THE TRUTH.
...... YEAH.
I- I LIKE HIM...
IS THAT SO ...?
IN THAT CASE, I'LL FORGIVE YOU.

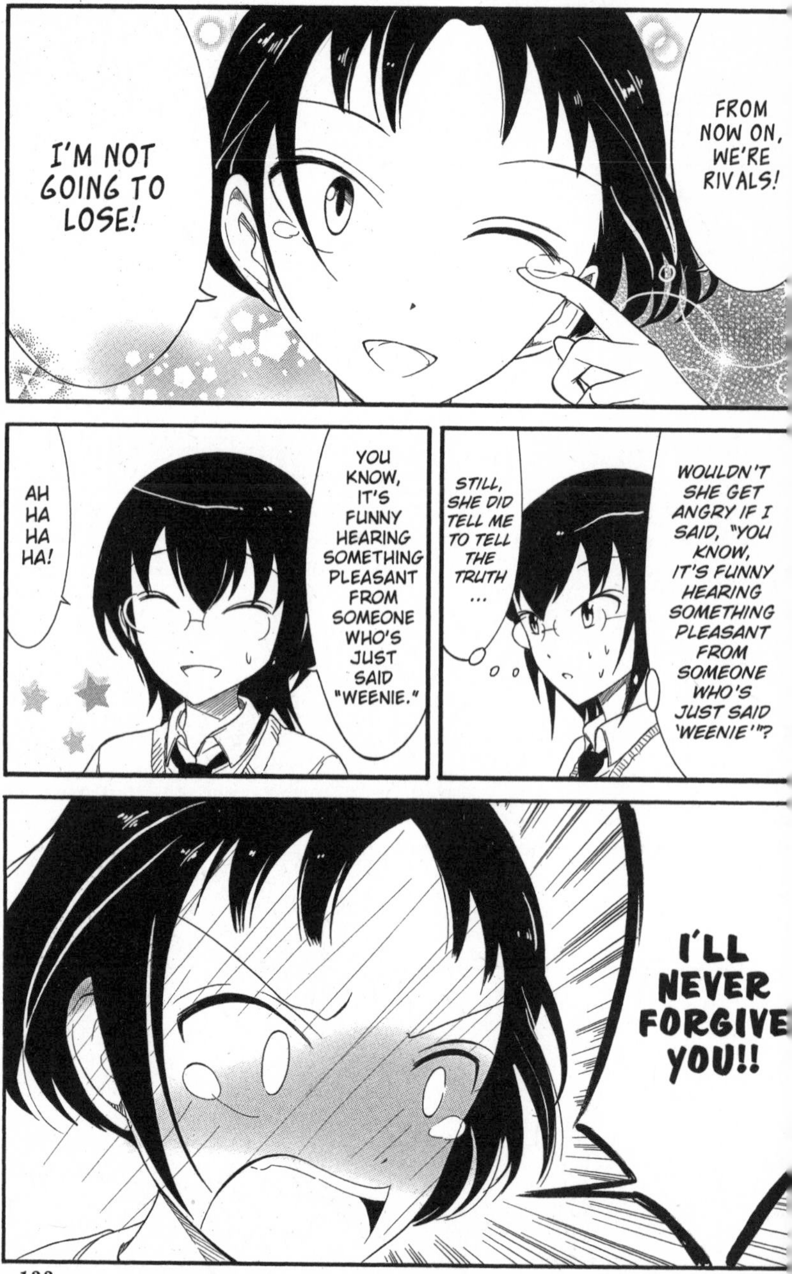
FROM NOW ON, WE'RE RIVALS!
I'M NOT GOING TO LOSE!
WOULDN'T SHE GET ANGRY IF I SAID, "YOU KNOW, IT'S FUNNY HEARING SOMETHING PLEASANT FROM SOMEONE WHO'S JUST SAID 'WEENIE'"?
STILL, SHE DID TELL ME TO TELL THE TRUTH ...
YOU KNOW, IT'S FUNNY HEARING SOMETHING PLEASANT FROM SOMEONE WHO'S JUST SAID "WEENIE."
AH HA HA HA!
I'LL NEVER FORGIVE YOU!!

No Matter How I Look at It, It's You Guys' Fault I'm Not Popular!

AFTERWORD

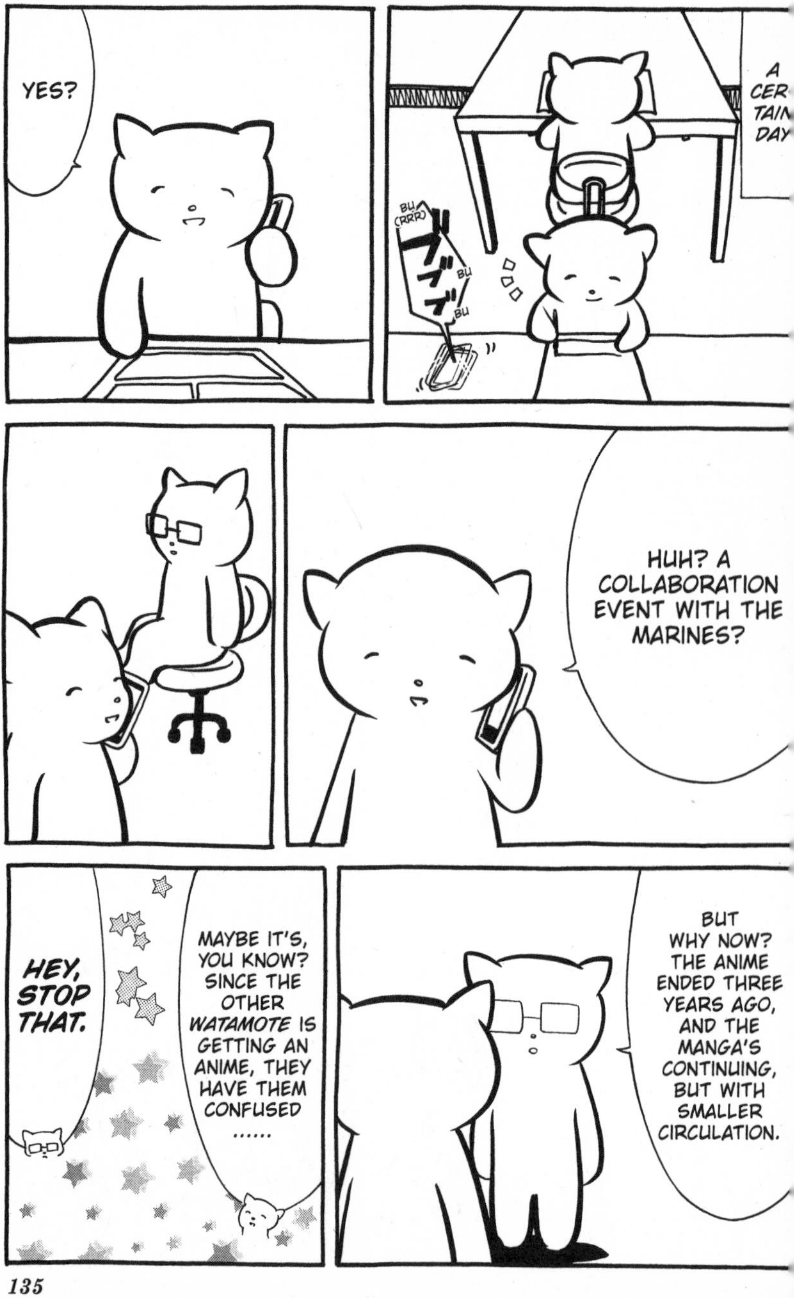
A CERTAIN DAY
BU (RRR)
BU
BU
YES?
HUH? A COLLABORATION EVENT WITH THE MARINES?
BUT WHY NOW? THE ANIME ENDED THREE YEARS AGO, AND THE MANGA'S CONTINUING, BUT WITH SMALLER CIRCULATION.
MAYBE IT'S, YOU KNOW? SINCE THE OTHER *WATAMOTE* IS GETTING AN ANIME, THEY HAVE THEM CONFUSED ......
HEY, STOP THAT.

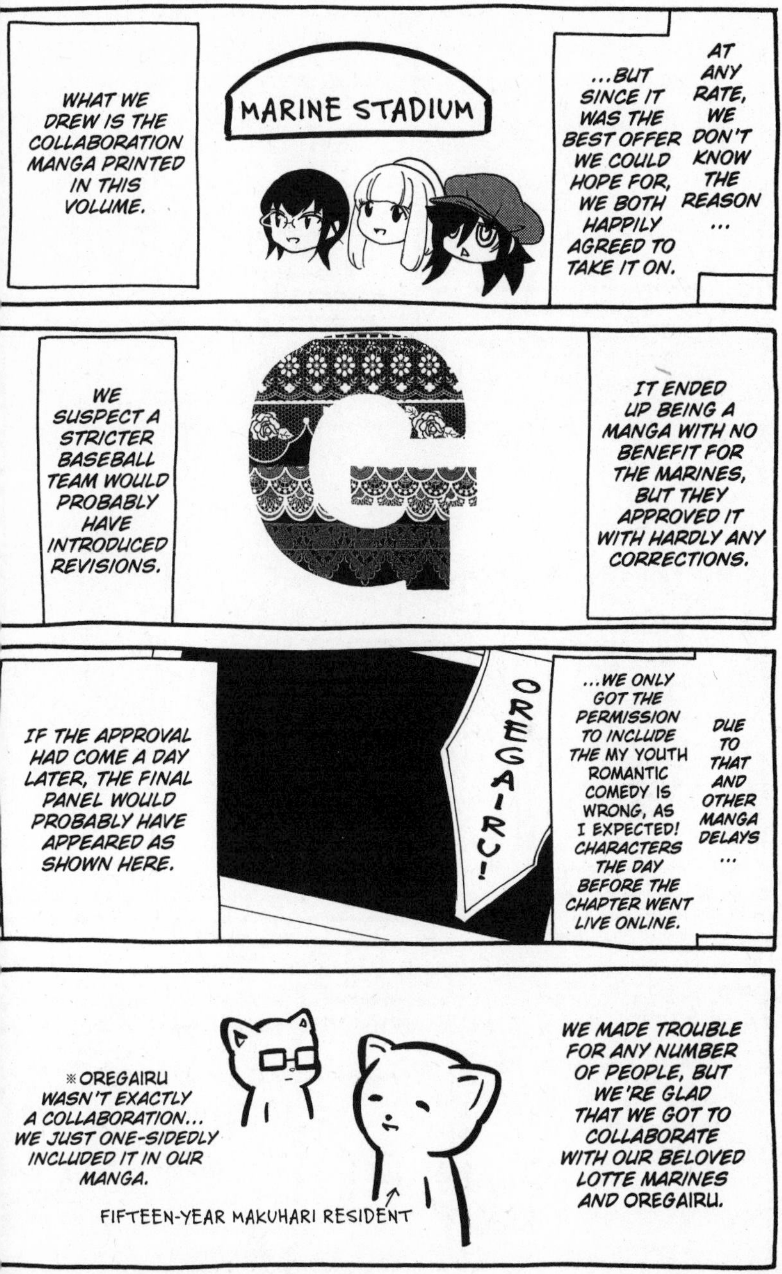
AT ANY RATE, WE DON'T KNOW THE REASON...
...BUT SINCE IT WAS THE BEST OFFER WE COULD HOPE FOR, WE BOTH HAPPILY AGREED TO TAKE IT ON.
MARINE STADIUM
WHAT WE DREW IS THE COLLABORATION MANGA PRINTED IN THIS VOLUME.
IT ENDED UP BEING A MANGA WITH NO BENEFIT FOR THE MARINES, BUT THEY APPROVED IT WITH HARDLY ANY CORRECTIONS.
WE SUSPECT A STRICTER BASEBALL TEAM WOULD PROBABLY HAVE INTRODUCED REVISIONS.
DUE TO THAT AND OTHER MANGA DELAYS...
...WE ONLY GOT THE PERMISSION TO INCLUDE THE MY YOUTH ROMANTIC COMEDY IS WRONG, AS I EXPECTED! CHARACTERS THE DAY BEFORE THE CHAPTER WENT LIVE ONLINE.
OREGAIRU!
IF THE APPROVAL HAD COME A DAY LATER, THE FINAL PANEL WOULD PROBABLY HAVE APPEARED AS SHOWN HERE.
WE MADE TROUBLE FOR ANY NUMBER OF PEOPLE, BUT WE'RE GLAD THAT WE GOT TO COLLABORATE WITH OUR BELOVED LOTTE MARINES AND OREGAIRU.
FIFTEEN-YEAR MAKUHARI RESIDENT
※OREGAIRU WASN'T EXACTLY A COLLABORATION... WE JUST ONE-SIDEDLY INCLUDED IT IN OUR MANGA.

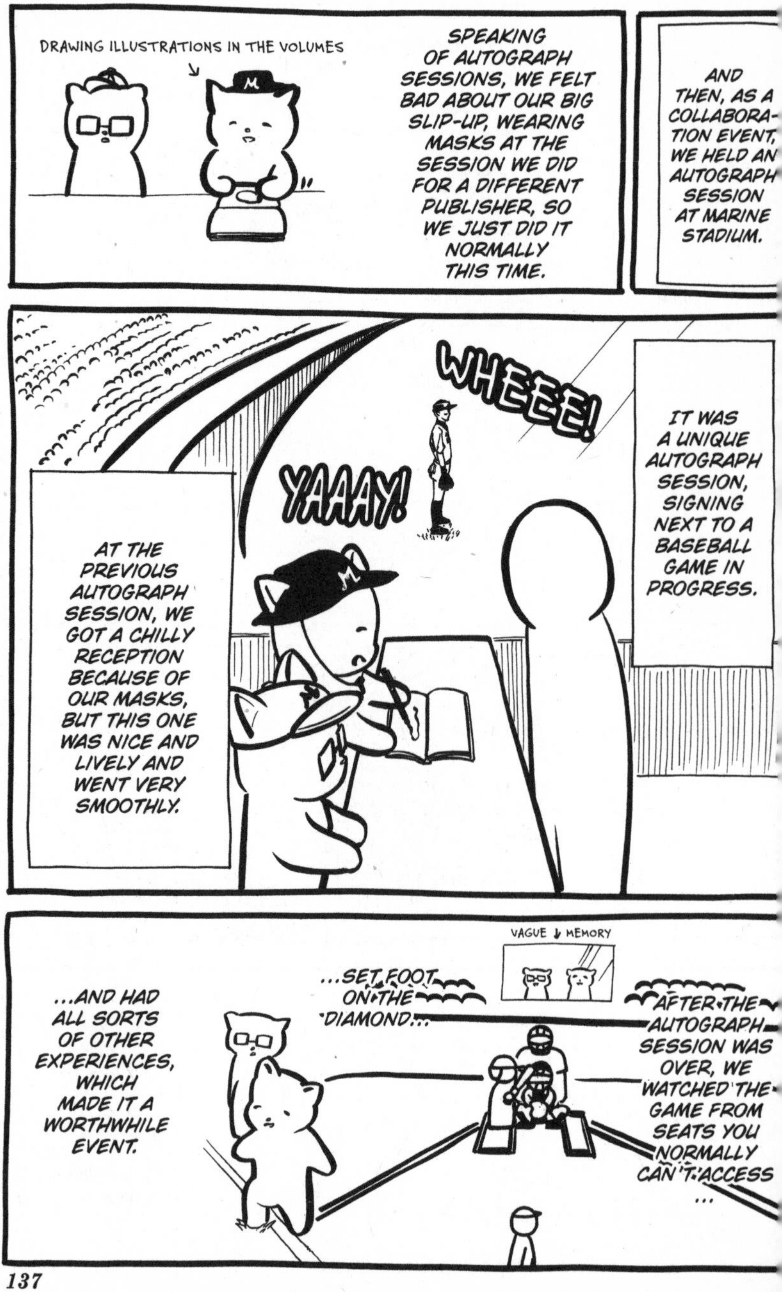
AND THEN, AS A COLLABORATION EVENT, WE HELD AN AUTOGRAPH SESSION AT MARINE STADIUM.
SPEAKING OF AUTOGRAPH SESSIONS, WE FELT BAD ABOUT OUR BIG SLIP-UP, WEARING MASKS AT THE SESSION WE DID FOR A DIFFERENT PUBLISHER, SO WE JUST DID IT NORMALLY THIS TIME.
DRAWING ILLUSTRATIONS IN THE VOLUMES
IT WAS A UNIQUE AUTOGRAPH SESSION, SIGNING NEXT TO A BASEBALL GAME IN PROGRESS.
WHEEEE!
YAAAY!
AT THE PREVIOUS AUTOGRAPH SESSION, WE GOT A CHILLY RECEPTION BECAUSE OF OUR MASKS, BUT THIS ONE WAS NICE AND LIVELY AND WENT VERY SMOOTHLY.
AFTER THE AUTOGRAPH SESSION WAS OVER, WE WATCHED THE GAME FROM SEATS YOU NORMALLY CAN'T ACCESS ...
VAGUE ↓ MEMORY
...SET FOOT ON THE DIAMOND...
...AND HAD ALL SORTS OF OTHER EXPERIENCES, WHICH MADE IT A WORTHWHILE EVENT.

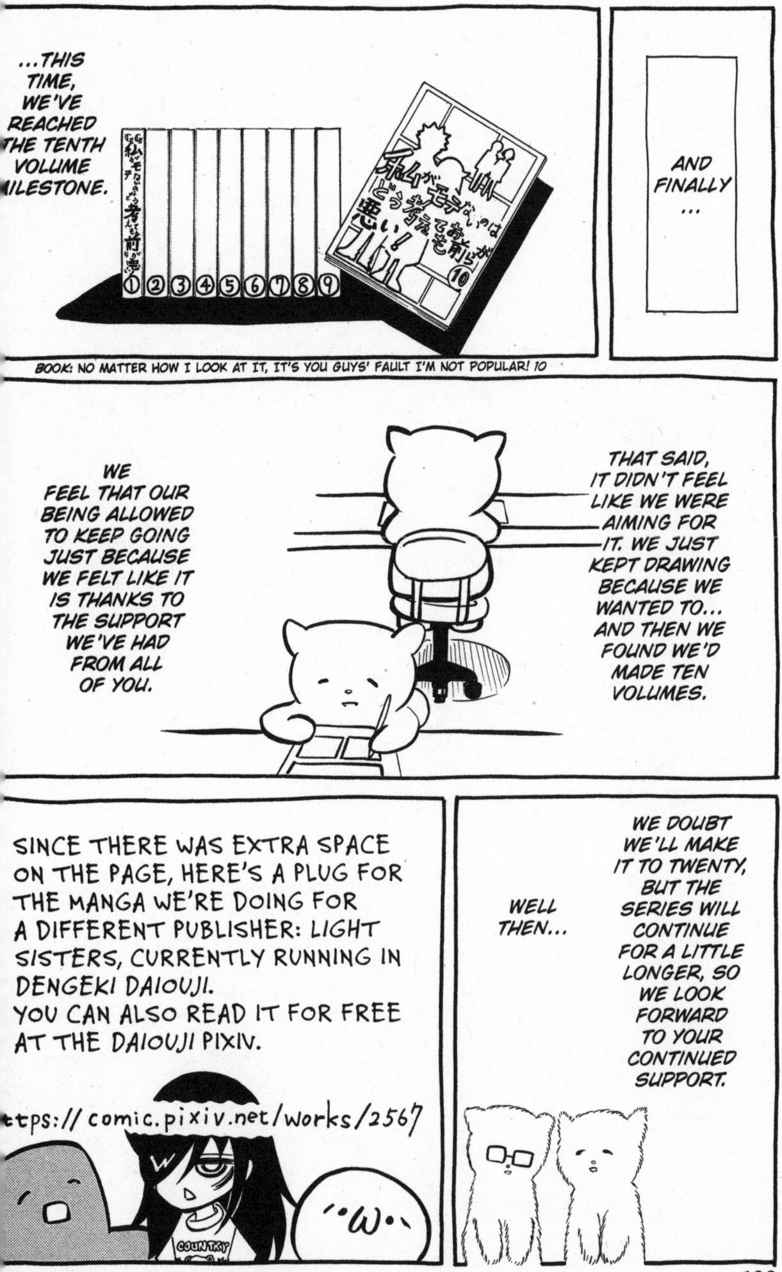
AND FINALLY...
...THIS TIME, WE'VE REACHED THE TENTH VOLUME MILESTONE.
私がモテないのはどう考えてもお前らが悪い!
10
BOOK: NO MATTER HOW I LOOK AT IT, IT'S YOU GUYS' FAULT I'M NOT POPULAR! 10
THAT SAID, IT DIDN'T FEEL LIKE WE WERE AIMING FOR IT. WE JUST KEPT DRAWING BECAUSE WE WANTED TO... AND THEN WE FOUND WE'D MADE TEN VOLUMES.
WE FEEL THAT OUR BEING ALLOWED TO KEEP GOING JUST BECAUSE WE FELT LIKE IT IS THANKS TO THE SUPPORT WE'VE HAD FROM ALL OF YOU.
WE DOUBT WE'LL MAKE IT TO TWENTY, BUT THE SERIES WILL CONTINUE FOR A LITTLE LONGER, SO WE LOOK FORWARD TO YOUR CONTINUED SUPPORT.
WELL THEN...
SINCE THERE WAS EXTRA SPACE ON THE PAGE, HERE'S A PLUG FOR THE MANGA WE'RE DOING FOR A DIFFERENT PUBLISHER: LIGHT SISTERS, CURRENTLY RUNNING IN DENGEKI DAIOUJI.
YOU CAN ALSO READ IT FOR FREE AT THE DAIOUJI PIXIV.
ttps://comic.pixiv.net/works/2567
COUNTRY

ITH HELP FROM ASSISTANT YUUJI ASAKURA-SAN

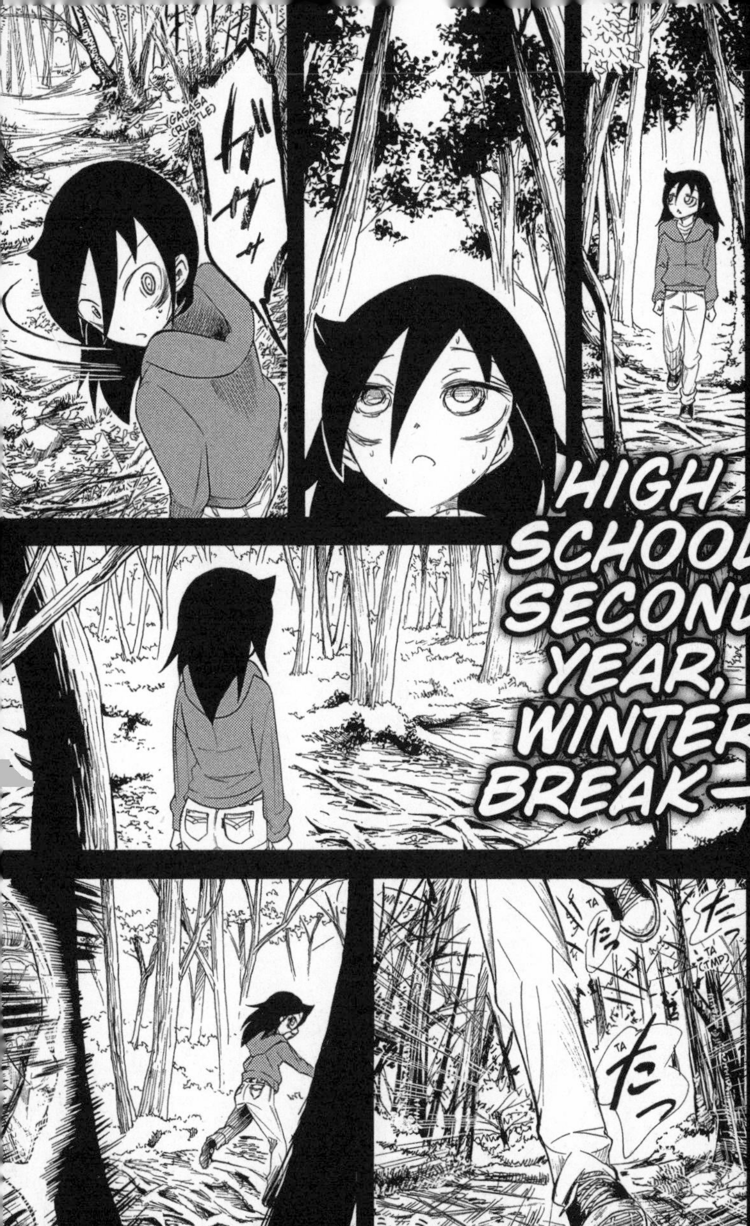
GASASA (RUSTLE)
HIGH SCHOOL SECOND YEAR, WINTER BREAK—
TA (TMP)
TA
TA

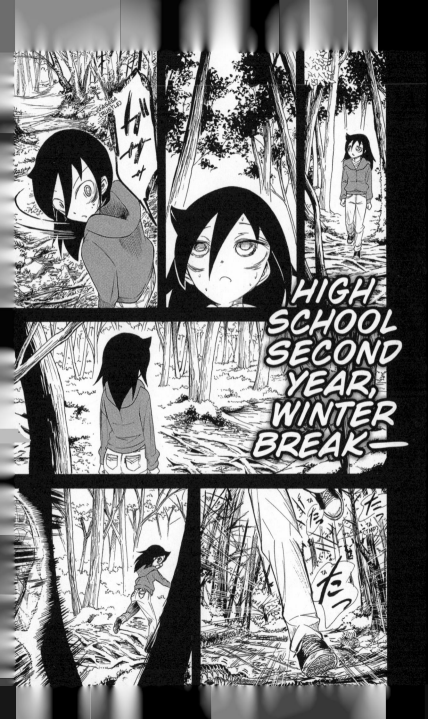

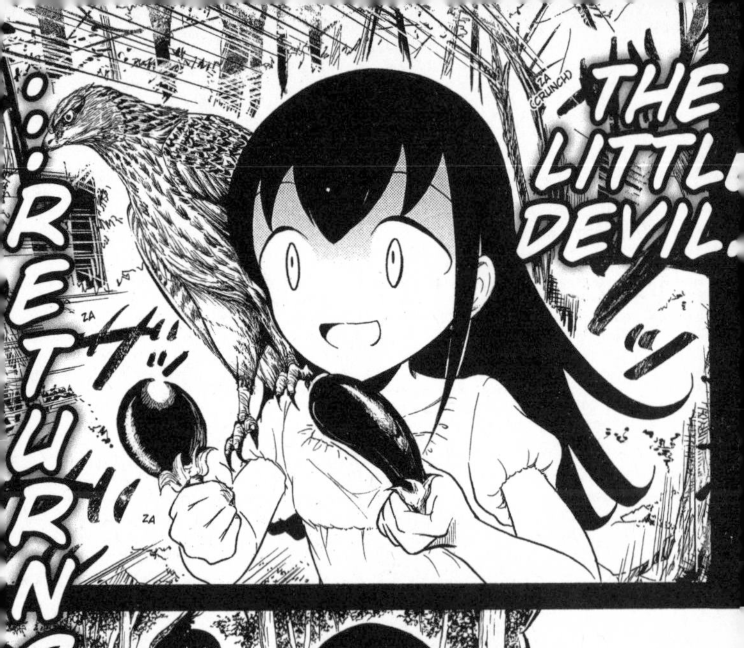
THE LITTLE DEVIL...
ZA (CRUNCH)
...RETURNS!!
ZA
ZA
UWAAAA-AAAAH!!

No Matter How I Look at It, It's You Guys' Fault I'm Not Popular! 11 COMING SOON!

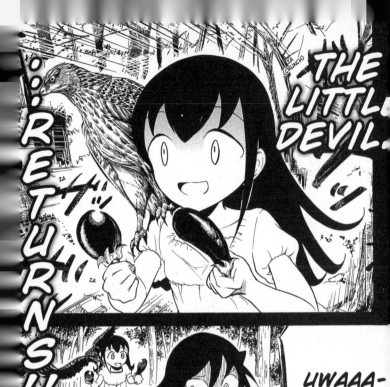

INSIDE COVERS

The **virgin conception** paper really exists! It was published in the December 2013 issue of the *British Medical Journal*, and its main conclusion is that "researchers may still face challenges in the collection and analysis of self-reported data on potentially sensitive topics."

PAGE 4

Asuko Okitegami's Testament by MisiOisiM (or HigasiOisiN) is a parody of the light novel *Kyouko Okitegami's Testament (Okitegami Kyouko no Yuigonsho)* by NisiOisiN. It was published in 2015 and is the fourth novel in the Forgetful Detective (*Boukyaku Tantei*) series. The parody author name in Japanese uses the word for "east" (*higas[h,j]i*) instead of "west" (*nis[h,j]i*).

PAGE 4

Uncommon Sense Advice (*Hijoushiki no Susume*) is a real book by longtime Chiba Lotte Marines catcher Tomoya Satozaki. He's also the "Archangel" mentioned on the other (real) book featured, **Chiba Lotte Marines: Anything's Possible 2**.

PAGE 5

Animage is an anime and entertainment magazine aimed at a general audience. Tomoko is looking at the December 2015 issue featuring Haruka and Makoto from *High Speed!* and *FREE!* on the cover. That issue would have come out the month before this chapter was serialized.

PAGE 15

Komi's glowing head is mimicking endorphin manipulation from the fighting manga series *Baki the Grappler* by Keisuke Itagaki.

PAGE 19

In Japan, students are also present at **parent~teacher~student conferences**, where parents meet with their child's homeroom teacher to discuss their progress and issues at school.

PAGE 22

maany Diapers is a parody of the actual diaper brand moony.

PAGE 22

NEET is an acronym for "Not in Education, Employment, or Training." It was first used in Britain but has been highly adopted in Japan to describe the increased number of people who are either unemployed or disengaged from the working world.

PAGE 22

The **Akutagawa Prize** is a Japanese literary prize awarded in January and July to the best recent work by a new or rising author.

PAGE 22

A **light novel** is a genre of novels aimed primarily at young adults. They contain comics-style illustrations and are often adapted into manga and anime.

PAGE 23

Hamada Kiyoshi is a parody of the Matsumoto Kiyoshi drugstore chain. Matsumoto and Hamada are the last names of the members of the influential Japanese comedy duo Downtown.

PAGE 28

The **Drama and Theater Arts major at Matsunaga University's School of Arts and Letters** is a parody of the Drama and Theater Arts major at Meiji University's School of Arts and Letters. The joke is that Meiji and Matsunaga are both major brand names for milk in Japan.

PAGE 29

"It turns out..." is a reference to the Japanese copypasta origin meme *"Yappari Kadokuratte kuso da wa."* ("It turns out Kadokura really is shit.") It's the end of an online comment that seems at first to be written in support of professional baseball player Ken Kadokura's pitching but ultimately insults him.

PAGE 45

SECA is a parody name for SEGA.

PAGE 45

The **Ghaliotte figure** is a parody of the character Nao Tomori from the 2015 anime series *Charlotte*.

PAGE 46

In Japan, **pachinko** has a relatively seedy reputation as a gambling game for adults, not kids, much like slot machines and video poker in the U.S. Even in a family-friendly arcade like the one Tomoko is visiting, the pachinko games are more likely to be played by adults to get cheaper practice on a new machine before going to a regular pachinko parlor.

PAGE 48

The **hanging-ring type** of crane game has the prize attached to a plastic ring with a flat base, which is then suspended from a rubber ball on the end of a rod. The friction between the plastic base and rubber ball is harder to overcome than one would expect.

PAGE 55

M[ ]P OUTLETPARK is a spoof of MITSUI OUTLET PARK in Makuhari, a branch of the Japanese outlet mall chain.

PAGE 56

Komi's **"Wowwie, it's a box of gems!?"** is *"Housekibako yan!?"* in the original edition, which is a catchphrase associated with humor celebrity and reporter Hikomaro.

PAGE 58

Tomoko's **"I'm gonna f•cking kill you..."** (*"Buchikorosuzo!"*) appears early on in the gambling manga and anime *Kaiji*. It's said by hall master Tonegawa aboard the ship *Espoir* when he abruptly stops being polite in reaction to the players' demands for more information.

PAGE 60

AWO'S STYLE is a parody of the Japanese lingerie chain AMO'S STYLE.

PAGE 64

STARTURRYS COFFEE is a combination of the Starbucks and Tully's Coffee coffee chains' names.

PAGE 68

"I squeezed lemon..." is a reference to a 2channel message board thread from June 2012 that featured hypothetical reactions to Saya-nee (idol Sayaka Yamamoto from NMB48) saying, "I squeezed lemon on your fried chicken."

PAGE 72

Matsudo Nittai, the opposing soccer team's school name, is a combination of the names of two other Chiba schools—Senshu University Matsudo and Nippon Sport Science (Taiiku) University.

PAGE 75

ROOMDECO, known as ROOM DECO KANETAYA in real life, is a furniture store located near Kaihin-Makuhari Station in Chiba Prefecture.

PAGE 77

TOMO is the shortened version of the moped brand TOMOS.

PAGE 77

The **UFO-like building** that Yoshida saw is an actual building in the Makuhari neighborhood of Chiba City called Hotel UFO, and it is in fact a love hotel, a short-stay hotel where people by and large check in to engage in sexual activities.

PAGE 79

Tomoko's phrase, **"change flippity-flap"** (*"tsurizeni pakapaka"*) comes from episode 6 of the comedy anime *Ai Mai Mi*, in which the character Ponoka is referred to as *Jihanbaiki Tsurizeni Pakapaka Jirou-sousui* (Vending-Machine Change Flippity-Flap Commander-in-Chief Jirou).

PAGE 86

The manga magazines *Weekly Shounen Jump* and *Young Magazine* both come out on Mondays, hence Tomoko's **Monday Routine**.

PAGE 91

In the original edition, Tomoko is looking up what kanji are used in the word *doukoku* ("wailing," "lamentation"). It's implied that this leads her to look at a walk-through site for the 1998 Sega Saturn game *Doukoku Soshite...*. The translation swaps out the original game for another 1998 Sega Saturn game called *Baroque*.

TRANSLATION NOTES 2

PAGE 93
In the original edition, Tomoko types in a Japanese slang word for the video-streaming site YouTube (**YooToob**) that sounds out the name as if it's four Japanese syllables — YO-U-T(S)U-BE.

PAGE 95
Tomoko's **"My body won't..."** line is actually spoken by Shadow Dunaway after being affected by the Insania virus in episode 19 of the sexy mecha series *Godannar*.

PAGE 97
Tomoko's hypothetical convenience-store lunches are as follows: At the upper left is a LUNCH PACK, a line of snacks made by the Yamazaki Baking Company that simulate a wide variety of dishes as sandwiches by putting a flavored sauce between two slices of white bread. The one shown is Tokachi pork and cabbage cutlets. The upper right package is a Pasco-brand donut with sweet beam jam and whipped cream filling. Down on the lower left is a *nori* bento (boxed lunch featuring dried seaweed) sold by 7-Eleven, while on the lower right is an *okaka onigiri* (rice ball with a bonito and soy sauce filling) also sold by 7-Eleven.

PAGE 100
Cafeterias in Japan often let you order by pressing a button for the food item you want on a machine at the entrance. The machine passes your request to the kitchen staff and gives you a **meal ticket** to claim that item.

PAGE 101
The Black Lady is a reference to the Japanese light novel *The Black Knight and the Red Lady* by Shiira Gou.

PAGE 102
The **udon coming out of Tomoko's nose** is an homage to the character Mammoth Nishi from the boxing manga and anime *Ashita no Joe*.

PAGE 105
PAD, or *Pazudora* in Japanese, is the shortened name for the popular mobile puzzle game *Puzzle & Dragons*.

PAGE 106
Attack on Kabane is a mashup of the titles of two violent manga/anime series, *Attack on Titan* and *Kabaneri of the Iron Fortress*.

PAGE 109
Normies, or *riajuu*, is Japanese Internet slang for someone who has a fulfilling life in real life (i.e. off-line).

PAGE 111
No Guard is one of the abilities possessed by certain Pokémon.

PAGE 115
Yoshida's flurry of punches refers to Kenshiro's "North Star Hundred Crack Fist" from the manga and anime series *Fist of the North Star*.

PAGE 121
The **Chiba Lotte Marines** are the baseball team for Chiba City, and candy conglomerate Lotte are their corporate sponsor. It's fairly common for people in Japan to call a baseball team just by their sponsor name, which is why you'll see Komi just call them "Lotte" a fair bit. Their home ballpark was called **QVC Marine Field** when this chapter came out in early 2016, but as of 2017, it is called **ZOZO Marine Stadium**. And yes, that's QVC as in the TV shopping channel.

PAGE 121
"But on TV..." is referring to a scandal that broke in late 2015 when three players for the popular Tokyo Yomiuri Giants baseball team were indefinitely suspended for illegally gambling on baseball games.

PAGE 122
In the first panel, the girls are by a set of food stalls located outside of the ballpark. The stalls shown include Tsukiji Gindaco, which sells *takoyaki* (octopus puffs); Kawashimaya, which sells *yakitori* (grilled chicken on skewers); and Gyutan Fukusuke, which sells grilled **beef tongue**. The **Bandit-style chicken** (*sanzoku yaki*) that Kawashimaya is advertising is generally grilled bone-in chicken legs with sweet garlic sauce.

PAGE 123
Komi is standing in front of two food sellers located inside the ballpark. **Senkyaku Banrai** is a food and sweets shop, and its name is a four kanji compound that means "flood of customers." The other is BIG INNING, which sells steak combos.

PAGE 123
Offal stew, or *motsuni*, is a general term for a stew that uses any innards of an animal such as beef, pork, or chicken. This is the dish that the Marines' ballpark is known for, and there are three places selling their own version of it inside the stadium.

PAGE 123
Tomoko is looking at a real **Seven Young Gulls** poster that was made to celebrate the seven Marines rookie players in 2016 and was based on the classic poster for the Akira Kurosawa film *Seven Samurai*. Tsutomu Io is the team manager, and the team mascot is a seagull.

PAGE 124
Gulls, not chickens! Originally, Tomoko thought the Japanese word written there was the one for "chicken" because *wakadori* is a common word for it, while *wakakamome* isn't normally something that'd be treated as one word. That, and the kanji for "seagull," or *kamome*, is much less commonly used and isn't one that students have to learn by the end of their schooling, unlike the kanji for *niwatori* ("chicken"). Komi probably knows the kanji well thanks to being a fan of the Marines.

PAGE 124
One of the signs you can see above the field has **TEAM26** on it. This is because number 26 has been reserved for the fans and is never given to one of the players. There's plenty of TEAM26 merchandise for the fans to buy as an official member of the Marines.

PAGE 125
The **Kanpai Girls** are a group of six female idol singers who also work as beer vendors in the stands at the stadium for the Marines. They started up in 2015 as a beer marketing strategy.

PAGE 126
The team the Marines are playing against is the **Saitama Seibu Lions**, who are based in Saitama Prefecture just north of Tokyo and have the Seibu railway conglomerate as their corporate sponsor.

PAGE 126
The name of batter **Ogino** might be familiar, since it's also the name of Tomoko's homeroom teacher. In fact, all the family names used in the series are names of Marines players because Nico Tanigawa are huge fans of the team. Most of the names are from the current roster, but Kuroki and Komiyama retired before the series began in 2011.

PAGE 127
In Japanese baseball, *sayonara* refers to the game ending instantly once the home team scores a winning run in the bottom of the ninth inning. The chapter was published March 17, 2016, before the season actually began, so the scores and events are merely hypothetical/plausible for a Marines win.

PAGE 128
Much like how this series is also known by the shortened name *WataMote* in Japanese, *OreGairu* is the abbreviated name for the light novel/manga/anime series *Yahari Ore no Seishun Rabukome wa Machigatteiru* by Wataru Watari (*My Youth Romantic Comedy is Wrong, As I Expected!*)

PAGE 135
The **"other WataMote"** refers to the manga *Watashi ga Motete Dousunda* by Junko, which is published in English under the title *Kiss Him, Not Me!*

PAGE 136
The big **"G"** in the middle of the page refers to the Tokyo Yomiuri Giants baseball team, which is much better known and would be much stricter on how they're portrayed.

NO MATTER HOW IT'S YOU GUYS' FAULT I'M NOT POPULAR! ⑩

Nico Tanigawa

Translation/Adaptation: Krista Shipley, Karie Shipley
Lettering: Bianca Pistillo

This book is a work of fiction. Names, characters, places, and incidents are the product of the author's imagination or are used fictitiously. Any resemblance to actual events, locales, or persons, living or dead, is coincidental.

WATASHI GA MOTENAI NOWA DOU KANGAETEMO OMAERA GA WARUI! Volume 10 © 2016 Nico Tanigawa / SQUARE ENIX CO., LTD. First published in Japan in 2016 by SQUARE ENIX CO., LTD. English translation rights arranged with SQUARE ENIX CO., LTD. and Yen Press, LLC through Tuttle-Mori Agency, Inc., Tokyo.

English translation ©2017 by SQUARE ENIX CO., LTD.

Yen Press, LLC supports the right to free expression and the value of copyright. The purpose of copyright is to encourage writers and artists to produce the creative works that enrich our culture.

The scanning, uploading, and distribution of this book without permission is a theft of the author's intellectual property. If you would like permission to use material from the book (other than for review purposes), please contact the publisher. Thank you for your support of the author's rights.

Yen Press
1290 Avenue of the Americas
New York, NY 10104

Visit us!
⚊ yenpress.com
⚊ facebook.com/yenpress
⚊ twitter.com/yenpress
⚊ yenpress.tumblr.com
⚊ instagram.com/yenpress

First Yen Press Edition: July 2017

Yen Press is an imprint of Yen Press, LLC.
The Yen Press name and logo are trademarks of Yen Press, LLC.

The publisher is not responsible for websites (or their content) that are not owned by the publisher.

Library of Congress Control Number: 2013498929

ISBNs: 978-0-316-43971-8 (paperback)
       978-0-316-47338-5 (ebook)

10 9 8 7 6 5 4 3 2 1

BVG

Printed in the United States of America